The Politics of Memory: Truth, Healing and Social Justice

edited by Ifi Amadiume and Abdullahi An-Na'im

Zed Books
LONDON • NEW YORK

The Politics of Memory: Truth, Healing and Social Justice was first published by Zed Books Ltd, 7 Cynthia Street, London N1 9JF, UK and Room 400, 175 Fifth Avenue, New York, NY 10010, USA in 2000.

Distributed exclusively in the USA by St Martin's Press, Inc., 175 Fifth Avenue, New York, NY 10010, USA.

Cover designed by Andrew Corbett
Set in Monotype Ehrhardt and Franklin Gothic by Ewan Smith
Printed and bound in the United Kingdom by Biddles Ltd, Guildford and King's Lynn

A catalogue record for this book is available from the British Library

Library of Congress Cataloging-in-Publication Data

The politics of memory: truth, healing, and social justice / [edited by] Ifi Amadiume.
    p. cm
    Includes bibliographical references and index.
    ISBN 1-85649-842-5 (cloth) – ISBN 1-85649-843-3 (pbk.)
    1. Human rights. 2. Reconciliation. 3. Social justice
  I. Amadiume, Ifi, 1947–

JC571.P642 2000
323.1–dc21

99-087433

ISBN 1 85649 842 5 cased
ISBN 1 85649 843 3 limp

Zed Titles on Globalization

Globalization became the new buzzword in the late 1990s. Despite the very different meanings attached to the term and even more divergent evaluations of its likely impacts, it is clear nevertheless that we are in an accelerated process of transition to a new period in world history. Zed Books' titles on globalization pay special attention to what it means for the South, for women, for workers and for other vulnerable groups.

Nassau Adams, *Worlds Apart: The North–South Divide and the International System*

Samir Amin, *Capitalism in the Age of Globalization: The Management of Contemporary Society*

Asoka Bandarage, *Women, Population and Global Crisis: A Political-Economic Analysis*

Michel Chossudovsky, *The Globalization of Poverty: Impacts of IMF and World Bank Reforms*

Peter Custers, *Capital Accumulation and Women's Labour in Asian Economies*

Bhagirath Lal Das, *An Introduction to the WTO Agreements*

Bhagirath Lal Das, *The WTO Agreements: Deficiencies, Imbalances and Required Changes*

Bhagirath Lal Das, *The World Trade Organization: A Guide to the New Framework for International Trade*

Diplab Dasgupta, *Structural Adjustment, Global Trade and the New Political Economy of Development*

Graham Dunkley, *The Free Trade Adventure: The WTO, GATT and Globalism: A Critique*

Bjorn Hettne et al., *International Political Economy: Understanding Global Disorder*

Terence Hopkins and Immanuel Wallerstein et al., *The Age of Transition: Trajectory of the World-System, 1945–2025*

K. S. Jomo (ed.), *Tigers in Trouble: Financial Governance, Liberalization and the Economic Crises in East Asia*

Hans-Peter Martin and Harald Schumann, *The Global Trap: Globalization and the Assault on Prosperity and Democracy*

Harry Shutt, *The Trouble with Capitalism: An Enquiry into the Causes of Global Economic Failure*

Kavaljit Singh, *The Globalization of Finance: A Citizen's Guide*

Henk Thomas (ed.), *Globalization and Third World Trade Unions*

Christa Wichterich, *The Globalized Woman: Reports from a Future of Inequality*

David Woodward, *Foreign Direct and Equity Investment in Developing Countries: The Next Crisis?*

For full details of this list and Zed's other subject and general catalogues, please write to: The Marketing Department, Zed Books, 7 Cynthia Street, London N1 9JF UK or e-mail: sales@zedbooks.demon.co.uk

Visit our website at: http://www.zedbooks.demon.co.uk

Contents

List of Contributors   vii

Abbreviations and Acronyms   xiii

Introduction: Facing Truth, Voicing Justice   **1**
Ifi Amadiume and Abdullahi An-Na'im

1 Memory, Truth and Healing   **21**
Wole Soyinka

**2 The Politics of Memory: Biafra and Intellectual
     Responsibility**   **38**
Ifi Amadiume

**3 Biafran War Literature and Africa's Search for Social
     Justice**   **56**
Akachi Ezeigbo

**4 Social Movements Revisited: Mediation of Contradictory
     Roles**   **68**
Abdullahi An-Na'im and Svetlana Peshkova

5 Post-Biafran Marginalization of the Igbo in Nigeria   **90**
Nnaemeka Ikpeze

**6 Towards a Social History of Warfare and Reconstruction:
     The Nigerian/Biafran Case**   **110**
Axel Harneit-Sievers and Sydney Emezue

7 Latin American Experiences of Accountability   **127**
Juan E. Méndez

**8 Truth in a Box: The Limits of Justice through
     Judicial Mechanisms**   **142**
Julie Mertus

**9   Justice for Women Victims of Violence: Rwanda after
the 1994 Genocide**   **162**
Binaifer Nowrojee and Regan Ralph

10 The Truth According to the TRC   **176**
Mahmood Mamdani

11 Conclusion: The Cause of Justice Behind Civil Wars   **184**
Francis M. Deng

Index   **201**

List of Contributors

Ifi Amadiume recently served as Chair of the African and African-American Studies Program in addition to holding a joint appointment in the Department of Religion and the AAAS Program at Dartmouth College. Her role as Director of the Ford Foundation project 'Reconceptualizing African Social Movements: Gender, Religion, Culture, Politics and Cross-Cultural Interactions' characterizes Dr Amadiume's political academic interests. She was active in local British politics and throughout her academic studies at the University of London, and she eventually became editor of the *Pan-African Liberation Platform* (*PAL Platform*), an educational journal on human rights. During her education at the University of London, she received a BA with honours in Social Anthropology and Hausa (African language) as well as a PhD in social anthropology. Having held the positions and titles of researcher, lecturer, professor and academician, she is also an award-winning writer and poet, writing her own books and contributing to chapters in books, encyclopaedias and journals. Some of her publications include *Daughters of the Goddess, Daughters of Imperialism: African Women, Culture, Power and Democracy* (Zed Books, 2000); *Re-inventing Africa: Matriarchy, Religion and Culture* (St Martin's Press, 1998); *Male Daughters and Female Husbands: Gender and Sex in an African Society* (Zed Books, 1987); *African Matriarchal Foundations: The Igbo Case* (Karnak House 1987); *Passion Waves* (poetry, 1985), and *Ecstasy* (poetry, 1995). Dr Amadiume has worked on several projects funded by the Ford Foundation, including the project on The Health and Reproductive Rights of Women in Nigeria, directed by the late Professor Claude Ake. She also worked on the international project African Social Movements with leading Africanists, including Dr Thandika Mkandawire, Professor Ernest Wamba di Wamba and Professor Mahmood Mamdani. Dr Amadiume is currently part of a collaborative research project on The Civil Status of God with COD-ESRIA, in Dakar, Senegal, which is a major research institute in Africa.

Abdullahi An-Na'im, citizen of Sudan, permanent resident of the USA, is Charles Howard Candler Professor of Law, Emory University, Atlanta, GA, USA. He is the author of *Toward an Islamic Reformation: Civil Liberties, Human Rights and International Law* (translated into Arabic, Indonesian and Russian). An-Na'im is editor of *Human Rights in Cross Cultural Perspectives: Quest for Consensus*; *Human Rights in Africa: Cross-Cultural Perspectives* (with Francis Deng); *The Cultural Dimensions of Human Rights in the Arab World* (in Arabic); *Universal Rights, Local Remedies: Legal Protection of Human Rights under the Constitutions of African Countries*; and *Proselytization and Communal Self-Determination in Africa*. He has also published some forty articles and book chapters on human rights, constitutionalism, Islamic law and politics. Dr An-Na'im is the director of two major research projects, funded by the Ford Foundation and being implemented out of Emory Law School, one on women and land in Africa, and the second a global study of the theory and practice of Islamic family law throughout the world.

Francis M. Deng has served as Sudan's ambassador to Canada, the Scandinavian countries and the USA, and as minister of state for foreign affairs, in addition to academic appointments in his home country, and in several universities in the USA. He was the first Rockefeller Brothers Fund Distinguished Fellow, a senior research associate at the Woodrow Wilson International Center for International Scholars and was appointed as the Jennings Randolph Distinguished Fellow of the United States Institute of Peace. He has given seminars on law and nation-building in Africa as a visiting lecturer for several years at Yale Law School, where he also received his PhD in law. In 1989, he joined the Brookings Institution as a senior fellow and he helped to establish the African Studies branch of the Foreign Policy Studies programme, which he heads. Following the imprisonment of General Olusegun Obasanjo (now released and currently head of state of Nigeria) who was and founder of the African Leadership Forum, Deng assumed the position of acting chairman of the forum. Deng has also authored and edited over twenty books in the fields of law, conflict resolution, human rights, anthropology, folklore, history and politics.

Sydney Emezue is on a doctoral programme at the University of Nigeria, where he received his BA and MA degrees. He teaches history at Abia State University and his thesis is on 'Pre-colonial Igbo warfare'. He has frequently travelled giving lectures at universities including the Department of History, University of Hamburg; the Institute of African Studies in Humboldt; and the University of Berlin. He also participated in a summer institute hosted by Professor Paul Lovejoy at York University, Canada, in 1999 and gave a well-received paper entitled 'Warfare and slaving in 19th-century Igboland'. Having lived through the Biafran war as a teenager, he has an abiding interest in studying the Nigerian civil war. In 1997 he co-edited a book entitled *A Social History of the Nigerian Civil War: Perspectives from Below*. The book is based on oral interviews conducted in all the war-affected eastern states as well as in Kogi in the north. He is also the author of numerous professional papers and articles.

Akachi Ezeigbo is an associate professor in the Department of English at the University of Lagos, Nigeria. Her publications include *Fact and Fiction in the Literature of the Nigerian Civil War* (1991); *Gender Issues in Nigeria – A Feminine Perspective* (1996); three collections of short stories – *Rhythms of Life* (1992), *Echoes in the Mind* (1994), *Rituals and Departures* (1996); a novel, *The Last of the Strong Ones* (1996); and children's fiction – *The Buried Treasure*, *The Prize*. She was awarded a Commonwealth Fellowship spent in 1989–90 at SOAS, London, as visiting Commonwealth fellow. She is the vice-president of Women Writers of Nigeria (WRITA). She is presently in South Africa where she has been awarded a research fellowship from August 1999–July 2000 at the University of Natal, Pietermaritzburg, in the School of Language, Culture and Communication (EnAgish Studies Unit).

Axel Harneit-Sievers has been a research fellow at the Center for Modern Oriental Studies, Berlin since November 1993. His current research project is on 'Locality, Ethnicity and the State in Southeastern Nigeria: Igboland since 1880', with a special interest in non-professional local historiography and post-colonial chieftaincy. His work includes various field-trips and research-related travel to Nigeria, Namibia, Uganda and Mozambique. Born in Germany, Dr Harneit-Sievers studied history, political science and philosophy at the University of Hanover. He received his first degree (similar to an MA in the US system) from the Department of History at the University of Hanover in 1984. Around this time, he also engaged in a study of development and politics of the SWAPO of Namibia, 1959–84. In 1990, he received his PhD from the Department of History, also at the University of Hanover, on Nigerian businessmen and colonial politics, 1930s to 1950s. Since then, he has done research work on the history of the Nigerian civil war and the reconstruction process after 1970.

Nnaemeka Ikpeze was educated at the University of Ibadan, University of Nigeria and Columbia University, USA. He began a career in lecturing and research in economics at the University of Nigeria in 1971 and progressed to the rank of full professor in 1991. His main research interests and publications focus on public policy and development management, industrial development and policy, and human resources development and management. Professor Ikpeze is currently country team leader (Nigeria) for an IDRC-sponsored research project in economic policy-making and implementation in Africa ('A Case Study of Strategic Trade and Selective Industrial Policies').

Mahmood Mamdani is the Herbert Lehman Professor of Government and Director, Institute of African Studies, Columbia University, and President (1999–2002) of the Council for the Development of Social Research in Africa. He is the author of *Citizen and Subject: Contemporary Africa and the Legacy of Late Colonialism* (Herskovits Award, African Studies Association, 1997) and *Politics and Class Formation in Uganda* among other books. He was founding director of the Centre for Basic Research in Kampala, Uganda and is a member of the African Academy of Sciences.

Juan E. Méndez has been the executive director of the Inter-American Institute on Human Rights (IAIH) in San José, Costa Rica since 1996. From 1994 to 1996, he was general counsel for the New York-based Human Rights Watch after being the executive director for Human Rights Watch–Americas, in Washington, DC. Professor Méndez's academic positions include: professor of law, Georgetown University, 1992–96; visiting professor at the University of Notre Dame, 1996; visiting faculty at the Oxford University Summer Programme on International Human Rights Law, 1997–98; and visiting fellow, Kellogg Institute, University of Notre Dame, 1996. Additionally, he is the author of several articles and book sections on accountability for past human rights violations, the right to truth, the relativism and universality of human rights, the inter-American system of human rights protection, and related topics.

Julie Mertus has written dozens of articles and several books on racism and conflict, human rights, refugees and gender issues. Her most recent books include *Kosovo: How Myths and Truths Started a War* (University of California Press, 1999) and *The Suitcase: Refugees' Voices from Bosnia and Croatia* (University of California Press, 1999). She teaches law at Ohio Northern University and serves as a consultant with the Women's Commission for Refugee Women and Children and the Humanitarianism and War Project at Brown University. She was formerly counsel to Human Rights Watch, a MacArthur Foundation fellow, a Harvard Law School human rights fellow, a Fulbright scholar, and a visiting professor at Emory University School of Law. In a more traditional lawyering role, she was an attorney with the American Civil Liberties Union and assistant corporation counsel for affirmative litigation for the City of New York.

Professor Mertus has been a commentator on CNN International, a frequent contributor to the *Washington Post* and has spoken at such institutions as Yale, Harvard, Columbia, University of Michigan, George Washington University, the University of Miami, West Point, Moscow State University, and the School of International Affairs in Hanoi, Vietnam, as well as at the annual meetings of the American Society of International Law, the American Political Science Association, and the Canadian Council of Lawyers.

Professor Mertus graduated from Yale Law School and Cornell University.

Binaifer Nowrojee, a lawyer from Kenya, is counsel with Human Rights Watch's Africa division. She graduated from Columbia Law School with a JD degree and Harvard Law School with an LLM degree. She has written numerous reports on human rights violations in several African countries, including Rwanda, Kenya, Tanzania, South Africa, Ghana, Gambia, Nigeria and Liberia.

Svetlana Peshkova is currently a PhD student in socio-cultural anthropology at Syracuse University (Syracuse, NY). She received her BA and MA in foreign languages and linguistics in 1996, from Pyatigorsk State University of Linguistics, Russia, and her masters in theological studies from Emory University (Atlanta, GA) in 1999. In 1994–95, she worked for a regional branch of the Peace Foundation (Pyatigorsk, Russia), and she worked at Eastern Mennonite University (Harrisonburg, VA) in 1995–97. In October 1998 Svetlana coordinated and participated in the project on the Future of Chechnya sponsored by the Andrey Sakarov Foundation (NYC, NY) and Andrey Sakarov Museum (Moscow, Russia). She also worked as a researcher for the Islamic Family Law Project of the Law and Religion Program, Emory University in 1997–99. Her current interests are in political Islam and conflict transformation with the regional focus on Central Asia and the Caucasus.

Regan Ralph is the executive director of the New York-based non-governmental organization Human Rights Watch/Women's Rights Division. The Women's Rights Division of Human Rights Watch monitors violence against women and gender discrimination around the world.

Wole Soyinka is an acclaimed playwright, essayist, poet, novelist, theatre director and political activist. He received the Nobel Prize for Literature in 1986. Educated in Ibadan, Nigeria and Leeds, England, where he obtained an Honours Degree in Literature, Soyinka has held fellowship and professional positions in theatre and comparative literature at the

Universities of Ibadan, Lagos and Ife (Nigeria), Legan (Gambia), Sheffield and Cambridge (England), and Yale, Cornell and Harvard (USA). He frequently lectures as visiting professor/distinguished scholar in other American, European and African universities. Currently, he is the Robert W. Woodruff Professor of Arts at Emory University in Atlanta, Georgia. In addition to his many civic honours, including Commander of the Federal Republic of Nigeria, Soyinka has received numerous honorary degrees and fellowships from universities worldwide. Soyinka has supported the production of literature in Africa by instituting numerous literary awards and using the Nobel Prize to build a global writers village in Nigeria. As a political activist, he has been in the forefront of the struggles for justice and democratic ideals in his native Nigeria and other African countries. He was imprisoned during the Nigerian civil war from 1967 to 1969. In 1992 he formed the African Democratic League to put an end to the reign of dictators in Africa. Soyinka has been in exile since November 1994, when he fled the brutal government of Nigeria's military dictator, General Sani Abacha. Tireless in his campaign in support of Ogoni environmental activists and Nigerian political prisoners, particularly the late Mashood Abiola, he was charged in March 1997, *in absentia*, with treason, which carries the sentence of death. As a playwright, essayist, poet and novelist, Soyinka writes primarily in English. His works are distinguished for their exploration of the African world view and are steeped in Yoruba mythology, imagery and dramatic idioms.

Abbreviations and Acronyms

BOFF	Biafran Organization of Freedom Fighters
CODESRIA	Council for the Development of Social Science Research in Africa
ECA	Economic Commission for Africa
ECOWAS	Economic Community of West African States
FAR	Forces Armées Rwandaises (Rwandan Army)
ICC	International Criminal Court
IGADD	Intergovernmental Authority on Drought and Desertification
NATO	North Atlantic Treaty Organization
NGO	non-governmental organization
NIF	National Islamic Front
NLF	National Liberation Front (Rwanda)
OAU	Organization of African Unity
RPF/A	Rwandese Patriotic Front/Army
SADCC	South Afrcan Development Coordinationg Committee
SPLM/A	Sudanese People's Liberation Movement/Army
STF	Special Task Force
TC	truth commission
TRC	Truth and Reconciliation Commission
UN	United Nations
UNESCO	UN Educational, Scientific and Cultural Organization
UNHCR	UN High Commission on Human Rights

Introduction: Facing Truth, Voicing Justice

Ifi Amadiume and Abdullahi An-Na'im

This selection of essays brings together a distinguished group of academics, scholars, policy-makers, equity workers and social activists in a creative engagement with issues of human rights in relation to truth, reconciliation and social justice in societies that have experienced serious internal conflict and war. We consider this impressive collection of such a diverse combination of interests a truly historic achievement, as all the authors tackle what sadly is a most urgent question for today: recognizing the power of memory, what are the best strategies for achieving post-conflict reconciliation?

Methodology and Scope

These essays from Nigeria, Senegal, Uganda, Sudan, South Africa, Latin America, Europe and the United States create an opportunity for collaboration with Africa-based scholars. We find this inter-regional and interdisciplinary approach a useful way to examine new questions, methodologies and theoretical models that current events in Africa and research on Africa are raising in a global context. By encouraging fresh thinking on issues and the use of accessible language that is uncluttered by heavy academic references, it is our objective to cross the historical borders that have separated the academy from the world, and intellectual labour from economic and political labour. We consider the involvement of non-academics, including community workers and activists, crucial to the success of a transformative cross-cultural discourse on the politics of memory.

It is therefore not surprising that we have adopted a more complex approach to Africa, situating events in both their local contexts and global interactions, with a view to begin to rethink and revitalize the study of Africa for the twenty-first century. It is a position that calls for the challenging and reformulation of old theoretical models. We are specifically critical of the Cold War model of a Balkanized Africa, which resulted in a marginalization of African Studies within academic communities, especially in the United States. We also see the experiences of Africans as contributing critical insights into local and global processes, since Africa's political, economic and cultural borders have continuously shifted, allowing for numerous exchanges of people, resources, ideas and cultures. As such, new ideas for the study of Africa require a multi-disciplinary, trans-subject, comparative and border-crossing approach. New thinking on Africa demands collaboration with African and Africanist scholars from abroad to cross and dismantle the additional borders of intellectual isolation and deepen our different communities' engagement with African Studies. Such serious efforts can provide avenues for strengthening institutional support for African Studies. We hope that this book will define a new basis for studying Africa in local and global contexts and generate ideas, collaborative research projects and new institutional frameworks for future collaborative and comparative research work in African Studies.

The importance of a comparative method is crucial and informs our editorial policy on gender, scope, themes, and the role of Biafra in defining this book.

Gender We believe that women's perspectives are extremely important, and we suggested that all authors incorporate women's perspectives in their essays. In our view, the tendency to leave women's issues usually to women authors is counterproductive. Men and women should highlight and emphasize women's perspectives in an integrated manner because they are central to every conceivable issue or theme of concern.

Scope Issues of truth, healing and social justice concern social movements. However, we choose not only to consider social movements as progressive (in the sense of resisting oppression) but also to look at those that are repressive and do not liberate. We should revisit this new reality. Genocide in Rwanda was caused by a social movement, even if an ugly one. The same could be said for some Islamic fundamentalist movements, for example, in Sudan. To discuss the best strategies for achieving post-conflict reconciliation means that there should be a balanced reference to other countries in Africa and comparisons with other regions – for example, other countries in Africa, comparisons to countries outside Africa such as Latin America and Bosnia, and the post-communist countries in Europe. However, there is a problem with including too much and losing focus, hence the choice of a deeper engagement with case studies such as Biafra.

Biafra Biafra was the first expression of massive suffering inflicted on society by an internal African war. Great trauma resulted from it. To what extent and how that trauma was healed is a central question for the authors as it is extended to later conflicts. In that sense, Biafra is a metaphor for South Africa, Rwanda, Mozambique and other areas of conflict. Biafra is symbolic, because it was so early, so bloody and because in the past few years we seem to have forgotten that Nigeria is so important. A return to the Biafran war forces a reconsideration of how people re-create communities fragmented by war and violence, and an examination of one historical experience that can inform new perspectives and paradigms. Biafra provides a comparative focus on the causes of needless civilian deaths. Why do more civilians than soldiers die in African wars? How can we arrive at policies that safeguard civilian lives? Biafra provides an opportunity to study what is generally believed to have been a remarkable reconciliation following the war. Nevertheless, 30 years later, the ghost of Biafra haunts the discourse on social justice and national security in Nigeria, and even the ethics of US foreign policy and double standard on human rights.

Methodology: case study versus thematic approach   We are in favour of a thematic approach, but believe that it should be carried out through essays on case studies that encourage comparison. The comparative perspective presents contrasting paradigms for exploring the tension between justice and reconciliation in situations of deep internal conflict. Rwanda, for example, exemplifies a trajectory of justice without reconciliation; South Africa illustrates one of reconciliation without justice. Biafra is presented as a success story in reconciliation with no talk of justice. Each situation illuminates the other, raising numerous questions and considerations that illustrate the richness of a comparative study.

The book is organized under the following themes.

Chapters 1 to 3 consider social justice. Is it both ends and means of healing and reconciliation, considering that conceptions and mechanisms of realizing social justice vary among countries, societies and cultures, and even perhaps gender and class?

Chapters 4 to 6 consider the nature of conflict. To get to 'healing and social justice' issues, we need to understand the nature, context and consequences of conflict in Africa and elsewhere in the world. We need to revisit social movements in terms of actors, contexts, processes and outcomes, in order to examine the social processes that force us to consider the other themes, and to clarify the varieties of and perspectives on social movements and their roles.

Chapters 7 to 9 consider legal accountability as an approach to healing and social justice. Similar questions are extended to truth.

Chapter 10 considers truth commissions. Do they function similarly all over the world? Do they serve as an approach to healing? Is it at the expense of social justice?

How can we reflect on these problems to raise issues of theory, methodology, policy and future research?

Social Justice

It is important to look at different situations that generate conflict, such as national interests to maintain unity, local determination to separate, and international economic and political interests. Conflicts in Africa over the past 30 years have led to labels such as 'permanent emergencies', 'complex humanitarian emergencies' and 'permanent transitions', which in themselves indicate the problems of considering truth, social justice and healing in such contexts.

The current crisis in the Congo is a case in point, for the euphoria over the removal of one dictator is soon replaced by anxiety over a new one – first Mobutu, now Kabila. In view of this, are the new developments of democracies in South Africa and the Great Lakes Region cause for optimism about the revival of the spirit of liberation and re-engagement with the pan-African movement? The new realities certainly put squarely on the agenda the importance of the diaspora connection in our concern with revitalizing African Studies, and, even more so, the need to address the cultural politics involved in the framing of diasporic identities by both intellectuals and activists, and the many questions raised in the attempt to define the boundaries of Africa, the rights of the African diaspora, and alliances for liberation, human rights and democratization in Africa.

Current perceptions and definitions of human rights raise questions on their limitations and call for a broader, more balanced concept that does not separate and privilege civil and political rights from and over economic and social rights. There is a simplistic assumption that social movements are unquestionably for civil and political rights. Yet social movements are not always progressive, in the sense of resisting oppression: there are also those that are repressive and do not liberate, resulting in genocide, for example. We can compare several cases, including Uganda, Sudan, Rwanda, South Africa, Nigeria, Latin America and Yugoslavia, because they all raise questions of successful or unsuccessful reconciliation with or without social justice, and failed or successful cases of legal accountability or truth commission or human rights commission.

Transition in South Africa came about from a negotiated settlement, a political compromise. Thus we can ask if reconciliation can be achieved between blacks and whites who have experienced very brutal atrocities, since unanswered questions remain in the areas of racial and economic equity. In this new agreement, reconciliation is dependent on amnesty, yet the security of the old order remains intact. Not surprisingly, there is criticism that amnesty prevents the punishment of crime. Amnesty is not equal to justice. Also, the Truth and Reconciliation Commission (TRC) memory is limited to only 30 years. The TRC does not deal with the blaming of the system of apartheid itself, since the national government would not have negotiated on those terms. What this proposes is restorative justice. Social justice is not necessarily retributional, yet the TRC opens wounds and the whole process is precarious. Wole Soyinka responds to this by pointing out that social justice is not restitution, but a bridge to reconciliation (Chapter 1).

We do need to admit that truth is a worthwhile aim to pursue, but also that it takes time, and that we cannot take for granted that democracy and economic success necessarily need truth about the past. Comparing TRCs and judicial prosecutions, it is not necessarily clear which of them one should prefer in terms of efficiency of revealing the truth and in terms of legitimacy. It has been quite convincingly argued that the war crime tribunals of recent years mainly serve the interests and political and moral needs of the international community, and possibly certain sections of the local public, rather than local needs (see Chapter 8). They do not necessarily yield results in compliance with local concepts of justice, however difficult this is to define. The same argument could be made about the TRCs (see Chapter 10). All of these institutions, by their very nature, proceed according to formal legal rules that may have little to do with common-sense understanding of what is right or wrong. Certainly, the international community supporting TRCs or tribunals has to follow international law – but the question is whether the international community might not also be able to support or encourage more local, less abstract processes of moving towards justice about the past. On the other hand, there is also the thinking that leaving this purely to local dynamics might involve the risk of lynching or mob 'justice' – this should be reason enough to think further about these issues.

Memory is an interdependent process of remembering and forgetting. Should we agree with the solutions presented by the truth commissions that are brought in by outsiders? Are they the best solutions? What happens if they do not work? There is a widespread impression that 'truth', 'peace', 'democratization' and 'economic success' are linked, and support each other. This represents the South African model of dealing with the past. We don't know yet whether it will really work.

In the case of South Africa, there are other commissions dealing with other issues in society, and there are global issues affecting South Africa as the TRC is going on. This is not denying that local initiatives get hijacked by NGOs and the international community. The reality is a clash of two paradigms – African countries are not given help and empowerment by the international community, unlike Western countries such as Bosnia, so that foreign intervention is still a major issue. It is not surprising that history (long memory) is so central in the chapters by Africans.

Wole Soyinka's contribution (Chapter 1) stretches the imagination and extends the scope of discourse simply by posing the question 'How far back should memory reach?' Responding to his own question, he defiantly asserts that memory is not governed by statutes, yet one cannot stick too much to the past. If we are concerned with truth, restitution and reconciliation, surely reparation is a prerequisite of healing racial injustice, since vestiges of the past sometimes militate against putting aside the burden of memory. Soyinka thus undertakes the task of resurrecting our memory of the slave trade, a theme one might, in a simplistic narrowness of historical memory, suppose to be unrelated to our theme. This history, he argues, remains a fact of the failure of European humanism. A similar logic was behind European colonialism and Arab colonialism in Africa. How far back indeed should memory reach?

Memory ought to serve as a corrective, and in this sense, reparation is not necessarily monetary recompense. In fact memory can cease to be a burden, as Soyinka demonstrates in his description of his visit to a slave site and his experiential empathy with those who suffered enslavement. These huge historical atrocities are not lost to the past since there are internal continuums of an external violation, be it in the military tyrants in Nigeria or the perpetrators of genocide, and rights-abusing governments in Africa. By not excusing anyone over time and over geographical space, Soyinka gives all of us, in our shared humanity, the moral responsibility of knowledge and acknowledgement. In this sense, reparation is a metaphor for global healing.

Soyinka reconceptualizes struggles for separation in Africa by arguing that these should be seen not as retribalization, but as movements for renationalization – an idea that poses a challenge to Abdullahi An-Na'im and Svetlana Peshkova in Chapter 4 as they revisit social movements from the perspective of the mediation of contradictory roles and other contributors on social justice, legal accountability and truth commissions.

The possibility of social justice as both end and means of healing and reconciliation is examined in the light of the fact that conceptions and mechanisms of realizing social justice vary among countries, societies and cultures, and even perhaps gender and class. In Chapter 2 Ifi Amadiume explores the situation in Nigeria, citing the Igbo-led Biafran movement for separation following experiences of genocide as a lesson in the potency of memory. The war that followed led to the death of over three million people, with, it would seem, no lessons learned. Citing the South African Truth Commission and the criminal tribunals for genocides in Bosnia and Rwanda as instruments of truth and justice, she condemns the policy of silence and denial of memory about Biafra, since present atrocities and human rights abuses can be traced to the same military who not only supervised the genocide, but executed the war that was fought against victims of genocide. In this case, victims were denied the healing power of truth; they have not been allowed to tell their own truth.

Since the Biafran war was the first attempt to break the neo-colonial dictatorship of imperialism, Amadiume argues that it is necessary to look again at the politics of memory and to use Biafra to revisit the question of intellectual responsibility. She points out the need to re-analyse the vanguardist intellectual leadership of Wole Soyinka, who opposed the Biafran separation and the resultant war on moral grounds, and has continued to oppose military tyranny and injustice in Nigeria. Her assessment of aspects of the post-Biafran war intellectual debate and the nature of memories of experiences of the war shows the extent to which the failure of public debate and intellectual discourse on Biafra is responsible for the pattern of alignment of forces during the post-Babangida period, especially in 1994, and in 1998 following the deaths of General Sani Abacha and Chief Mashood Abiola. The simple truth is that Nigeria has not escaped the ghost of Biafra, and she concludes that Nigeria has had its own Rwanda and its own Bosnia, and must learn the lessons of history by facing the memory of Biafra.

Amadiume presents women as central to the nurturing, management, survival and rebuilding of the communities during and after the Biafran war. During the war, although gender politics became more intense, women were risk-takers and were enlisted in civil defence forces.

Amadiume concludes that discourses on Biafra go beyond claims of Igbo marginalization, showing that memory can be used for a greater cause, for although one can forgive past evil deeds, it is impossible to forget. However, law is not necessarily an instrument of healing, thus raising the question whether truth commissions by themselves heal the wounds of injustice. International law courts and truth commissions seem to work only for Western societies, since indigenous communities, their values, philosophies and cultures are marginalized.

Africans do not lack ideas about peace and reconciliation. Writing on social justice as a means of social healing from the perspective of literature and gender, Akachi Ezeigbo in Chapter 3 takes a quote from Wole Soyinka to argue the place of art in the service of social justice. Artists, such as writers, are the voice of vision in African societies. She points out that although women are the greatest victims of war, they are also the greatest survivors. In African literature, for example, in the work of Soyinka, old women and Earth-derived metaphors represent the forces of healing and regeneration. Similarly, in Achebe's concern with the problem of bad leadership women are again represented as the main hope of the future as they reconcile belligerent groups and society itself. Social justice is therefore a means of maintaining peace and stability. Africans need to look at their past and learn from their mistakes. In place of reckless dictatorship, what is needed is democracy. Nation-building is therefore a collective task for both men and women.

The Nature of Conflict

Our interest in the nature of conflict is to re-examine social movements, to look at the nature, context and consequences of conflict in Africa and elsewhere in the world. Our goal is to examine the question of how civilians deal with wars and human agency in war and post-war situations.

Abdullahi An-Na'im and Svetlana Peshkova see social movements as midwives of change that can be positive or negative, which means that there is a tension in our topic, since one issue does not lead directly to the other. In short, truth does not necessarily lead to healing, and reconciliation does not mean that there is social justice. Their rethinking of social movements is all-embracing, as they look at social movements from several angles, including, as non-elite people using destructive means in trying to build a social order, as an element of seeking to redefine society, the right of self-determination. From whichever perspective, movements contain notions of contentious collective action to promote their objectives. They challenge opponents. They have solidarity and leaders can mobilize on shared identities and interests such as ethnicity or religion.

Since civil society is the environment in which social movements operate, the character of the state is crucial to our understanding of social movements. As An-Na'im and Peshkova put it, social movements for better or worse are about what prevails in society, which can be good or bad. They intensify or mediate conflict. This is how we should look at genocide in Rwanda, for example. We are wrong to be concerned with numbers or proportion rather than the moral wrong of killing even one person. In addition, they support Soyinka's rethinking of the nation space by arguing that we ought to think in regional terms when we look at migration and consider the dismantling of boundaries because of the limited space for the large populations.

We can see Rwanda as having a refugee movement problem, and that whole complex should be looked at as the Central Lakes Region. Movements are in fact across state boundaries, so that we need new theoretical models that redefine the state. In Sudan for example, religion is co-opted into ethnicity and northern identity, and we need also to look at the choices people make in selecting identity.

An-Na'im and Peshkova take a realistic position in seeing social movements as unavoidable because they are the instruments people use to articulate and realize their demands for political, economic and social change. As such, they are desirable for empowering people to exercise their right to self-determination, which cannot be pre-empted by a predetermination of whether others accept or reject their outcome. Social movements are necessary agents of the generation and intensification of conflict and injustice, as well as of sustainable conflict mediation. Accordingly, strategies for the promotion of sustainable mediation, healing and justice should be founded on a clear understanding of the sources and dynamics of the role of social movements in these processes.

The question of human agency is raised by Ikpeze and Axel Harnet-Sievers and Sydney Emezue in Chapter 6; they argue that it was necessary for survival during and after the Biafran war. They show the role of myth-making as a survival strategy. They look at Biafran propaganda to demonstrate the conflicting representation of the roles of the Organization of African Unity (OAU), saboteurs and mercenaries, as Biafrans grappled with explanations of defeat. If victory is not good for reconciliation, perhaps there is usefulness in creating a stalemate. In which case, there is a psychological as opposed to a practical benefit to misremembering.

It would appear that both the psychological and practical considerations in myth-making are relevant to the problematic question of violence against women in war situations. Although Harneit-Sievers and Emezue acknowledge sexual violence of conquering soldiers against women of the enemy side to be general in all wars, they argue that a distinction should be made between the systematic and large-scale rape of Bosnian Muslim women by Serb soldiers and sexual violence against women in the Nigerian civil war. They see rape in Bosnia as a systematic attack on Muslim Bosnian culture, but argue that women cannot be perceived as mere victims in the Nigerian case because the category of 'violence' does not cover the variety of relationships between women and soldiers, which involved proactive and reactive negotiation for survival. They prefer to analyse the relationship between women and soldiers in the context of relations between the military and the civilian population, since interviewees themselves lump all the acts of military aggression together – murder, robbery and rape. While some women were victims, others profited from their relationship with Nigerian soldiers and carried a social stigma in the immediate post-war period. Yet informants appear reluctant to point at or detail specific cases, preferring to speak in general terms and using the term 'war marriage' instead of rape.

Conflicts in Africa show a repeat of history and one may well ask the question: why are we not learning a lesson from the past? Some therefore argue the importance of focusing on Africa and talking among ourselves, rather than studying other conflicts. Some would also suggest learning lessons from the past to prevent future conflicts. Countries being ruled by dictators, for example, need a power change to avert violence that is waiting to happen. The 1998 bombing in Kenya is perhaps an example of violence that could have been averted. On 7 August 1998 a car-bomb explosion outside the American embassy in Nairobi, Kenya, killed 216 and injured over 5,000 people. The trauma reached far and wide, and the number of victims is far larger if we include widows and relatives who are emotionally and economically affected. This is an example where prevention would have worked since there were warnings before the bombing. Innocent Africans suffered external invasion because this was an attack against the USA. How can these victims seek truth and justice? Is the $38 million humanitarian aid package for Kenyan victims approved in 1998 justice for victims, or the legal action for $1.5 billion in damages brought against the US government by 2,300 Kenyan victims justice?

Truth and social justice are not things we face only after violence has occurred. We must also deal with social justice and truth before violence happens. A concern with truth involves seeing conflicts as generated at different levels, which interlink in complex ways. During the Cold War the question of conflict in Africa was compounded by both superpowers, with the United States and the Soviet Union supporting at different times regimes in Africa for strategic regions. This foreign resourcing of regimes encouraged conflict rather than peace-seeking – a problem that has not gone away in the so-called post-Cold War era.

Judicial Accountability

In judicial accountability, our focus is on legal accountability as an approach to healing and social justice. Contributors tackle the complex issues raised by the positions that truth is healing versus truth is social justice. In Chapter 7 Juan Méndez argues that Latin America's experiences of passage from military rule to democracy depended on the ability of civil society to go beyond the limits imposed by military conditions. Society had to deal with the wounds of violations that are the responsibility of the state, whether perpetrator government or successor government. It follows that on the question of crimes against humanity, the state owes each victim a right to truth, which is to be open and official, and a right to justice and reparation. It is the right of society to see that those unwilling to participate in such a project are not part of new governments.

Méndez does not see truth commissions as an alternative to justice. For him, international law is the basis of justice because it provides the right to a remedy, which leads to the right to see justice done. It also provides non-derogatable rights that lead to rights that have gone beyond Nuremberg rights. Méndez's definition of civil society provides new functions of NGOs in democratic orders – for example, human rights organizations. He further explains that there is a difference between knowledge and acknowledgement that would enable us to tell the victims that they are not forgotten and are valuable, as demonstrated in civil society's efforts at accountability and the UN's responsibility to take on cases. In the end, the object is reconciliation, even with the TRCs that have amnesty as their goal.

Julie Mertus, who writes on Bosnian victims of genocide in Chapter 8, does not fully see international law as the basis of justice. In her view, constituted legal instruments of punishment of war crimes – such as tribunals – are necessary, but insufficient since international and local expectations are contradictory. With distinct categories of prosecutors, violators and victims, all these groups benefit differently because victims are the prop in this drama as survivors act as conduits of prosecutors. The international community benefits more than the victims. As a means of naming crimes, law is too cold, technical and sterile. Even as a means of blaming, it does not work if the perpetrator is a paramilitary group. If it is used as a means of recording history, one still faces the choices of history as experience and history as myth.

Binaifer Nowrojee and Regan Ralph write in Chapter 9 on women's rights and violations of humanitarian law in civil war situations. They point out that issues of justice for women victims of genocide expose limitations of the war crimes tribunals. In post-conflict societies, a majority of survivors are women and women have the responsibility to rebuild. Generally, there is a taboo against violated women. In Rwanda, thousands of women were raped, yet there is no justice for women in Rwanda. Genocide investigators are not trained to investigate women's violations, which should be tackled differently. Nowrojee and Ralph enumerate shortcomings in the working of the Rwanda Tribunal, which include discriminatory attitudes, tribunal members belittling rape and being reluctant to collect evidence on rape, lack of skill in evidence collection, not enough women sitting on tribunals, unwillingness of the tribunals to work through women's groups acting as interlocutors. In their view, there is need for gender parity in the tribunal, particularly for collecting rape testimonies. There is also a need for witness protection. Tribunals need to provide safety before witnesses are targeted. In coming forward witnesses put themselves at risk, and Nowrojee and Ralph believe that these women are doing us a favour in bringing their stories to tribunals.

In the case of Latin America, continuous witnessing by relatives of victims explains the success of the Mothers of the Disappeared in putting and keeping the matter on the agenda (see Chapter 7). It matters that the tribunals should be appreciated by the local people. However, pointing to a double standard, unlike in Yugoslavia, the 'big fish' in Rwanda have been arrested because of information collected from witnesses. We must also acknowledge that in Rwanda, the National Tribunal has become a means of revenge. Rwanda's victims took justice as revenge, which raises the question of differences between international and customary law, and different methods of justice that can address the concerns of the people. Some have argued that there has been no justice for Hutus.

Testimonies serve the future too, yet many victims cannot tell, will not tell, have not told, so the wounds remain open. If this is so, can one think of reconciliation and healing? There are differences in experiences of women in TRCs, which have no punishment for rape, and international trial tribunals, where there is at least the possibility of punishment. The rule of law is important for democracy, but in which context can we make exceptions? The function of the judiciary is to individualize guilt and minimize collective guilt. There should be no impunity no matter what you are wearing, even if it is military uniform. The West German experience after the Second World War shows that the relationship between all these issues is certainly not a straightforward or simple one.

In post-Second World War West Germany, 'truth' was, to some extent, publicly established by the Nuremberg war crime tribunals, but at the same time, these tribunals seriously limited the scope of responsibility: in the tribunals, a few major culprits were singled out. This allowed the rest of society (among them numerous quite important members of the Nazi administrative and technical elite and the military) to excuse themselves as people who had just obeyed orders, or as people who had been involved only in subaltern functions (the German term is *Mitlaeufer* – 'co-runners'). This was partly direct lying about the past, partly self-deception, and it also reflected the need of the Allies, especially the USA and Britain, for people able to run post-war Germany.

For many years, this 'big lie' (and resulting silence) about the Nazi past, and the involvement of so many people in it, formed the basis of post-war West Germany, its economic miracle, and also its democracy (and it was a democratic society, no doubt). Of course, there was always a certain degree of debate about the Nazi past, but it gained momentum only in the mid-1960s, in the context of students' movements and the general turn towards the left. In effect, it seems to have needed a whole generation to get the debate running. And it is going on very intensely today, more than fifty years after the end of the war (cf. the debates in the USA about

Stephen Spielberg's film *Schindler's List*, about Daniel Goldhagen's book, *Hitler's Willing Executioners*,[1] and about the planned monument for the murdered European Jews, to be established in the centre of Berlin). In this context, one can recall interesting comments on the recent post-unification German past – a famous critical sentence by one former East German opposition activist, expressing much dissatisfaction with post-1990 developments in Germany: 'We wanted justice, but what we received was the rule of law' (in German, the two terms *Gerechtigkeit* – justice – and *Rechtsstaat* – rule of law – use the same word root, *Recht*).

Truth Commissions

Do truth commissions function similarly all over the world? Do truth commissions serve as an approach to healing? Is it at the expense of social justice? What is the relationship between TRCs and democratization?

Mahmood Mamdani explains in detail both the history and structure of the South African TRC, pointing out the difference between the Amnesty Committee, which focuses on perpetrators, and the main Commission, which deals with victims. Both committees are obviously unequal as amnesty for apartheid leaders was part of the political compromise in the transition from apartheid. In Chapter 10 Mamdani argues that the TRC's process of institutionalizing truth turned a political compromise into a moral compromise, obscuring the larger truth to serve the purposes of the new regime. Such moral and intellectual compromise may backfire. South Africa needs a social debate if it is to face the harsh truths about the beneficiaries of apartheid.

Nuremberg seen as the victor's justice is a wrong metaphor for South Africa, since whites and blacks in South Africa are not the same as Germans and Jews in terms of being bound to building a common society after conflict. The Nuremberg analogy was dropped and the Latin American analogy of dictatorship and human rights abuse was adopted in the thinking behind the TRC. But this analogy did not capture the colonial nature of apartheid, in which there were perpetrators and beneficiaries. In the case of South Africa, victims are the majority; they are social communities, not just individual political activists. In the short period between 1960 and 1982 there were about 3.5 million people forcibly dispossessed and removed from their communities. Where is their truth? The TRC focused on torture, murder and rape and ignored the apartheid legal machine of systemic violence. Mamdani insists on the exploration of alternative forms of justice and holds that truth is a prerequisite for justice.

In creating community in Bosnia after the Dayton Peace Accord it appears that the Truth Commission for Yugoslavia has been widely unsuccessful (see Chapter 8). The Nigerian example shows that free and fair elections cannot be held when perpetrators are out at large (see Chapter 2). It was argued by Western governments, particularly the US government, that the war crimes tribunal in Yugoslavia was the last choice for the Western powers after other options had failed. Yet the main perpetrators have not been indicted. Individuals were indicted for sexual assault, but the indictments were removed. It was left to Bosnia to try to create a domestic truth commission to provide a voice for victims, to provide accurate records of crimes and sacrifices, and to meet the need to deny collective guilt. There are four such truth commissions in Bosnia and a number of individuals have been prosecuted by the Bosnian government.

There is the claim that truth commissions were intended to break the cycle of violence and to provide accurate history, and that amnesty is needed in this process to get stories from perpetrators. This raises such questions as: how do you protect victims and witnesses? How do you work accountability and cathartic stories? How far back do you go in history? Yet, in order for Bosnia to develop a collective memory, there is a need to integrate tribunals, truth commissions and the media with civilian compensatory mechanisms. The lessons of truth commissions as a tool for rebuilding will be learned in the future – we don't yet have the answers.

In considering the value of talking, we are reminded that silence is not forgetting. Some have asked: why the sudden option of truth commissions in countries with long histories of violence and large external intervention? Also in these countries there is an absence of punitive democratic traditions. In South Africa, for example, apartheid has escaped punishment. Weighing the options of trials or equal redistribution of justice and truth commissions, it can be argued that truth commissions are to be preferred because if we hold trials, the old guards will be defensive and no democratization will result. Justice is often out of reach because there may be too many perpetrators to punish and too little evidence. Trials lead parties to suppress the truth and so healing is not achieved. Some think that trials are adversarial, unlike truth commissions, which, they argue, encourage community. All this raises the question of whether truth commissions, since they don't deal with the real problems, get in the way of other means or strategies of struggle. Truth is necessary, but might not heal. Healing did not happen in post-war Germany, but democratization did.

Since truth commissions have a narrow mandate, we should also consider the damage that can be done by this imperfect method. We are reminded that Archbishop Desmond Tutu declared that the TRC's function is to promote reconciliation, not to achieve it. But we are also reminded of Nigeria, where the late General Sani Abacha set up a National Reconciliation Committee that drew no response because of silences on the past;

this is inhibiting democracy in Nigeria. Tutu had a better chance of achieving success with a truth commission because of his status in the Church and the international community. The situation in Nigeria is not conducive to success because of those in power. If this changes, then it will be possible to call for a permanent truth commission to which the military should be a signatory. Truth commissions are important because they break the silence and mark the beginning of probing into other issues, as for example in Uganda, where there is an inquiry under way into inequalities concerning land and other matters.

In South Africa, if the TRC is opening wounds for whites, then for blacks, it would be a healing process. The TRC closure on 31 July 1998 was just a cut-off point, since there is provision for extension. There is a need to ask more questions about the role of other perpetrator institutions and groups in the crimes of apartheid – the role of education, the health sector, the media, churches, not necessarily individuals. Systemic institutions need to give account in some form.

It is, however, clear that there is no support for any programme of radical redistribution; support is only for TCs. African nations have their own way of achieving resolutions – for example, the use of rituals. Why do they have to go to TCs? Democracy in Africa is not possible where there is poverty and where people are fighting basically for survival. Tribunals and TCs do not address cultural differences and would need to be re-organized. The international community and the media prioritize conflicts differently, so that we need to re-address such issues as, for example, how many resources should the international community put into Sierra Leone versus Bosnia.

Cultural differences, resources and prevention are also major issues in resolving the current problems in the Balkans. In Yugoslavia, the post-1945 federalism with limited autonomy given to the provinces has failed, with demands for cultural autonomy or self-government given to small ethnically based units fearing Serbian domination. Talks about regional security in the Balkans again involve discourse on separation. They also involve perpetrators and victims of genocide. Yet these issues are not separate from the issue of economic equity. In the continuing nationalism and ethnic conflict in Yugoslavia, lessons are not learned from past mistakes. The principle of no impunity requires the commitment to punish perpetrators. Taking individual perpetrators to court creates less suffering for the masses and prevents a repetition of war crimes.

If we look at the examples of Iraq and Yugoslavia, the answer to how to deal with one individual (for this is how these conflicts were presented) is not to demonize him in order to justify hi-tech war. These specific wars led to the destruction of the infrastructure of a sovereign country, the creation of refugees and mass suffering, and the destabilization of a region by those who claim humanitarian intervention and by forces that claim to be peacemakers. The destabilization of one province destabilizes the whole nation, other provinces, nearby communities and the whole region.

In the Kosovo conflict, months of NATO air bombardment did not weaken the Yugoslav leader, President Slobodan Milosevic. They instead produced popular outrage and a strong sense of nationalist pride and resolution in a country under siege from foreign intervention. Citizens have rights too. With a weakened state in Yugoslavia, the NATO peacekeeping force in its observer mission is now becoming a sort of colonial presence, seemingly maintaining a ceasefire, settling disputes and punishing offenders as outside foreign countries fight over loans and contracts to rebuild that which they destroyed in the first place. Economic stabilization through policy commitment to equity would generate the language of cooperation and social justice that goes towards healing and reconciliation.

Conclusion

All the major themes covered in this book lead to the more important issue of prevention. What are the real bases for reparation and prevention? We should look at Biafra and come up with concrete ways of social healing, reparation and the prevention of atrocities. In this context we can point to the importance of sustainable mediation of conflict and the awareness of no permanent solution. We also favour the defining of social justice to emcompass all possibilities of conflict. This means that it might be too early to judge South Africa's TRC, since in South America it took two years to test the success of truth, thus allowing time for judgement. We owe something to inherent right and dignity as a basis of society, so that each society must come up with its own ethics of truth-telling as a way of prevention.

One example of truth-telling as prevention is lifting the silence on Biafra so that the past can be a lesson for the present. We should criticize foreign intervention and the US State Department, which has supported or promoted military dictatorship in Nigeria. To promote the principle of no impunity, even if wearing a military uniform, there is a need for international involvement in seeking legal accountability against perpetrators in Nigeria. We can extend this principle to the African diaspora, where there has been no reparation and no accountability on injustices in American history itself. Even the truth of America's engagement with South Africa has not been told in the TRC. We need truth-telling to be organized at all levels in society as venues for political accountability to stem violence.

Prevention demands memories. There are lessons to be learned from the Holocaust, such as creating a record. We do not have to live in the same country, but we all exist in the same world and have a stake in healing, restitution and forgiveness. Even if the real witnesses of genocide cannot witness because they are dead, memory is passed on. Prevention demands a role of bystanders, who have a responsibility as non-experts and non-citizens to tell the stories, sharing and not distancing ourselves as outsiders. We therefore have a responsibility of witnessing to ourselves, witnessing to the testimonies of others, witnessing to the processes of wit-nessing itself and mediating conflicts. Prevention also means that people ought to feel secure enough not to act on negative genocidal feelings. Since conflict is a part of human nature, we should therefore focus on prevention, employing the creative and therapeutic benefits of art as a means of coping with and preventing conflict.

We may well ask if there are crimes too big for accountability, for example slavery and colonialism. Yet, when there is silence and voices are not heard, wounds stay open. With the Holocaust, it took 30 years before memory and voices were allowed to come out. Truth commissions are like mirrors and can be useful against dictators in Nigeria and elsewhere. Silence on Biafra and the marginalization of Igbos from power enabled Nigeria to present the crisis as a small problem. It is an illusion to think that Nigeria is on the brink of proper democratic governance. The fact that Nigerians were talking about secession in 1998 is worrying and not indicative of positive development. There are ethnic riots and killings in Nigeria at the time of writing, in July 1999. The silence on Biafra means that people do not see the link between the 1998 situation and the events leading up to Biafra in 1966 and 1967. There were external economic interests behind the Biafran crisis, therefore we should use Biafra as a lesson to avoid repetition. These are legitimate concerns, and the message of no help for minimal conflicts encourages violence on a larger scale. It is easier to deal with small flames than with a wild fire.

Chapter 11 by Francis Deng brings a coherence to these chapters by raising issues of policy, stating that we are facing a major problem due to post-Cold War changes that shifted conflict resolution responsibility to the local powers, who do not have the means to resolve them. This might not be a bad thing, since there is a need for solutions from within, a need to empathize with each other's situations, and a need to seek equitable remedies. Deng points out the need for overriding human values to guide us, as he sees violent conflicts and dictatorships as currently the major problem areas.

Crisis of identity is one major source of conflict that needs attention – for example, in Sudan people and groups face a crisis of identity within themselves, in their self-perception and in classification by others. We need to find common norms other than European values for resolving conflicts. We need new guidelines for solutions since the UN principles of self-determination did not go far enough, and it is important to recognize the use of indigenous cultures for political and economic development. Management of conflict also involves the question of governance, which makes it necessary to look outside for help in a stalemate with internal leaders. This is a major lesson that has been learnt from internal displacements, which have wider consequences at the national, sub-regional and continental levels. If you cannot do it for yourself, call on the international community.

This comparative perspective presents contrasting paradigms, local, cross-territorial, cross-cultural experiences and multi-layered memories and voices from Africa and its diaspora, the United States, Europe and Latin America on the tension between truth, justice and reconciliation in situations of deep internal conflict. This book covers issues of theory, methodology, policy and future research, and raises many questions and considerations that illustrate the richness of a comparative local–global study. The success of this perspective supports the proposal that the revitalized study of Africa requires a multi-disciplinary, trans-subject and comparative approach.

In putting together these essays by scholars and policy-makers from Africa, Latin America and Europe, we hope that this book will contribute to intellectual and institutional efforts to build African Studies resource materials that will be invaluable to those conducting research in history, government, literature, religion, culture, migration, science, film, drama, media, African political history, Holocaust, refugees, women, peace and war studies.

By way of acknowledgement, we thank all those who have made this project the tremendous success it is – all the effort that went on behind the scenes, all the thinking and the contributions and the passion that came across so strongly. Our appreciation and gratitude to all those who made this possible – all the supporters, contributors and funders. We want to express a deeply-felt gratitude to the Ford Foundation, especially Program Officer Toby Volkman and the larger project funded through the Ford Foundation's 'Crossing-Borders: Revitalizing Area Studies' initiative. Thanks also to key Dartmouth College institutions such as the Rockefeller Foundation, the Class of 1930 Fellowship and the Dickey Center for International Understanding.

Thanks to the following who participated in a round-table discussion on this topic and made it such a wonderful experience – Akbar M. Virmani, Alice C. Wright, Julie Mertus, Janet Lord, Joan Kakwenzire, Lynda Boose,

Chika Okeke, Yulisa A. Maddy, Robert J. Chapman, MD, Maina Kiai, Errol Hill, Barbara Soros, Margaret Parrott, Julia Hikory, Babatunde Lawal, Juan Méndez, Francis M. Deng, Megan Brown, Akachi Ezeigbo, Irene Kacandes, Marianne Hirsch, Leo Spitzer, Eluemuno Blyden, Sydney Emezue, Meredeth Turshen, Judith Byfield, Tshikala Biaya, Obiora Udech-ukwu. Last, but not least, we want to thank the staff at Zed for their determination to secure a subsidized African edition and distribution of free copies of this book to a selection of academic and public libraries in Africa.

Note

1. Daniel Goldhagen, *Hitler's Willing Executioners: Ordinary Germans and the Holocaust* (New York: Alfred A. Knopf, 1996).

Memory, Truth and Healing

Wole Soyinka

At the back of our minds, confronted by the trilogy that makes up the overall theme of this book – Truth, Healing and Social Justice – is surely the question: how far back should memory reach? How deeply into the recesses of the past? The answer that springs spontaneously to mind is that memory is not governed by the statute of limitations, and that collective memory especially is the very warp and weft of the tapestry of history that makes up society. Unravel and jettison a thread from that tapestry and society itself may become undone at the seams.

And yet, the opposite is also true. Cling too passionately to those threads in the fabric, even to the designs that they have spun out of events, and society may lose itself in the labyrinths of the past. Then, like the millipede that stopped to count the number of filaments that propelled it, we find that we have lost the will or the ability to walk again.

One experiment in contemporary times that has attempted to put this dilemma behind its society is the work of the Truth and Reconciliation Commission of South Africa. It is an imperfect proceeding, one that provokes some disquiet, elements of which I have tried to address in a collection of essays – *The Burden of Memory and the Muse of Forgiveness*. In those essays, I propose a missing element in South Africa's formula, the insertion of which then offers us a trilogy that shares, as it happens, an identical spirit with the framework of this book, namely truth, restitution and – reconciliation, restitution, social justice, reparations – whatever name we choose to give to it but, very definitely, a process of recompense for loss, for denial and violation. But even that formula still brings us back to the question: how far into the past should memory reach?

Memory and Truth

There was an individual who held passionately to the belief that – as I earlier suggested – memory, especially collective memory, is vitiated by any notion of limitations or, indeed, by claims of mitigation through intervening relationships of a more harmonious order. It was in indirect acknowledgement of the conviction of this individual, of his passionate championing of the crucial place of racial memory, that I devoted a portion of those essays to the theme of reparations for a global wrong that the world is inclined to absorb, or dismiss as a mere incident in the course of history – slavery. His was the loudest voice on the African continent, or indeed within the diaspora, for the claims of racial memory and the justice of reparations. He poured his resources – both material and organizational – into that cause and I suspect that with his death, we shall hear less and less of that challenge to global conscience. Certainly, it was most noticeable that in the last four or five years of his existence, a period of total incapacitation when he was effectively shut off from the world, the voice of reparations had become muted, and the machinery that he had so obsessively placed in motion had ground to a halt. I refer of course to Bashorun M. K. O. Abiola, the late president-elect of Nigeria, who died in mysterious circumstances in prison, virtually on the eve of his release.

Perhaps this is just as well – even so, of course, would sigh a portion of the world, with undisguised relief. But then again, for the rest, perhaps not so well. We can argue over specifics but what refuses to go away is the underlying principle of reparations, restitution, social or racial justice or whatever presents itself as a prerequisite of healing and reconciliation. We cannot take refuge in amnesia. And we can do worse than explore the effects – both obscured and current – of that ancient but yet unexpiated wrong, as entry points into any evident malaise within societies, into an understanding of the eruptions that confound even our grossest projections of the capacity of humanity for unconscionable acts of violation against its own kind. Such a proceeding, and an objective assessment of the roles and responsibilities of the participants – both violators and victims – may enable us to anticipate or identify warning signs of impending repetitions of such collective derelictions in our own time.

Rwanda is, of course, the most chastening, truly benumbing reminder of such negative instructions. Admittedly, the sheer enormity, the meticulous comprehensiveness of this inhuman regression differs drastically from – shall we say? – the random or incidental slaughter that surely accompanied the hunt for slaves on that same continent between the sixteenth and nineteenth centuries, but the two conditions of mind, which relegate one section of humanity to an expendable status, fit only for expulsion from the immediate shared environment, are closely related. One group sees only 'cockroaches' – one of the expressions of depersonalization favoured by the Hutu organizers of Tutsi extermination. The other group also identifies an expendable commodity, lucrative if kept alive for a while.

Both have relegated the victim to a convenient, sub-human category. Memory serves to preserve intimations of the infinite possibilities of such regressions of the human mind – and the dangers they spell for the harmonization goals of our world.

Genocide

I had to visit Rwanda. In attempting to come to terms with the hitherto unimaginable, it was inevitable that I would seize an opportunity to step on the soil of Rwanda and see if any shred of humanity remained, was still jealously guarded by the survivors of that genocide. The 'land of a thousand hills' that gave its name to a radio that was put to such diabolical use – 'Radio des Milles Collines' – was still, as I remembered it after 30 years, breathtakingly beautiful, so pastoral and idyllic that it did not take too long to recall that it was the land of Rwanda that gave birth to Rider Haggard's *King Solomon's Mines*, and the legend of Prester John. On the way from the airport into Kigali, my guide pointed out the National Assembly building, holed by shells, where the Hutu militia had put up their last desperate stand. When I first visited Rwanda in the mid-1960s as part of a band of young, optimistic writers and artists, heading from a conference in Kampala, we had been obliged to spend a night in this same town, and there heard, for the first time, stories of sporadic mutual slaughter between the Tutsi and the Hutu, but those had been muted skirmishes, seemingly localized. Nothing at the time approached the horrors that would numb the world in the 1990s, when some Hutu leaders dreamt up their 'Final Solution' and methodically brought it to execution. That term – the Final Solution – was apparently invoked by some of the intellectuals who had organized this unspeakable crime, and the pattern of command and obedience had been modelled on the Nazi precedent. Only the tools and the methods were different.

Could any of us, in the 1960s, have suspected the possibility of this scale of massacre? I imagine not. Not even the brutality of the Katanga killings that culminated eventually in the death of Patrice Lumumba approached this level of a collective abandonment of humanity. Not even – coming nearer to the present – the rabid slaughter in Liberia, home of the poet Lenrie Peters, or the random killing in Sierra Leone of that urbane critic Eldred Jones had prepared us for this. Not the genocide in Nigeria that led to the secession war of Biafra in which the poet Christopher Okigbo lost his life, nor the agonies of Robert Serumaga and Okot p'Bitek's Uganda. Absent or participant, these were the representative voices that had dominated the Kampala conference. It was the humanism, the vision of their work that inscribed for us the new Africa. Now, where was that Africa? How does a nation like Rwanda overcome its recent history?

I visited slaughter spots, spoke to survivors and to some liberation fighters. The survivors included Hutu, accused of being Tutsi sympathizers – does this echo the pariah status of America's own 'nigger lovers' among their own white kinfolk? Many had lost entire families – those 'sympathizers' were, in some cases, treated with far greater vindictiveness than the Tutsis, but of course, it was the Tutsi that bore the full brunt of the killers' eradication policies.

One killing-ground was now a field of wooden crosses, bare of the luxury of headstones. There at least, the bodies were interred. Then I was taken to a memorial museum, an hour's ride on a pot-holed laterite road from Kigali. It had been conceived around the prospect of an optimistically named 'Peace Park', and it honoured the name of Nelson Mandela. The rough shelves contained only 5,000 skulls, only – because there was still the larger museum that we could not visit for lack of time, one that housed 50,000 remains of Rwandan humanity. After that particular slaughter, bulldozers had been commandeered to heap earth over the corpses. And so, following liberation by the army of exiled Tutsi and dissenting Hutu, bulldozers were again brought in to disinter them, then human hands cleaned the skeletons, pieced them together and recorded them. In the Mandela Park, a church had been preserved where the victims had holed up, seeking sanctuary. They were slaughtered in that building, and that is where their remains are kept, preserved where they fell until the skin and flesh fell off and only the blood-caked apparel remained as shrouds for the bones. Very few skulls bore bullet-holes; they were mostly panga-slashed. Embedded to the hilt in one child's skull, most eloquently of all, was a crude knife.

There was, apparently, a going fee for the privilege of being killed swiftly, by a bullet. For thousands who could not afford it, or who were simply not given the chance, it was painful, cruel death – limb by limb, disembowelment – sometimes the tendons were first severed to ensure that the victims remained in place as their torturers took time off to attend to others, or simply take a pause for a meal or a drink, orchestrating a drawn-out tempo for each victim in the dance of death. There were stories, there remained landmarks – and body scars – for nearly every tale, including tales of heroism and self-sacrifice. I understood then what he meant, that general from the United Nations peacekeeping force, who could only convey what he had witnessed in the words: 'I know now that there is God, because I have seen the face of the devil.'

In the early 1960s, at the gathering of our tribe of artists in Kampala, we also believed that there was good, because we had known the face of evil. But evil then wore the face of the Belgians (who are still inculpated in the Rwandan massacres), the faces of the British, the Portuguese, the Dutch, French, Spaniards and Arabs. That conference had placed us strategically in a region through which the trans-Saharan slave route had passed, once upon a not so remote time, a region where slave raids had consumed millions of black humanity – Zanzibar, Tanzania, Uganda, Congo – where our own kind had been hunted down, just as the Tutsi recently were, but only to feed that previous time the markets of Oman, Saudi Arabia, Yemen. Thousands of miles away in their own turn, the very existence and composition of the populations of the Caribbean islands, North and South America, survivors of the European transatlantic slave routes, remain far more eloquent than any history text in identifying to us, even long before then, what faces were responsible for the most quantitatively pernicious act of dehumanization that the world has ever known. We, however, represented the good, the descendants of those victims, those upon whose genetic template memory had embossed the words 'Never Again'. We saw our generation as the cubs of a continent's transformation waiting to spring – but only into creative vistas of a limitless future. No, we did not foresee Rwanda, or a strictly internalized replay of those slave hunts that devastated much of our continent.

In seeking explanations, however, even as events such as the Rwandan massacres cannot fail to trigger off relative scenarios of the past, so do they also interrogate parallels of lesser kinds in contemporary times, instituting mental courts of self-indictment, exposing evidence of internal complicities that lead, inexorably, to a recognition of a persistent pattern of criminalities that were once unthinkable. Such abandonment of our humanity is not new, and it is a good thing that memory continues to serve as a corrective to our moral complacencies, even to the dangers of an undialectical assumption of a victim status.

I have addressed myself to the possibility that this, perhaps, is what informs the superhuman, indeed near transcendental, principle of forgiveness that underlies South Africa's project of Truth and Reconciliation. In other words, that its generosity, its seeming accommodativeness, is an acknowledgement of a troubled memory, the memory of our own past complicities in our history of dehumanization, all the way from the slave centuries to the Rwandan massacres. In short, quite apart from the political considerations, the pragmatism that produced the agreements that ended apartheid, we cannot rule out the possibility that, in confronting the claims of strict justice, of the retributive instincts, there could also have been a background functioning of memory as a check against the assumption of the chaste separation of victims from the criminal status of violators. The dangers of such a retraction, especially its implicit – even though unintended – encouragement of the culture of impunity, undoubtedly receives more than adequate attention in debates by other contributors in this book.

Let us resume our attention to the claims that memory makes to a permanent space in the annals of racial encounters, and the unequal relationships that still plague our continent, both internally, and with the rest of the world. It is not difficult to establish an abundance of reasons why the history of slavery must continue to plague the memory of the world. Principal among these are the simple facts that the history of humanity is incomplete without this acknowledgement, and that the history of the African continent, including its economic history, would remain truncated without it. Next, objectively, the Atlantic slave trade remains an inescapable critique of European humanism. In a different context, I've railed against the thesis that it was the Jewish Holocaust that placed the first question mark on all claims of European humanism – from the Renaissance to the Enlightenment to the present-day multicultural orientation. Insistence on that thesis, we must continue to maintain, merely provides further proof that the European mind has yet to come into full cognition of the African world as an equal sector of a universal humanity – for if it had, its historic recollection would have placed the failure of European humanism centuries earlier, and that would be at the very inception of the Atlantic slave trade. This, we remind ourselves, was an enterprise that voided a continent, it is estimated, of some 20 million souls and transported them across the Atlantic under conditions of brutality that are yet to be equalled by any other encounter between races. The cry for reparations, therefore, from this point of view, as a structure of memory and critique, may be regarded as a necessity for the credibility of Eurocentric historicism and a corrective for its exclusionist world view.

More than qualifiable humanity was lost to that continent. The slave trade also ruptured the organic economic systems of much of the continent. It is a distortion – compounded later, of course, by the imposition of colonial priorities in raw materials for Europe's industrial needs and the advent of multinational conglomerates – that is surely partly responsible for the intractable economic problems of the continent.

Was the partitioning of Africa by the imperial powers simply a geographical violation of a people's right of coming-into-being as a nation? Only if we insist on believing that political instability within the so-called nations that make up the continent today owes nothing whatever to the artificiality, the sheer illogic of their boundaries. It is therefore appropriate to add partitioning to the wrongs that underlie the cry for reparations for Africa, and surely such a claim would be unanswerable.

The only problem with this is that African nations since independence have possessed it within their will to redress this particular wrong, even where evidently and bitterly contested, to launch their own internal reparations for the deprivation of organic identities and its costly consequences. Obviously, no outsider, least of all the original perpetrators of this misdeed, can be entrusted with such an undertaking – another Berlin Conference of former colonizers to redraw the present boundaries of the continent? That would transgress even the most generous boundaries of absurdity.

Beginning with the Organization of African Unity, which formally consecrated this act of aggression, reinforced by civil wars on varied scales of mutual destruction in defence of the imperial mandate, the continent as a whole appears to have swallowed intact this explosive seed of disunity under the ironic banner of unity. If only African leaders could become acquainted with how much – to illustrate the hollowness of such beginnings – the division of India and Pakistan, for instance, and the allocation of their respective boundaries, owed to the whimsical decisions of a mere civil servant imported straight from Whitehall. Someone who had never visited the Asian continent until then, but was selected for the objective distancing that that very ignorance was presumed to confer upon him, was given a deadline of a mere 28 days to complete his task in order to ensure that that continent was effectively divided before Independence Day. Such leaders and cheerleaders would be much less cocky about the many claims of national sovereignty. Much of the division of Africa owed more to a case of brandy and a box of cigars than to any intrinsic claims about what the boundaries enclose.

Reparation and Reconciliation

Cultural and spiritual violations – we may as well complete the catalogue – have left indelible imprints on the collective psyche and sense of identity of the peoples, a process that was ensured with savage repressions of coherent traditions by successive waves of colonizing hordes. The presence of these hordes was both physical and abstract. Their mission was not merely to implant their own peoples in any lands whose climates were congenial – East and Southern Africa in particular – but to establish outposts for surrogate controls where the environment proved physically inclement. West Africa owed much to its humidity and the mosquito, a fact that was often celebrated by the early generational wave of nationalists. One political party in pre-independence Nigeria actually selected the mosquito as its party symbol. The British were not amused and promptly proscribed it. The cultural and spiritual savaging of the continent, let us hasten to add, was not by the Christian-European axis alone. The Arab-Islamic dimension preceded it and was every bit as devastating, a fact that a rather distorted sense of continental solidarity leads some scholars to edit out at the expense of truth and reality. It is time we silenced this revisionist trend. Do we have, for instance, on that same continent – if indeed we do decide that reparations are essential for the enthronement of a new harmonized order of global relationships – do we have on that same land mass called Africa those from whom reparations should be demanded?

Not all African voices are united or are comfortable with these questions, but truth goes with reparation and reconciliation and there can be no evasion. Those who preach the gospel of reparations must be prepared to accompany their claim to its logical conclusion. At a conference on that very subject held in Abuja, the capital of Nigeria, in 1991, an uncomfortable moment was reached when the issue of Arab participation in the slave trade could no longer be evaded. The movement for reparations on the African continent was initiated, spearheaded and heavily funded by that maverick of a businessman turned politician, an early pan-Africanist, by the way, a fact about him that was very little publicized in his lifetime, but more pertinently, the late elected president of Nigeria, Chief Mashood Abiola. He died on 7 July 1998, after a debilitating four years in the dungeons of the dictator, Sani Abacha, for the crime of winning the 1993 presidential elections and insisting on his mandate. Abiola's campaign for reparations was taken up by the government of Nigeria at a meeting of the Organization of African Unity in Abuja in 1992. Since then, the reparations movement has become an intergovernmental project for the commission and the OAU. Now that provokes a number of ethical issues.

There has to be a moral foundation to all quests of equity. 'He who comes to the court of equity', says the Latin proverb, 'must approach with clean hands.' A crusade that is based on moral rights is obviously undermined by an impurity of conduct in its proponents. The complicity, both through active collaboration and through silence, of the majority of African nations in the death of this man, vitiates any cries for redress for crimes against the continent by the outside world.

To return to that conference, however, over which the late Mashood Abiola presided, the issue of Arab participation in the slave trade was finally addressed. Sitting on the commission was a member of the International Committee on Reparations, a Tunisian diplomat, an Arab. He found himself compelled to confront the paradox of his presence as a member of that committee. His response was a safe one – not original, but safe. Unlike some African apologists and, indeed, a handful of African-American scholars and ideologues of certain persuasion, he did not attempt a pointless denial of a historical reality. He simply countered with a proposition that, since we are all victims of colonial oppression, we should act together with solidarity against the common oppressor and obliterate that part of our divisive history. Of course, he then had to confront the logical follow-up, that the entire nature of the reparations movement should be changed, that it should even be renamed altogether – Reparations Movement for Victims of Colonialism, perhaps – but then this would dilute the original cause, require a totally different orientation and strategy. It would expand to embrace the indigenes of North and South America, Australia and New Zealand. In short, this is one way of ensuring that a manifesto for reparations ends up as a permanent study document on the tables of the United Nations.

So for now, at least, let us restrict ourselves to that burden of memory that a continent seeks to exorcize through the strategy of reparations. We are obliged to proceed from facts, not sentiment, and the following facts are indisputable: that, from the West, the Euro-Christian armies of conquest, hard on the heels of missionaries and early adventurers called explorers, plundered and looted African civilizations, burning and smashing priceless carvings, which, from their point of view, were nothing but manifestations of idolatry and satanism. But some, of course, like Frebenius, had different tastes. They looted the shrines and sent their treasures home to museums as trophies. Conversion to Christianity was admittedly sometimes achieved by persuasion; often it was enforced through military conquests, terror of enslavement, and punitive economic controls. A world view that separated humanity into the saved and the dammed, the latter being qualified for mass deportation to distant lands as beasts of burden, provides at least a *prima facie* case for a preliminary hearing in the Court of Reparations. We can proceed to use it as a yardstick of criminal responsibility. Was the Orient of the Arab–Islamic record an improvement? Georges Hardy had this comment on its iconoclastic rampage, and it sums up that record impartially. He wrote, 'Islam began the work of destruction but Europe did a better job.'

The fate that overtook the arts was the same as that inflicted on society overall. From the west coast of Africa to southern Africa the story is the same – conversions for the glory of an equally alien deity. Nothing that the Islamic invaders encountered was sacred. All was profane except the sword and the Book of Allah. They set the precedent for compelling converts to shed their indigenous names, names that narrated their beginnings and conferred upon them their individual and historic identities. They inaugurated the era of slavery on the black continent for Arab slave markets. The routes of slave caravans began in the central and eastern heartlands of the continent, stretched through northern Africa to Saudi Arabia, passed over the waters by slave dhows from Madagascar and Dar es Salaam to Yemen, Oman, etc. Even today, you'll encounter ghettos in many Arab countries, peopled entirely by descendants of those slaves. And thus, we see that often it is the enduring vestiges of the past that constitute the greatest obstacles to the alleviation of the burden of memory, and this is one burden that not even the thesis of comparative humanism can alleviate.

For we do encounter sometimes intensely argued apologia from some of our own African and African-American scholars, who inform us that the condition of the slave under Arab slave-owners was far more humane than under the Europeans and Americans. That may be demonstrable. Presumably, such a search would involve, in the former instance, only those who did survive the trans-Saharan route. I do not imagine that evidence in the form of extant engravings of slaves on the caravan routes dying the slow death of thirst and floggings would bear this out any more than the clinical reports of losses by the merchant middlemen. The French would also dispute such a thesis, at least where the female slaves were concerned. To the French, slavery was all very well, but in the territory of exotic libido and its socialization, at least in those times, there was no question at all that a black woman was in every way the equal, indeed, the superior, of her white counterpart. The *signares* of Senegal, mistresses of French slavers, inaugurated a tradition of social acceptability that was even translated into French law, protecting the *café au lait* products of such liaisons and indeed guaranteeing unprecedented rights to the slave partner. From the *signares'* point of view, any claims to a greater degree of humanism by other slaving cultures would be simply laughable – equality in bed, backed by open domestic bliss, social acceptance and French law? What more could a slave desire?

But let the thesis stand. It simply appears to me rather presumptuous to attempt to offer absolution to the practitioner of a dehumanizing trade through an exercise in comparative degrees of abuse. In any case, we can leave that argument in the capable hands of the various revisionist schools of Cliometrics, Fogel and Company. To stir up those murky waters even more, hasn't the latest testifier, Keith Richburg, made a strong case for the opposing thesis? Such is the quality of blessing he accords to the deportation of his forebears and their luck in being selected for the American soil that his recently published book *Out of America* just stops short of proposing that Thanksgiving Day be shifted to the day that the first African slave – hopefully, his own direct ancestor – first set foot on American soil. That, of course, is only one in the variety of weaponry in the arsenal that is mounted directly or indirectly against the battle for reparations.

Warped though Mr Richburg's conclusion may be deemed, we must acknowledge as a valid corrective his endeavour to direct our attention to the cumulative effects of social mismanagement of the African continent – a catalogue of disasters that owe their origin to human criminality, lending persuasion to the position that the movement for reparations is untenable because it has become undeserved. Keith Richburg's contemptuous dismissal of the proponents of reparations is one with which I confess I feel more than a little sympathy. His book refers to reparations only in passing, but it does provide a partial critique that cannot be ignored. If we insist on the one hand that the issue is, at the very least, a useful critique of European historicism, we cannot in all honesty ignore the proposition that it also serves as a critique of African historicism. This latter is not an abstract issue but an immediate, accusing reality. This is why I, for one, can only express gratitude to Mr Richburg for his searing indictment not only of a continent that has abandoned its humanity and desecrated its memory, but of his own countrymen and women for conduct that confers legitimacy on the inheritors of the external career of enslavement, and thus obscures truthful apprehension both of memory and of our history in the making.

Let the following passage serve as a summation of our own bitterness and frustration and the thoughtlessness of our American relations. Mr Richburg is narrating a familiar scene of uncritical hero-worshipping that has become the trademark of black American leaders at any encounter with our continent's leadership froth. He writes about Captain Valentine Strasser, the former dictator of Sierra Leone:

> When Strasser entered the meeting hall, sporting his now trademark sunglasses and his camouflage battle fatigues, the crowd of mostly middle- and upper-class black Americans went wild with cheering, swooning from the women, some hoots and frenzied applause. Sitting in that hall you might be forgiven for thinking Strasser was a music celebrity instead of a puny dictator. Those black Americans were obviously more impressed with the macho military image Strasser cut than with the fact that he represents all that is wrong with Africa – military thugs who take power and thwart the continent's fledgling effort toward democracy. The chanting and hooting was a disgusting display and to me, it highlighted the complete ignorance about Africa among the American so-called black elite.

A people who do not preserve their memory are a people who have forfeited their history – I have adapted these words from Elie Wiesel and Danielle Mitterrand during a conference on Memory and Nations. It is therefore quite fitting that UNESCO has committed itself to the preservation of the slave route, establishing a scientific committee to document, preserve and open up the landmarks of the slave routes for posterity. That in itself constitutes an act of reparation – whether we like it or not, reparation is still reparation by any other name. Reparation is not monetary recompense.

Long before this undertaking, African-Americans made pilgrimages to the Isle of Goree, visited the forts and slave monuments of Accra, Cape Coast, Dar es Salaam and Zanzibar, entered the tunnels and dungeons where their ancestors had suffered and agonized about what gods they had failed to placate to have brought down such a calamity on their heads. I have myself partaken of such reminders, for these are as much a part of our history, we, the stay-at-homes, as much a part of our collective racial trauma, as they are of those who were forcibly displaced. But is that all it can be, should be – an evocation of trauma several centuries removed, an immersion in accusatory and guilt-ridden history? Every landmark is a testament of history and, in our own indelible instance – from Goree to the slave ports of Ghana, Zanzibar – all the forts and stockades, increasingly turned into museums, are filled with grim evocations of this passage of our history. They are indices of truth, an essence and a reality that offer any people, however impoverished, a value in itself, a value that, especially when rooted in anguish and sacrifice, may dictate a resolve for redemption and strategies for social regeneration. To act in any way that denigrates the lessons, the imperatives of that truth, for demagogic or opportunistic reasons, is to pollute a people's source and declare a new round of exterior control of a people's heritage.

That comment is inserted as a repeat of an earlier warning, provoked by the demagogic and influential black nationalist school of revisionism, earlier hinted at, in the United States, which has tried to place the responsibility for our slavehood passage squarely in the court of one racial group – the Jewish – through a singular feat of historic distortion, elusion and manipulation. We can only plead with them, 'Please do not tarnish our collective memories.' Undeniably, within that convenient scapegoat group (and what racial group totally escapes intact from participation at some commercial or ownership level or the other in the degrading traffic?) records do exist of individuals who indeed owned slaves and traded in them. But those who are embroiled in an anti-Semitic agenda should at least hold inviolate the authority of our shared history, and not engage in distortions of a proven reality for their private warfare. We have not yet even arrived at a unanimity over the viability of the project of reparations, and yet here we have a tendency that is determined to divert the history and heritage of millions into a futile cul-de-sac of racial or political animosities and alliances.

Truth and Forgiveness

As a humanist actively engaged, for most of my mature existence, in confronting all encroachments on or distortions of the self-retrieval of my kind – and this centres on a truthful, but critical embrace of our past –

I find these games simply insulting to racial intelligence and contemptuous of the humanity that exercises such intelligence. In addition, do they conceal an agenda of distraction? It is not possible for us to ignore the actuality of brutal conflicts on our own continent, some as blatantly race-derived as those between Senegal and Mauritania within this decade and even the more intractable ongoing conflict in the Sudan – a conflict that has entailed over three decades of carnage, with the possible consequences of social disintegration of an enduring nature. The indigenous culture of Sudan is totally imperilled as never before, but by whom? Does it matter? Have we a duty to be concerned or threatened?

Let us briefly digress and examine the general implications of these diversionary antics for the rest of the continent. In consonance with other contributory factors to Africa's seeming destiny of instability, such as the yoke of colonial boundaries, there is this issue of internal cultural retention and a straining towards a reharmonization with the past. By this I mean simply this: if we succeeded in leapfrogging backwards in time over the multiple insertions of the contending forces of dissension, be they of the West or the Orient, and with all their mutually destructive schisms and fragmentations of ideology, religion and so on, and by this process we were able to regain a measure of anterior self-knowledge, it may be possible to regard religio-cultural interventions as possibly no more than disruptive illusions whose ramifications hold the future in thrall. In any case, how recent in the history of mankind are some of these intrusions?

Of course, there is no suggestion here that the accretions of such interventions be abandoned on all fronts, not in the least. One does not shed the weight of centuries simply as a snake sloughs off its winter or harmattan skin. Our proposition is simply one of recollection or, to go back to our commencing code, that of memory, the need for the preservation of the material and spiritual properties by which memory is invested, the acceptance of both its burdens and triumphs, or better still, its actuality, the simple fact of its anterior existence and its validity for its time. Within such a frame of mind, we begin to recognize the irrationality of mutual destructiveness on behalf of any values whatever, however seductive – cultural, ideological, religious or race-authenticated – that intervened, and obscured or eroded those multiple anteriorities, of whatever kind, from which our being took its definition. These for us remain the warnings and lessons of the Sudanese conflict or the Rwandan.

In our own time in Sudan, a culture is being raped, as if Africa had regressed to the battlefronts of the thirteenth and fourteenth centuries. There have been other, less publicized, but no less bloody race- and religion-inspired conflicts in other parts of the continent. We cannot sincerely address these sobering eruptions on our continent without recourse to the suspended questions of memory, and without interrogating the agenda, disguised or overt, of those whose distortions of history prevent a proper apprehension of that history by the rest of the world, and especially among our own kind – the captive impressionable audiences seeking visible, identifiable targets for their immediate predicament, upon whom the mentors exercise their will to populist authority. Like it or not, imprecise and speculative although it may appear to those ensconced in the security of academia, the memory and vestiges of slavehood relations lie at the heart of a number of these conflicts and, until the enthronement of truth and the fulfilment of the imperatives of its recognition, the possibility of reconciliation remains a chimera.

Unlike the idealists of history, for whom history is an impersonal totem, a Utopian projection thrust into the future by the unstoppable potency of some abstracted, extrapolated will and, nearer still, unlike the materialist, Marxist revision of that persuasion whose restitution of the human entity to history is no less reductive of that very entity, the human entity, rendering it subservient to its own Utopian vision, we insist on the determinant and purpose of history as the human entity in and for itself even as asserted by W. H. DuBois. 'It is easy', Dubois writes, 'to lose ourselves in details in endeavoring to grasp and comprehend the real condition of a mass of human beings. We often forget that each unit in the mass is a throbbing human soul. It loves and hates. It toils and tires. It laughs and weeps in bitter tears and looks in vague and awful longing at the grim horizon of its life.'

It would be false to claim that I recollected those words as I first stood on the beach of embarkation at Ouidah on the slave route in present-day Benin. But unquestionably, there were such echoes in my mind, echoes of innumerable reminders of this most elementary truth of the human condition, one that does not permit the luxury or the arrogance of abstractionist games in the quest for a humane order. Of all the landmarks of slavery that I have ever traversed, none, not even in the grim tunnels of Goree, Cape Coast, once smoothed by the yet echoing slaps of feet on the passage into Hell, could match the eerie evocation of the walk towards the embarkation point on the coast of Ouidah in the Republic of Benin, then known as the Kingdom of Dahomey. I clearly felt the inadequacy of words as I tried to set down what was clearly a collective experience of that day. Still, the following did aspire to be a faithful record of that experience. I wrote:

We traversed the actual route taken by the slaves on their way to embarkation, stood on the spot from which they cast their last look on homelands, over the grounds where thousands of the weak and the ill and thus, commercial handicaps had been slaughtered and buried. We stood also on Suicide Point where hundreds had broken their bonds and plunged to a kinder death than what the unknown threatened in their imagination. We visited slave museums, passed by the ancestral home of the descendants of a slave merchant, a Portuguese who had settled down to a polygamous existence and fathered numerous mulattos. We ran our fingers over antiquated cannons, metallic restrainers and other instruments of torture, passed over flat stones once smoothed by the boots of slave owners and the bare feet of slaves. In the museum were original sketches and water colors of slave bazaars, royal ceremonials at which slaves were ritualistically beheaded, open air receptions for the officers of merchant vessels, scenes from slave raids and weepy embarkation scenes from which the artists, all European, had attempted to extract the maximum pathos.

No experience, however, could match the long walk through clumps of mangrove and palm, in which clutches of huts and palm fronds encased compounds in pristine preservation, along the only safe path through treacherous marine ponds and mangrove swamps. As if by common consent, we breathed gently as if we feared to disturb a somnolent air that had lain on the earth, seemingly undisturbed for centuries ... and so all the way to Embarkation Point and the place of no return. Those who know only the dictionary meaning of pilgrimage experienced its essence that morning. It was sobering, reflective and paradoxically devoid of all feelings of hatred, vengeance, not even indictment. There was only a quiescent residuum of history, as palpable reality, as truth.

Now it is possible that some wrongs have a magnitude that transcends feelings of vengeance, even desire for redress in any form – a kind of crimino-critical mass after which wrongs and suffering are transmuted into a totally different state of sensibility from which can only derive a sense of peace, a space of truth that overawes all else and chastens the human, moral dimension. It is not a surrender to evil, not a condoning of wrongs. Perhaps it is akin to a balm that comes after a cataclysm of nature, even when clearly of man's making. It overrides grief and despair, diffuses rage, infuses one with a sense of purgation, the aftermath of true tragic apprehension. At such rare moments memory ceases to be a burden. It becomes a quiescent stock-taking, an affirmation of existence in the present and a resolve in defence of unborn generations.

We remain conscious of and must build on our heritage of glories, but the self-inflicted passages of ignominy also remain to indict our present. Scenes of African slave-lords decapitating their own kind for the delectation of officers from slave-ships provide some of the most chastening images for us in the archives of slavery. Of course, even our own oral history provides unambiguous testimonies on the fatal delinquency of our own kind. The conduct of traditional rulers in thrall to new military enslavers is therefore only a bitter reprise of our history.

Conclusion

My own Nigeria, always at the forefront of such obscenities, is again criss-crossed today by sycophantic trails of slime along which crawl the erstwhile majesties of obis, abas and emirs in homage to the new slave-masters in military uniform. One after the other, they slither and slide, tumble over one another, grapple with one another by the trail of their robes and royal sceptres in an effort to be first at the ritual of self-abasement at the feet of some thug with a swagger stick. The tradition of withdrawal and seclusion in the face of superior forces is abandoned as are their people, for the brief replenishment from contracts and preferments. Not for them the silent symbol whose absence speaks volumes and infuses resistance with more than mystic blessing.

Are these the kings of whom the griots sang? Are these their descend-ants? We do not know them but we know from which lines – between those who resisted and those who fawned upon the presence of their enslavers – the majority of these are descended. We know the difference between Oba Ovevhamwen, whose defiance of the British led to the sacking of Benin in the eighteenth century, and the present incumbent of his throne. Ile-Ife, the cradle of my own people, the Yoruba, indeed of the black races all over the world, is today an alms-house tenanted by a mendicant, who surely makes his ancestors drown the heavenly rafters with their tears. If, in a freak teleological reversal, the world were to follow Napoleon's example and reinstate slavery after its abolition – maybe our planet is invaded and the United Nations is subjected to a new definition of humanism by superbeings from outer space – we recognize among us those who would be first in line to offer up their own kith and kin as slaves; their genealogy is branded on their foreheads like the mark of Cain. The righteous armour of demand for ancient wrongs is therefore sadly dented.

The ignominious role of the ancient rulers continues into the present, serves to remind us of their complicity in the cause for which reparations are sought. Without their collaboration, with their commitment to the protection of their kind, the slave trade would have been stemmed at source. Even if the African continent had been devastated as a consequence – well, why speculate? We only know that the continent was devastated by their choice and that their complicity, echoed today in the politics of power, clouds what should have been a clear division between victim and violator. Nevertheless, the principle of recompense can be elicited both from objective criteria and from the regard of the European and Asian worlds towards their own histories. We cannot dismiss a process that boasts the virtue of calling flawed historicism into question and enables us to criminalize the internal continuum of an external violation.

We can and must exorcize the burden of memory, but only by such strategies that do not sanitize the residuum of an unexpiated past, be this of external inflictions or the culpability of internal collaborators. In this context, therefore, the call for reparations remains a potent instrument for that internal awakening into an era of global healing, ushering in an era of a reconciliation that is surely the hope of humanity in this new millennium.

Bibliography

DuBois, W. E. B. (1992) *The Souls of Black Folks*, in John Hope Franklin (ed.), *Three Negro Classics*, New York: Avon Books.

Hardy, G. (1927) *L'Art Negre*, Paris: Edition H. Laurens.

Richburg, K. B. (1997) *Out of America*, New York: Basic Books, p. 17.

Soyinka, W. (1999) *The Burden of Memory: The Muse of Forgiveness*, New York: Oxford University Press.

2

The Politics of Memory: Biafra and Intellectual Responsibility

Ifi Amadiume

The international elite may celebrate the charisma of globalization, and not surprisingly oppressed Third World peoples see the logic of globalization in their experiences of imperialism and capitalism. Today, Nelson Mandela is presented as a model of reconciliation and peace, yet it was the same repressive logic of apartheid that denied public space to Mandela because of its totalizing agenda, which forbade free movement and free speech. Passports were seized, voices, books and thought banned, civil organizations repressed and crushed. There was therefore a multiple assault on memory. In the standardized rhetoric of global human rights, we have deviated very much from the more authentic position that saw truth and reconciliation as squarely linked with social justice.

On 24 March 1998, a CNN report of President Bill Clinton's visit to Africa informed us that Africa is three times the size of the United States of America, and then followed this statement with images of disease, chaos and war. This was darkest Africa! It prepared the grounds for Clinton to shine the light, contradicting claims that the visit was intended to provide a positive image that would correct the negative portrayal of Africa in the United States. Truths were mixed with false statements. One truth was the admission that Africans were pawns in the Cold War, while America pursued a policy that enriched repressive dictators and impoverished the mass of African people. Even this truth is again falsified by the claim that aid bred dependency, hence a policy change to trade, and not just aid. These statements on changed US policy on Africa were marked by a deafening silence on Nigeria.

US policy on Nigeria has been under review for over three years ever since the United States rejected the general call for full sanctions on the Nigerian military, following the framing, imprisonment and hanging of Ogoni environmental activist Ken Saro Wiwa and eight of his fellow activists. Since 1962, the USA has spent $32 billion in specific places like

Somalia and Liberia. Not much came out of it, and now the USA wants to facilitate business interest and entry, particularly private money. Clinton's 1998 trip was therefore seen by Africans as motivated by American economic interests rather than a genuine commitment to democratization or human rights, areas in which African activists accuse the USA of a double standard.

African activist writer Wole Soyinka is again a leading voice for justice. He is perhaps one of the most engaging intellectual activists of our time. You could almost say that resistance and struggle are his life. I want to focus on Soyinka to examine critically the question of justice in the context of Biafra and the responsibility of the intelligentsia to lead by voice and action in conflict situations.

Biafra, Soyinka and Social Justice

I begin with these quotes from his prison notes.

Books and all forms of writing have always been objects of terror to those who seek to suppress truth.

The man dies in all who keep silent in the face of tyranny.

In any people that submit willingly to the 'daily humiliation of fear', the man dies.

Wole Soyinka, 14 December 1971 (*The Man Died*, 1975)

In his personal narrative on the Nigerian crisis, Soyinka (1996) warned that the possibility of civil war or separation was again real in Nigeria. Not only was this real, it was in fact the popular discourse, and Soyinka argued that this went back to long before Nigerian independence in 1960. The northern Nigerian counter-coup makers of July 1966, leaders of different ethnic groups and General Yakubu Gowon, all declared that there was no basis for unity. But only the Igbo-led Biafran movement, which included other ethnicities and all classes, actually took a decisive action to end its own involvement in what was and still is seen as a glaring unequal and forced union.

As a result of the denial of the 12 June 1993 electoral victory to Chief Mashood Abiola, Soyinka, who was opposed to the Biafran separation, insisting on a unified Nigeria, now took a different position: 'I frankly could not advance any invulnerable reason for my preference for a solution that did not involve disintegration' (Soyinka 1996: 31). He went on to pronounce what, with the sudden and suspicious death of Chief Abiola under prison conditions on 7 July 1998 came to haunt us as an ominous prophecy: 'Alas, if that election of June 12 proves indeed to be ancient history, then – and do take this as prophecy – Nigeria as a nation has no future history' (ibid.: 131–2). I believe what Soyinka is saying is that the democratic mandate of the people is a divine one. It cannot be annulled or invalidated by tyrants, or the very basis of nationhood is denied.

If the quest for justice cannot be totally suppressed by tyrants, then, there is no escaping the burden of the memory of Biafra, and Soyinka admitted it then in 1967 when he reasoned that the departure of the Igbos would expunge the Nigerian nation of the guilt of genocide. He was presumably saying that the Igbos should stay in the union to serve as the moral conscience of the nation. He again recalled the memory of Biafra in 1996 as he ridiculed those who wish to suppress or erase the factual national importance of the history of Biafra. I want to quote Soyinka in full on this matter, since he admitted unambiguously the continuing relevance of the Biafran experience. With satire, he wrote,

> There are of course those dissenting biographers and historians, the Establishment record-keepers who insist on writing and speaking of Biafra in inverted commas, in a coy, sanctimonious denial of a reality. We should even encourage them to write it *B—ra* or invent any other childish contrivance, like a literary talisman programmed to create a lacuna in a history that dogs our conscience and collective memory; every day still reminds us that the factors that led to Biafra neither were ephemeral nor can be held to be permanently exorcised. (Soyinka 1996: 32)

In the face of current events in Nigeria, the regression from military dictatorship to fictitious, political ethnicity, we must look back to Biafran history. The current situation amounts to a tragic admission that 3 million people died[1] in vain, since, 29 years after the end of the Biafran war, we are still where we started – military dictatorship and the insistence that only a northern-led clique and its southern collaborators and stooges, who include self-appointed so-called Igbo leaders, must hold political power at the centre. No wonder, then, the general change of position and current challenge to the unimaginative and formalized rhetoric of 'non-negotiability' of Nigerian unity that is contradicted by process. The talk is either non-negotiability or a controlled power-shift to favoured individuals, regardless of popular opinion.

In spite of the mystification of reality by the state, the fact remains that material experiences resulting from economic and social decline since the end of the war in 1970 provide practical knowledge that contradicts claims made in Yakubu Gowon's victory speech. On 15 January 1970, Gowon claimed that the federal objective was the preservation of the territorial integrity and unity of Nigeria, on the grounds that only unity would guarantee peace, rapid economic development, a dignified future and respect in the world. Nothing could be further from the truth: Nigeria is presently one of the most reviled nations in the world. Another falsehood was also pronounced when Gowon went on to say:

> The so-called rising sun of Biafra is set forever. It will be a great disservice for anyone to continue to use the word Biafra to refer to any part of the East Central State of Nigeria. The tragic chapter of violence is just ended. We are at the dawn of national reconciliation. Once again, we have an opportunity to build a new nation. (Yakubu Gowon 1970: 37)

Especially because the Biafrans were defeated, prohibiting an open discourse on the Biafran war was a bad policy: it denied ordinary civilian victims a chance to express their suffering, grief and anger. They were denied the right to tell their own truth and expose the wounds of the past, which remain hidden in Nigeria's body politic. The unvoiced suffering of trauma continues to surface at critical moments. Biafra remains an unfinished business. At the political level, there is no closure, hence its potency as a political instrument, with intellectuals, the military and politicians indulging themselves in the politics of amnesia and selective memory of the Nigerian civil war, the official Nigerian term of reference.

Since those on the Biafran side were gagged by defeat and fear, one must ask what prevented intellectuals on the federal side from having a dialogue on a home war that saw so much civilian suffering and so many casualties.[2] What is the responsibility of the intellectuals? How did they remain silent and allow the generals, the perpetrators of war, to monopolize the recording and telling of this story?[3]

In the case of South Africa, the Truth and Reconciliation Commission (TRC) is a vehicle of revelation and reconciliation for crimes under the apartheid system, but is deemed not adequate for serious criminal trials, like the war crime tribunals for the genocides in Bosnia and Rwanda. I believe the question has been raised: why blame the system in one case, and punish the victims in another? Punitive action and casualties only strengthened the resolve of the Biafrans, because for them it was a matter of human pride and survival, having continued as victims of genocide to victims of war. Biafrans were subjected to a second humiliation when the federal government waged a war against the Eastern Region from 1967 to 1970.

Power-sharing or Secession

Nigeria came into being as a British colonial invention at the beginning of the twentieth century[4] and gained independence in 1960. Today, with over 120 million people, Nigeria has the highest population in Africa. Its economy now ranks fourth in size behind South Africa, Algeria and Egypt. In spite of rich oil and mineral resources, its average GNP has declined to an estimated US $310. With 36 states and 706 local government councils, its urban population is about 20 per cent; over 80 per cent dwell in the rural areas.

Nigeria is multilingual with over 395 languages; multi-ethnic, with over 250 ethnic groups; multi-religious, with diverse expressions of Islam, Christianity and African religions; and multi-class, with a diversity of interest and power groups. It is a highly developed nation in civic political consciousness and trade union activism, where every interest vies for power, including organized women's groups. Yet, at the formal level of power, in its 38 years as an independent nation it has been ruled by a civilian government only twice – the government of Tafawa Balewa and that of Shehu Shagari. Both were Muslim northerners and both were accused of corruption by the military in rationalizing a military takeover of government. The majority 28 years have been under the rule of military dictators who took power by a violent coup. Therefore, civil injustice and the abuse of human rights are structural in the Nigerian state system, and have their genesis in colonial violence. Much as contemporary scholars and activists appear to have suffered some loss of memory, the cause of justice was behind the Biafran secessionist movement.

The Biafran secession was the first attempt to break the neo-colonial structural arrangement, since it insisted on equal participation and power-sharing or separation. For this reason, the Western powers and the OAU, whose policies were seen as more interested in protecting imperialism and capital than democracy or human rights, saw Biafra as a threat. Instead of supporting the cause of justice in equal participation and equitable re-distribution, they defended colonial boundaries in the name of unity.

In reality, what did unity translate into? Economic interest for the West. R. G. Armstrong, on 1 September 1967, gave a policy advice article to the US State Department. The Nigerian embassy arranged for the same article to be published in the *Morning Post*, Lagos on 16 and 23 September 1967. Armstrong was advising on how to transform the Biafran conflict into a pure ethnic one by isolating the Igbos. The strategy was to whip up anti-Igbo sentiment and strengthen the Eastern and Midwestern minorities against the Igbos, and prevent the Biafrans from consolidating possession of the oil resources. He wrote: 'Most of the proven oil lies on non-Ibo land. Some of the very best wells are on Ikwerri land, which also includes the city of Port Harcourt. Although the Ikwerri language may be related to Ibo, one must ask whether linguistic affinity is a title to land, including especially oil-bearing land (Armstrong 1967: 11).

By then, it had been discovered that Nigeria was going to be a major world oil producer. An anthropologist turned State Department informer, Armstrong said that he was writing as an American citizen. American interest was thus foremost in his mind when he wrote: 'The Nigerian crisis is a struggle for very high stakes: popular control of the national and local bureaucracies, the protection of great economic resources, access to education, and access to full status in Nigerian society' (ibid.: 5).

Armstrong advised the American government to sell arms to the federal side, that is, the Nigerian government, and 'avoid acts and statements which seem to tend to give recognition to rebellion. And we must avoid appearing to encourage others to recognize rebellion' (ibid.: 16–17). Even though his pro-federal article also saw the issue of the Biafran war as a problem of structural inequality that should be addressed to end the war, in spite of the massacre of Igbos and people of many other southern ethnic groups, he insisted on seeing beyond such categories as tribal warfare, pogrom, feudalism and genocide, since the refugee problem was negotiable and could be compensated through generous reparations. A moral position against ethnic violence was compromised in pursuit of American economic interest.

Thirty years later, in the current discourse on correct or incorrect US policy on Nigeria, the focus is once again on whether to protect US oil interests or to insist on a policy shift and support democracy, not tyranny. The softly, softly policy of the Clinton administration has been criticized by Walter Carrington,[5] who was United States Ambassador in Nigeria from 1993 to 1997 and personally experienced the brutality of the military regime. Carrington had supported the call for a tougher policy, especially a full economic sanction against the military leaders. This was rejected by the State Department. The logic of calculated profit in cheap oil should now be a huge source of shame and embarrassment to the American people, because it is a policy that is dependent on genocide and tyranny.

For the Igbos, unity meant genocide and marginalization. Debunking false claims about reconciliation, Igbo scholars are also again raising the issue of marginalization. Chapter 5 details areas of economic and political marginalization of the Igbos in post-war Nigeria; areas that include revenue allocation, enrolment into institutions of higher education, and real every-day social issues. As I remember it then, the Igbos re-entered legitimate citizenship of Nigeria in May 1970 with all their assets frozen. They were given only 20 Nigerian pounds for families; for single people, it was just 5 pounds, and many had no capital whatsoever. This was their mass punishment, which was hidden behind the federal rhetoric of reconciliation.

Gowon's slogan of 'No victor, no vanquished', which he supported with his declaration of a programme of Reconciliation, Rehabilitation and Reconstruction (known as 3Rs), simply proved to be an instrument of corruption. During the Biafran war the National Rehabilitation Commission, which was set up by the federal government in 1968 and lasted until April 1970, served only a limited purpose. Its mandate was to bring relief to war victims, settle refugees, see to property compensation, and reconstruct damaged public infastructure such as markets, government offices, roads and bridges. The Commission concerned itself with repairing physical damage to government structures and did not have the mandate to heal personal and social wounds of war. In this case, where there was no war crime tribunal or truth commission, would a formal war crime hearing have served as a watchdog to protect Igbo victims of war from economic marginalization and exclusion from power-sharing?

In a 1997 BBC interview, asked about the status of Igbos 30 years after the Biafran secession, Emeka Ojukwu, who had led the Biafran secession and was the Biafran head of state, replied: 'The Igbos are not in a strong position. Their position comparatively has become much weaker. In every way in Nigeria there is a sort of glass ceiling. The Igbo situation economically is bad. We are reduced today to living almost outside the legitimacy of nationhood.'[6] What is different is that Ojukwu, the then rebel leader, now collaborated with the unpopular military governments of General Ibrahim Babangida and General Sani Abacha, believing in the corporate unity of Nigeria. Even as he admits a strong possibility of another civil war, he claims to believe in talking as a means of conflict resolution.

If for the West unity meant a managed condition for exploitation against the wishes of the governed, it meant corruption for the Nigerian power elites under General Yakubu Gowon, whom Wole Soyinka in 1971 accused of power profiteering from the war and pronounced guilty of causing the war. In 1967, Soyinka claimed that he had documents to prove that the dictatorial power of the military was consolidated on the genocide against the easterners. In his view, it was this intransigent tyranny of the army that brought about both secession and war. It was the military and their civilian stooges who profited from the war.

Both the pogrom against easterners and the war gave the army a reason to stay in power. The suggestion here is that only the military machine and the war industry profit from wars. It makes sense, especially if we recall, for example, the specific interests and governments that are opposed to the ban on landmines. Wole Soyinka had foresight and was uncompromising in stating the truth of military entrenchment when he wrote these words in 1971, a year after the Biafran war ended:

> Whatever the factors that made a dictatorship inevitable in the first place, those factors no longer exist. The present dictatorship is a degrading imposition. It is additionally humiliating because, in my knowledge and yours,

this dictatorship has exceeded a thousandfold in brutish arrogance, in repressiveness, in material corruption and in systematic reversal of all original revolutionary purposes, the worst excesses of the pre-1966 government of civilians. This is a shameful admission but it is the truth. (Soyinka 1975: 15)

Soyinka, it seems, has been at the centre of politics and intellectual leadership from the beginning of electoral politics and of military coups. In the above passage, he was accusing Gowon of counter-revolutionary repression and going against the revolutionary actions and agenda of the 15 January 1966 coup-makers. He offers some prophetic insights in his prison notes written 30 years ago that are relevant to current issues on truth, healing and social justice in other war and serious social conflict situations.

Justice or Genocide

Soyinka is again extremely active and prolific. We do need to reassess his philosophy of intellectual leadership as manifested in his actions. Soyinka wrote in his prison notes: 'For me, justice is the first condition of humanity' (Soyinka 1975: 96). Let us call it going back to basics in the quest for justice in a situation of mass genocide. Soyinka had first to lay claim to the right to be treated as human, having personally experienced inhuman treatment under prison conditions – what he called humiliation. He vividly recorded the appalling treatment of Igbos that he witnessed in the different prisons throughout the duration of the war. Under a different consciousness and sensibility as a result of shared pain and suffering, Soyinka was able to empathize with the victims of genocide and adopt a principled position. Although he condemned the 1966 pogroms against easterners in northern Nigeria, and the general 'Igbophobia', his position on the mechanism of dealing with extreme forms of oppression was unclear and problematic *vis-à-vis* Igbo masses.

Following the massacres of 1966 and Gowon's punitive measures in 1967, the easterners, top Igbo intellectuals and poets, including Christopher Okigbo, a close friend of Soyinka's, truly believed that without Biafra they would have been exterminated (Okafor 1998). There was a strong likelihood of extinction, since the federal government began its so-called police action against the newly declared state of Biafra by positioning troops and attacking first. Yet Soyinka, although he was imprisoned for his trip to Biafra, was against secession as a solution to the conflict and did not support Biafra. He totally opposed the war, believing it to be morally unjustified. He took a vanguardist view of intellectual leadership, denouncing the war in the press, visiting the East, attempting to 'recruit'

Nigerian intellectuals at home and abroad to form a pressure group fighting for the ban on arms sales to both sides, and in his own words, 'creating a third force which would utilize the ensuing military stalemate to repudiate and end both the secession of Biafra, and the genocide-consolidated dictatorship of the Army which made both secession and war inevitable' (ibid.: 19). In his view, it was the evidence he provided of the Gowon government's policy of genocide that resulted in the authorities framing and nearly eliminating him.

Soyinka certainly believed that Nigeria had in place a mechanism for settling the conflict resulting from the genocide that would make war unnecessary. This was one of his reasons for attacking Gowon's hypocrisy. The judicial system was in place and was used to protect or excuse the aggressors, and not the victims of genocide. Examples of this are instances in northern and western Nigeria when murderers of Igbos were caught by courageous citizens and dragged to court and the army would intervene to release the murderers. This led Soyinka to conclude, 'the very presence of law and justice in the entire federation were subverted to the doctrine of justifiable genocide!' (ibid.: 21).

Soyinka consequently demanded that the judiciary of the Western Region government be independent of the Federal Courts, and that laws be passed in the Western Region making tribal and religious molestation a crime. As a westerner, he took responsibility for the wrong-doing in the West, comparing the situation to the mass-murder in My Lai, Vietnam and the US government protection of the guilty officer. Soyinka's position was to insist that the murderers and the forces behind the genocide must be named and condemned and later stand trial. To him, the Nigerian experience at that time 'was the most comprehensive, undiscriminating savaging of a people within memory on the black continent' (ibid.: 24). Little did he know that this would be the pattern of future conflicts, thus raising the question: what happens when the judicial system is corrupt and talking does not work for the oppressed? The question is even more important, particularly if the leaders do not represent the popular voice.

Memory and Intellectual Responsibility

Much as I admire Wole Soyinka, I hope also to point out some unclear areas in his intellectual engagement with Biafra that remain unresolved and, I believe, still block an honest intellectual dialogue on Nigeria's current deepening crisis, and by extension other comparative experiences of conflict situations and their resolution. They also raise the question of intellectual leadership in social movements.

Since Biafra is still important in the national political discourse as a wound that has not healed, an issue of conscience in our collective memory, I find it difficult to understand why Soyinka, in criticizing Ojukwu's lack of support for 12 June and Abiola's mandate for president, now presents Ojukwu as an embodiment of Biafra, so that his attack on Ojukwu appears an attack on Igbo masses, the victims (Soyinka 1996: 40–7). Ojukwu may have been the leader of the Biafran state, but he was surely not the sole embodiment of the complex struggle that the movement for secession brought together. It is an intellectually weak argument to use the excuse of 'the human factor' to respond to one of the most cogent questions put to Wole Soyinka – the failure to follow the logical route of effecting an alliance of progressive forces. Surely, Soyinka knows that even progressive Igbo elements have always considered Ojukwu a reactionary, as they also see through the treachery behind the present manoeuvring for the presidency. By focusing on Ojukwu, Soyinka continues to exclude the voices and alliance of the Igbo masses. This, I believe, was also the case during the Biafran war and becomes a weakness in his prison notes. It is one thing to empathize with individual victims, but as a collective people experiencing genocide and fearing extermination, what should they do? There is an Igbo proverb that says: 'Those who fail to chart their own destinies are doomed to have others do it for them.'

One can refer back to an area of unclarity in Soyinka's intellectual activism 30 years ago in the secret and mystery that surrounded his reference to a 'Third Force', which he then saw as an alternative to genocide and war. He wrote: 'For there existed then, and exists even now in spite of its reverses a truly national, moral and revolutionary alternative – Victor Banjo's Third Force' (1975: 95).

I have read again, word by word, Soyinka's conversation with Banjo and Alele on this alternative called the Third Force, and it suggests that there was a national movement planning a revolution that had a base in the West long before the 15 January coup that also had ideas of a revolution. Both plans were aborted. What therefore was the base for Banjo's Third Force, given the splintering of all these movements by the full-blown war? Is it not time for the disclosure of the full names of those military officers involved? Why did Soyinka and his revolution planners not see solidarity with Igbo masses as a progressive base that demanded their full loyalty and support, rather than a counter-invasion by Banjo's Third Force?

The inability of Soyinka and his allies to separate Ojukwu's destiny from that of the Igbo masses acounts for this confused reading of priorities in the Biafran war as they insisted on ideology in the head as well as a gun in the hand. On the one hand, their memory of history served them right as the question was asked, 'How do we get rid of the alliance of the capitalist adventurers and a bourgeois military after the war? Didn't all the intellectuals know their history?' (Soyinka 1975: 180). Yet history, it seems, will judge their intellectual leadership more harshly, especially as the commanders of the Biafran forces attribute the reason Biafra lost the war partly to the sabotage generated by Banjo's Third Force.[7]

This is not to say that Banjo was not personally sympathetic to the Igbos. The proof of Banjo's sympathy and solidarity with the victims of genocide was expressed time and time again as he accused Yoruba intellectuals of silence in the face of injustice: 'But what happened to all you people in the West? Otegbeye and all those people who are never off the pages of the newspapers. Not a word of condemnation from anyone. No protest to Gowon, not even a student demonstration, not one act of solidarity with the victims. How did the rest of the country expect them not to feel cut off?' (ibid.). Soyinka's point was that the war had no programme of reform or redefinition of purpose, as such victory would be declared on the basis of the immoral values on which the war was fought. It means that the post-Biafran national identity in Nigeria is an immoral one based on the gains of genocide. The grand narrative is a festering sore that only truth can heal.

The Politics of Managed Justice

As already mentioned, Soyinka certainly believed that Nigeria had in place a mechanism for settling the conflict resulting from the genocide that would have made war unecessary. The judicial system was in place and was used to protect or excuse the aggressors, and not the victims of genocide.

There were mechanisms that could have been used to try the perpetrators of genocide. Following the May 1966 massacre of easterners in northern Nigeria, the then military head of state Major-General Agui Ironsi had set up a commission of inquiry into the May massacre. Soyinka accused Gowon of only paying lip-service to the work of the commission when he seized power in July 1966, since he privately rendered the commission defunct. Yet, the national mass genocide of August–October 1966 was reason enough for Gowon to set up an atrocities commission, instead of which he appealed to the northerners to behave more responsibly, but was clever enough to provide them with a reason for their actions – the January coup killing of their civilian and military leaders. However, Gowon was quick to set up an atrocities commission in the mid-west following its recapture from the Biafrans in November 1967. The commission, known as the Omo Ebih Atrocities Tribual, sat in Benin to try and terrorize those who had collaborated with the Biafrans, and deserting federal soldiers.

The commanders of the Biafran army are consistent in reporting the atrocities of the federal commanders and their troops during the war, and we can see how the metaphor of rape speaks the language of the victor's war. The federals used mostly artillery to pound their way through. They raped women, killed and didn't care to keep prisoners of war. They burned captured villages. These atrocities are vividly captured in Buchi Emecheta's (1982) social historical novel through the horrific experiences of her main character, Debbie Ogedemgbe, a Western-educated member of the elite, who represents all the contradictions of the war. Many of these war-front commanders never faced a war crime tribunal, and have since become heads of state of Nigeria. Perhaps for them the war never stopped and the perverted and corrupt culture of war never changed. This might explain the suffering that Nigerians have experienced under an entrenched military dictatorship.

What of the generals, the perpetrators? There is currently a discourse on key players and alliances as individual memories of Biafra are questioned. Did Ojukwu act out of self-interest, sacrificing millions of civilians for his own personal ambitions, or was he pushed to declare secession on 30 May 1967 by the punitive federal actions, such as the declaration of a food blockade against the Eastern Region in October 1966 and the creation of twelve states on 26 May 1967 to isolate the Igbos? Is Ojukwu's current preference of talking over war a sort of admission of his mistake? He says he and Gowon were then 33 years old.[8] Does this explain why negotiations to end the Biafran war failed? Why did Gowon and Ojukwu fail to communicate? Why was the human cost of that war not taken up after the war? Since there was such a high body count and casualties, why have both leaders not admitted mistakes and apologized?[9]

Twenty-nine years after the end of the war, the hunger for vengeance and the need for criticism and admonition are still very strong, mainly because of government silence on Biafra. Perhaps this is why a particular article, written with irony and satire by a non-Igbo in 1996 at the height of General Abacha's reign of terror, proved so populpar among Igbo scholars that it was xeroxed and widely distributed. In 1996, Dele Sobowale wrote an article in his column titled 'Gowon's Call for Prayers', in which he took a moral stand in response to retired General Yakubu Gowon's call for several days of national prayer in the face of General Abacha's terror against all opposition and the deepening of the Nigerian crisis. Sobowale took a swipe at Gowon and his leadership in the past. In his words, Gowon's

> slow reaction to the pogrom leading to the death of 300,000 Igbo men, women and children must weigh heavily on his conscience. The civil war that followed was just another instance of might crushing right. The Igbos were the aggrieved party. So in leading the prayer, General Gowon should

start with a long prayer for the forgiveness of his own sins, which are grievous. Perhaps at 27 years, and fired by ambition, spilling blood meant nothing to him. Today, with the benefit of maturity and perhaps being reborn as a Christian, he needs to ask for forgiveness of every Igbo person he meets. Without cleansing himself, he cannot lead any meaningful prayer that will be acceptable to God. A hand soiled with the blood of the innocent cannot be raised in a supplication to the crown of thorns or to the man of Calvary. Gowon should know that better than anyone ... Prayer without the will and courage to reorder our lives to enthrone justice and fairplay will yield nothing. Here in Nigeria, God's work is really our own. And right now we seem not ready to do it. General Gowon's announcement, however, had a touch of desperation to it, when he announced his willingness to die for the sake of Nigeria. Is the old General, perhaps, thinking of the possibility that the situation in the future might degenerate to the point of people making self-sacrifice for the fatherland? I certainly hope not. We have had enough of blood sacrifice. (*Sunday Vanguard*, 20 October 1996, p. 7)

The internet is an information super-highway that the Nigerian military dictators cannot police. This is where polemics of admonition have grown intense and passionate in oral accounts as computer websites become sites for shared memory. There are extensive discussions on memories of Biafra on Igbo-Nets. As the possibility of an independent international war crimes tribunal was being discussed, discourse on Biafra extended to details of the atrocities committed by the war generals who were never tried and who ever since have been actively involved in politics. It requires intellectual leadership to explore this possibility of the international court as a strategy of forcing accountability on the Nigerian military and getting them out of politics and back into barracks, so that true civil healing can begin.

Self-determination and Process

The continued marginalization of the Igbo masses in post-war Nigeria raises the question: what kept these people going during and after the war? Where did their determination come from? Answers to these questions include the moral sense of a just war, precisely because of these unjust measures. There is also a possible explanation in inner strength and collective determination drawn from cultural resources. In the face of injustice and rejection, Igbos say, '*Onye ajulu ana ju onwe ya?*' – when others reject or abandon you, you don't also abandon yourself. Igbos pursued those areas that needed only their determination – education, trade and the informal sector. Many academics and professionals left the country (Amadiume 1997b).[10]

One of the most important points made about survival strategies during the Biafran war and in post-conflict reconstruction is the role of the informal sector and women. This is also detailed in Chapter 6 of this book. Women continued even more vigorously their roles as nurturers, cooking and caring for home and the war front. Women continued as risk-takers, crossing into enemy territory in long-distance trade, known as *ahia attack* (attack trade). Women continued as defenders by being enlisted into civil defence forces such as the Biafran Organization of Freedom Fighters (BOFF) and the Special Task Force (STF). Women continued to be matriarchs, administering the towns and villages in the absence of men and their sons. They continued to use their formal organizations to challenge increased patriarchal oppression on all fronts. Gender politics became more intense during the war in the activities of town unions, which replaced government institutions (Amadiume 1987: 147–59; 1997a: 125–39).

Memories of Biafra are therefore not expressed only in the discourse of marginalization, or in the discourse of victimhood of having been massacred, blockaded, outgunned and starved to death and defeat. Biafran discourse includes what people have done for themselves as distinct from and in spite of marginalizing government policies. There is also the discourse of black pride in self-generated science and technological advancement, again another pride in a David having stood up to the Goliath of imperialism and international oil interests. Pointing to a racial dimension to the war, Dubem Okafor writes, 'For Biafra was neither a tribe nor a village but a metaphor for a people's resistance to last-ditch attempts by imperialism to maintain a strangle-hold on the economic-political throat of Black Africa' (Okafor 1998: 119). Inspired by the philosophy of Black Consciousness, Biafrans saw themselves as fighting for political and psychological independence. Biafra took a stand against the much-hated Berlin Treaty-invented African nation-states that Soyinka is now calling nation spaces. Enumerating their achievements under great odds, many Igbos believe they were better off outside the present federal dispensation.

Then again, many Igbos have also refused to be frozen in time, and have recommitted themselves to being part of a broader progressive alliance in popular struggles for justice. I think this is equally important because it represents a different political expression in forgiving and not forgetting. As Emecheta writes in her foreword to *Destination Biafra*, 'it is time to forgive, though only a fool will forget' (Emecheta 1982: vii). It suggests a political use of memory for a greater cause.

Politically conscious Igbo activists and trade unionists continued their unfinished struggle by breaking away from the forced ethnic reclassification to join broader alliances. This politics of memory was at its high point in the complex political manoeuvring of 1994: the different identities that were assumed and the alliances that were forged around the question of Igbo leadership, electoral zoning, occupation of the presidency, relations with other interest and ethnic groups, participation in the constitutional conference, an agreed position on the military and a democratic agenda for civilian rule. There are realignments currently going on as the same problems involving the presidency and control of the centre are revisited following the deaths of Abacha and Abiola. The facts suggest a dynamic process.

Conclusion: Law and Reconciliation

May not truth commissions and legal accountability heal the war wounds of shattered communities and broken lives at the expense of social justice, and is social justice not both the ends and means of healing and reconciliation? How can we impose globally accepted standards when conceptions and mechanisms of realizing social justice vary from country to country? Is the newly agreed international court for war crimes to be used as an instrument of forced globalization or in the cause of justice?

From the perspective of traditional African values, truth commissions and legal accountability seem to work from the Western logic of sin that needs absolution. Indigenous Africans might think that the intention is to ascribe evil to some higher power, when for the Africans evil is in the social system in the guise of inequality and oppression. According to this African logic, guilt is collective; Africans turn to their own social mediators, healers and reclassifiers, such as diviners and prophets, whom they themselves know how to control and who they are controlled by. It is a modern arrogance to assume that courts are instruments of healing.

In truth, law has no monopoly on the definition of evil and human rights. Good and evil are not mutually exclusive. For many African peoples who sanctify unity and to whom disharmony is witchcraft or evil, something in society but external to the community, prolonged legal accountability would be institutionalizing permanent conflict, which only perpetuates the climate of evil and witch-hunting. It is to insist on continued perverted liminality in place of healing and closure. We are dealing with societies that recognize both violence and evil as necessary and inevitable and control and channel these impulses to social use through ritual performance or play. These mass killings that we are now experiencing appear to be something modern for Africans.

This indigenous African perception of conflict and chaos as perverted liminality contrasts with the legal system in the way it has functioned as a system of accountability in post-war situations. The legal system appears to be capable only of providing a control mechanism by imposing 'a non-chaotic' context in which the formal discourse is the formalized language of legal experts and policy consultants over and above the genuine voices of victims of war and conflict, the civilians. This controlling legal mechanism is very similar to the so-called transition programmes devised to end military rule that have led to a political impasse or what Nigerians call 'a log-jam'.

The legal experts in this volume have described the workings of these war crime tribunals, their structures and mandates, and their assumptions of a consensual global or international community. What, then, when 'global' is quite specifically local, such as the interventionist power of the US State Department, the gun lobby or the Christian right? This should also include the International Monetary Fund and its structural adjustment programmes as instruments of direct fiscal management and capitalist transformation of the development of the southern hemisphere. When sectional ideological interest is defined as the international community, might it be that this new rhetoric of the rule of law is itself in denial of the very truth of social conflict in any condition of contradictions? Even in American democracy, we are witnessing the paucity of imagination when truth is reduced to collection of information, the gathering of facts. The unimaginative, simplistic mind of law is posed against complex social issues.

In South Africa, the apartheid system exploited and forced poverty on the black population. Peace in reality is dependent on the narrowing of the gap between rich and poor, irrespective of colour. Nelson Mandela may talk about forgiveness and rebirth, but he cannot enforce forgetting. In Mandela's 10 May 1994 inaugural speech as president, he said. 'The time for healing of the wounds has come. The moment to bridge the chasms that divide us has come. The time to build is upon us' (Martin 1997: 521). The point he made was not to forget, but to face the truth of the apartheid era through public accounting of the atrocities, crimes and injustices. Here, reconciliation and pardon are dependent on a full admission of crime.

In Mandela's Nobel Prize speech in 1993, he also emphasized the human birth of prosperity for all as the normal condition for democracy. Democracy, justice, peace, non-racism, non-sexism, prosperity for all, a healthy environment, equality and solidarity are the normal condition for human existence in a democracy. The goodness of human beings is like the flame of freedom and of memory, which can be hidden but can never die. The demand of freedom is prison for both the denied and denier. Echoing Frantz Fanon, Mandela writes: 'The oppressed and the oppressor alike are robbed of their humanity' (Mandela 1994: 544).

This is why Soyinka maintains that justice is the first condition of humanity. Politics calls for selective memory, and I doubt that the past is ever completely put behind. The Biafran civilians did not have a war crime tribunal and court records. What they have is a different truth of the creative imagination in oral history and literature, which mostly are where the war experiences are being revisited and recorded. They can look back with some detachment and comment on the situation as the need arises. Their own truth commission is a situational one, lived in process, and as such, although there is no political closure, individuals have been achieving closure by themselves.

At the end of the Biafran war, Nigeria was generally believed to have achieved a remarkable reconciliation. Thirty years later, that assumption is being challenged, as memories of Biafra are again central to questions of social justice and national security. In facing the current crisis, Nigerians do not have to be warned of another Bosnia or Rwanda, because we have had our own Bosnia and our own Rwanda. Narratives of the Biafran war provide a lesson of history to Nigeria, and remain a challenge to researchers and policy-makers who are concerned with truth, healing and social justice.

Notes

1. Alexander Madiebo mourns this tragedy as he writes: 'In the end, the whole excercise of splitting and reuniting Nigeria cost us over three million lives. The question is how could anyone ever justify the loss of so many lives in order to gain political control of his country? What alienated Biafrans most during the whole violent period is that even if one were to admit that the May and July killings of 1966 were necessary for the successful carrying out of Gowon's counter-revolution and as a revenge for the elimination of some Northern Nigerian leaders in the January Revolution, what happened the subsequent October could be described as sadism, to say the least' (1980: 388).

2. Concrete statistics on the casualties of the Biafran war as far as I can tell have not been universally agreed on. The online *Encyclopedia Brittannica* (http://eb.com) states that between 500,000 and several million people were killed.

3. Obasanjo 1980 is a personal account of the Nigerian civil war from one of the Federal Government's top commanders. It contains a survey of the war's political background from 1960 to its outbreak, the military operations of both sides throughout the war and an analysis of foreign involvement and aid. Ojukwu 1969 contains thoughts and speeches of General Ojukwu, who led the Biafran secession, and chronicles the events of the war to contextualize thoughts and speeches; so also does Gowon 1970 provide important dates and events from the federal viewpoint.

4. Occupying an area of 357,000 square miles (924,000 sq. km), the nation-state known as Nigeria was created by the British colonialists in 1914 with the amalgamation of three separate colonial entities – the Northern and Southern Protectorates and the Colony of Lagos.

5. See Shenon 1998.

6. See Obadina 1997.

7. See Madiebo 1980 and Njoku 1987.

8. Gowon was born in 1934 and Ojukwu in 1933.

9. 'Wounds from Nigerian civil war begin to heal', *Los Angeles Times*, 1 December 1991, p. A10, records the first time in 25 years that Gowon and Ojukwu shook hands.

10. In a study of socio-cultural activities of Igbo immigrants in the USA (Amadiume 1997b), I show from statistics of the US Immigration and Naturalization Service that there was a large increase in the number of Nigerian immigrants into the USA between 1974 and 1983, following the end of the Biafran war. I also show that political and economic instability in the home country increased the immigration of highly qualified professionals and their families.

Bibliography

Amadiume, I. (1987) *Male Daughters, Female Husbands: Gender and Sex in an African Society*, London and New York: Zed Books.

— (1997a) *Reinventing Africa: Matriarchy, Religion and Culture*, London and New York: Zed Books.

— (1997b) 'Igbo', in David Levinson and Melvin Ember (eds), *American Immigrant Cultures: Builders of a Nation*, vol. 1, London: Macmillan.

Armstrong, R. G. (1967) *The Issue at Stake: Nigeria 1967*, Ibadan: The University Press.

Emecheta, B. (1982) *Destination Biafra*, London: Allison and Busby.

Gowon, Y. (1970) *Important Records on Nigerian Civil War: The Nigeria War Diary, 1966–1970, Dates of Events in Nigeria*, J.C. Brothers Bookshop.

Madiebo, A. A. (1980) *The Nigerian Revolution and the Biafran War*, Enugu: Fourth Dimension.

Mandela, N. (1994) *Long Walk to Freedom: The Autobiography of Nelson Mandela*, New York: Little, Brown.

Martin, M. (1997) *Nelson Mandela: A Biography*, New York: St Martin's Press.

Njoku, H. M. (1987) *A Tragedy without Heroes: The Nigeria–Biafra War*, Enugu: Fourth Dimension.

Obadina, T. (1997) 'Ojukwu warns on another civil war, says Nigeria could still break up', *Post Express*, 2 June.

Obasanjo, General O. (1980) *My Command: An Account of the Nigerian Civil War 1967–1970*, London: Heinemann.

Ojukwu, C. O. (1969) *Biafra: Selected Speeches and Random Thoughts*, New York: Harper and Row.

Okafor, D. (1998) *The Dance of Death: Nigerian History and Christopher Okigbo's Poetry*, Trenton, NJ: Africa World Press.

Shenon, P. (1998) 'U.S. policy on Nigeria could hinge on results of an autopsy', *New York Times*, 9 July.

Soyinka, W. (1975) *The Man Died: Prison Notes of Wole Soyinka*, Harmondsworth: Penguin.

— (1996) *The Open Sore of a Continent: A Personal Narrative of the Nigerian Crisis*, Oxford and New York: Oxford University Press.

Biafran War Literature and Africa's Search for Social Justice

Akachi Ezeigbo

Our history hasn't hurt us enough or the betrayals would stop, the streets would erupt, till we are overcome with the inescapable necessity of total self-transformation – we burn for vision – clear, positive vision – for vision allied with action – for want of vision my people perish – for want of action they perish – in dreams – in dreams begin responsibility – for we have become a people of dream-eaters, worshipping at the shrines of corruption – we can't escape our history – we will dwindle, become smaller, the continent will shrink, be taken over, swallowed, pulped, drained by predators, unless we transform – in vision begins – in vision begins responsibility ... (Okri 1996)

The renowned Nigerian playwright and social activist Professor Wole Soyinka once said that justice is the first condition of humanity. This chapter is premised on the fact that social justice is both the means and the end of healing and reconciliation. However, the analysis will underscore the point that concepts and mechanisms of realizing social justice vary from one writer to another.

The Background to Civil Anarchy in Africa

In the last one or two decades, many countries of Africa have witnessed some deterioration in their economies. The economic setback suffered by these nations is partly a result of the political crisis that engulfed them. In a speech delivered to members of the South African National Assembly in Cape Town on Monday 1 June 1998, Chief Emeka Anyaoku, the secretary-general of the Commonwealth, stressed the importance of stability in sustaining Africa's economic growth and output. Chief Anyaoku identified instability as the greatest scourge of sustained economic growth, particularly in a society in which 'a section feels it does not belong or perceives itself to be permanently excluded from an effective say in government'.[1]

Over the years, the crises in Nigeria have been influenced and aggravated by the differing perceptions brought to bear on the gamut of political events by the various ethnic groups. For instance, the 1965 crisis in Western Nigeria led to two military coups in 1966. The January 1966 coup, which was initially viewed as a necessary and positive move, was subsequently perceived and interpreted by some ethnic jingoists as an 'Igbo coup'.

Okwudiba Nnoli's (1972) theoretical analysis of the concepts of 'perception' and 'image' (developed from Kenneth Boulding's book *The Image*, 1956) is a most adequate reference point for a discussion of the contradictions inherent in the interpretations accorded the 15 January coup and subsequent crises in Nigeria. As Nnoli rightly stated:

> Human beings are constantly coming into contact with new experiences and new realities, as events unfold in their lifetime. It is through these perceptions of reality that people build an ordered image of reality for themselves. The image becomes the motivating force for the people's action. (1972: 119)

In other words, people's images of happenings in the world are what they believe to be true. Indeed, it is this image that largely governs the bulk of human behaviour.[2] Accordingly, it should be noted that where diverse and contradictory perceptions and interpretations of events exist, conflict is often inevitable.

From the foregoing, it is quite clear that the armed conflicts experienced in Africa and in other parts of the world are caused by human action – sometimes deliberately and at other times inadvertently. The recurrence of communal conflicts and civil wars in parts of the world has necessitated the search for peace and harmony among the belligerent groups, with the support of regional and world bodies such as NATO, the OAU and the UN. Many writers, thinkers and human rights activists have considered social justice as a means of achieving healing and reconciliation among the peoples of Africa and the rest of the world's trouble spots. Crucial to the argument of this chapter is the incontrovertible fact that social justice is both means and end of healing and reconciliation.

In this chapter I shall attempt an evaluation of the imperativeness of social justice in Africa from the literary perspective. The aim is to explore the subtle approaches to social justice advocated by some African writers, such as Wole Soyinka, Chinua Achebe, Buchi Emecheta and Eddie Iroh.

Social Justice as a Means of Healing and Reconciliation: A Literary Perspective

It is valid to argue that art is as functional in contemporary African society as it was in traditional African society. Frankly speaking, the notion of 'art for art's sake' existed no more in the African past than it does in the present. The traditional oral artist or performer was conscious of the didactic or utilitarian function of his art and geared his performance towards achieving that end. Thus, in traditional African society, art was placed at the service of society. The modern African artist is a product of this tradition. Wole Soyinka believes that 'the artist has always functioned in African societies as the record of mores and experience of his society and as the voice of vision of his own time' (1968: 21).

Many African writers have aimed to bring to the awareness of society their perceptions of the injustices and moral failings that plague their nations. Chinua Achebe (1975: 45) believes that the writer 'should march right in front' in 'the task of re-education and regeneration that must be done' and that the artist is 'the sensitive point in his community'.

The Soviet critic G. V. Plekhanov (1979: 5) appears to have echoed most African writers when he stated that 'the function of art is to assist the development of man's consciousness, to improve the social system'. The writer's primary concern is with social justice as a means of maintaining peace and harmony in society. With this in mind, our discourse here examines Soyinka's *Madmen and Specialists* (1974) – a play inspired by the events of the Nigerian civil war with a view to establishing its relevance to the search for social justice and its advocacy of a free, humane and moral society.

The three decades or so of political crisis in Nigeria, between 1966 and 1998, have compelled Wole Soyinka to become more actively involved in the country's politics, and more revolutionary in his idea of initiating social change and aggressively campaigning for social justice. In one of the poems in his collection based on the Nigerian crisis, *A Shuttle in the Crypt*, Soyinka exhorts his oppressed compatriots:

> Orphans of the world
> Ignite! Draw
> Your fuel of pain from earth's
> Sated core. (1977: 65)

The attack on excessive power and the call for justice that Soyinka makes in this poem are constant themes in literature all over the world and in all ages. His activism has taken him outside Nigeria in recent times, in search of external support to enthrone democracy and restore justice and equity in his crisis-ridden fatherland. In *Madmen and Specialists* (1974), he re-creates a society that has lost its moral and spiritual direction (like Nigeria) and then introduces the Earth Mothers, two old women, as agents of correction and healing, for the purpose of restoring wholeness and justice to the corrupt and spiritually debased society. Soyinka meant the old women to symbolize a positive force that intervenes as a last resort to save humanity from itself, root out evil, reconcile opposing forces and establish a humane, just and moral society (Ezeigbo 1991: 127, 128). In order to heal and reconcile society as well as restore harmony, the old women have to destroy Dr Bero, who represents evil, oppression and injustice.

In his novel *Season of Anomy* (1980), Soyinka explores his subsequent resolution to use art as a means of effecting revolutionary and egalitarian changes in society. The fair and just Aiyéró community is a symbol of social justice and operates the principles of communalism and welfarism – two systems of governance often identified with traditional African society in the works of writers such as Ayi Kwei Armah and Ngugi wa Thiong'o.[3] In the novel, Soyinka's vision is that the Aiyéró 'ideal' is to be transplanted to Cross-River in order to heal, rejuvenate and reinvigorate that morally debased and godless region controlled by the Cartel.

Soyinka, in his works, leaves no one in doubt as to his profound concerns with the restructuring of society to achieve spiritual health, freedom, justice and moral probity.

The old women in *Madmen and Specialists* and the Aiyéró community in *Season of Anomy* represent the 'morally incorruptible essence from the African past which was destroyed by the intrusion of foreign, excessively materialistic and exploitative ideologies' (Okonkwo 1980: 118). They are closely related to the earth and to the forces of healing and regeneration. It is through them and the forces they represent that Soyinka hopes to restore to his society its moral character and humane sensibility.

Wole Soyinka's vision in the two works is post-colonialist and Afrocentric in temper. Basing his discourse on the theory of post-colonialism, Soyinka breaks with the Western view that the solution to universal problems, including those of Africa, can be found only through Western initiatives. The Aiyéró ideal of 'communalism' and 'welfarism' and the healing and regenerative forces symbolized by the old women, Iya Agba and Iya Mate, are Afrocentric and best suited to solving Africa's problems.

Soyinka's unflinching determination to make a case for justice and human integrity compels him to explore themes involving human relations, social relations, economic and political situations and the agonies and anguish of people. His struggle for social justice can be seen as a constructive commitment to the propagation of peace, human dignity and liberty.

Interestingly enough, Chinua Achebe and Wole Soyinka seem to have identical attitudes regarding the writer's use of his or her 'trade' to advocate justice and freedom. For Achebe, as he has consistently stressed in his works, lectures and interviews, Africa's (and Nigeria's) greatest problem is bad leadership.[4] His thesis on the problem of leadership in his society is evident in *Anthills of the Savannah* (1987). The novel is set in an imaginary country called Kangan – a thin disguise for Nigeria that could also represent any other African country under a military dictatorship. It is the story of three former classmates. Sam is head of state and army commander-in-chief, Chris Oriko commissioner for information, Ikem Osodi editor-in-chief of Kangan's *National Gazette*. As Sam becomes more autocratic, he eliminates Ikem, whom he sees as a threat. Chris flees for his life but is killed at a checkpoint by a policeman whom he tries to prevent from raping a schoolgirl. The novel is a powerful book about leadership and the human condition in Africa and in the Third World countries, where military dictatorship has become the rule rather than the exception. It is a book that articulates and enunciates Achebe's pronouncements on the leadership predicament that has bedevilled his society since independence in 1960. The novel could be seen as Achebe's contribution to the search for social justice in a tyrannical and corrupt society. Adopting the postmodernist approach, Achebe privileges different strands of opinion in the novel, allowing various voices to make their feelings known. The novelist uses Ikem Osodi to highlight the democratic ethics in indigenous culture that the incursion of military dictatorships has almost destroyed. He believes that 'Dialogues are infinitely more interesting than monologues' and that 'whatever you are is never enough; you must find a way to accept something however small from the other to make you whole and save you from the mortal sin of righteousness and extremism' (1987: 154).

In Chapter 7 of the novel Achebe articulates his opinion, through Ikem Osodi, on the most effective way to end oppression and entrench freedom and reconciliation in society. Here 'reform' is considered superior to 'revolution' as a means of achieving social justice and bringing about lasting change:

> The sweeping, majestic visions of people rising victorious like a tidal wave against their oppressors and transforming their world with theories and slogans into a new heaven and a new earth of brotherhood, justice and freedom are at best grand illusions. The rising conquering tide, yes; but the millennium afterwards, no! New oppressors will have been readying themselves secretly in the undertow long before the tidal wave got really going.
>
> Experience and intelligence warn us that man's progress in freedom will be piecemeal, slow and undramatic. Revolution may be necessary for taking a society out of an intractable stretch of quagmire but it does not confer freedom, and may indeed hinder it …
>
> Reform may be a dirty word then but it begins to look more and more like the most promising route to success in the real world. I limit myself to

most promising rather than *only* for the simple reason that all certitude must now be suspect.

Society is an extension of the individual. The most we can hope to do with a problematic individual psyche is to re-form it ...

It had to be the same with society. You re-form it around what it is, its core of reality; not around an intellectual abstraction. (1987: 99, 100)

In *Anthills of the Savannah*, Achebe makes a case for a democratic system of government enriched by gender equality, while at the same time he inscribes his disenchantment with the military dictatorships that dominate his society and some other parts of Africa. In an interview he granted Anna Rutherford in London on 11 November 1987, he stated:

I think when the military first appeared in African politics they had programmes, they had ideas. Perhaps they were mistaken, perhaps we were mistaken in thinking there was a possibility that they could solve the problem. Today it has become so cynical. It's a case of 'OK, you've had your turn, now I want my turn'. We must really pray and work for the end of this. (Rutherford 1987: 6–7)

In the novel, Achebe explores the possibility of bringing military dictatorship to an end through the efforts of ordinary people and groups such as students and workers. In the interview referred to above, he further stated: 'We have seen in Africa, e.g., the situation where the students[5] in the Sudan rose up and told the military to go and it went' (ibid.: 7). There is every evidence in *Anthills of the Savannah* that Achebe regards it as the duty and responsibility of the people to rise up and say 'no' to bad governance, as a valid way to end oppression and enthrone social justice.

Women's empowerment and gender equity are given positive exposition in the novel. Beatrice Okoh is invested with strength and other qualities that enable her easily to assume a leadership position towards the end of the novel. David Ker rightly observes that:

The novel's two most lively and interesting characters are women: Beatrice Okoh and Elewa, and this role that Achebe has found for women should give all of us food for thought ... Everything about her [Beatrice] is meant to remove the prejudices that men have held about women. She is a complex character. Sometimes she is a priestess or prophetess, reminiscent of Chielo the prophetess of the hills and caves. She is able to predict the fate that befalls the men in the novel and generally is the one in control of all the major events ... Beatrice is a confident woman who knows what she wants, she is indeed the new emancipated Nigerian woman, bright, intelligent, career-oriented, tough and as committed to worthy causes as her male counterpart. (1998: 6)

Margaret Busby is also right when she observes that 'Achebe for the first time locates women centrally as perhaps the main hope for the future.'[6] Achebe's revisionary stance sees women in the novel as having a responsibility to put things right and sow the seed of social justice and healing in society.

This novel once more reveals Achebe's remarkable control of point of view and irony. The novel has a very complex narrative style – four narrators or witnesses – revealing the complexity of the people's experience in a dehumanized multicultural and multi-ethnic society. The multiplicity of points of view creates not only greater credibility but also greater grandeur or ornateness. In this novel, Achebe adopts the postmodernist and post-colonial theories that, by their radical nature, advocate dialogue and plurality of views and freedom – tenets or attributes that are indispensable for achieving social justice, reconciliation and healing in any system or clime. The military dictatorship symbolized by General Sam (Kabisa) is opposed to this flowering of dialogue, plurality of views and freedom, and this situation generates the conflict and the subsequent tragic occurrences in the novel. However, the positive force symbolized by the late Ikem Osodi and Chris Oriko, as well as by Beatrice and Elewa, is poised to bring about social change through the opposition building up against the dictator.

Achebe's *Anthills of the Savannah* negotiates a space for the women's perspective in the struggle to entrench social justice in Africa's plural society. But it is to Buchi Emecheta's *Destination Biafra* (1982) that we shall turn in order fully to appreciate the imaginative re-creation of women's struggle for social justice and reconciliation in Africa's war-ravaged and male-dominated societies. It is pertinent to state here that Emecheta explores women's experience from the feminist perspective. Feminism is one of the most prevalent gender theories in literary discourse today. It is an offshoot of postmodernism, from which it has benefited immensely in its radical conceptualization of ideas. Feminism posits that women should have rights and chances equal to those of men in every aspect of human experience: political, legal, economic, social. It challenges the male domination of society and, as a radical theory, it strives to emancipate women and empower them to gain more freedom and opportunity.

In *Destination Biafra*, the Nigerian civil war is the central concern. But Emecheta's vision of the war is directed towards exploring the new role women could play in the survival of a nation and in reconciling their war-torn communities. The greatest victims of war in the novel (as in real life) are women and children. Emecheta explores the ability of women to survive. From the courage, resilience and resourcefulness exhibited by many of the women in the novel, particularly the protagonist, Debbie Ogedemgbe,

Emecheta debunks the false notions of women's weakness, cowardice and dependency on men. As Grace Okereke rightly comments:

> By creating a self-assertive, politically-informed heroine like Debbie Ogedemgbe, Emecheta has successfully taken woman from the periphery of Nigerian politics and made her an active agent of history … Nigerian woman and indeed, the African woman, emerges from the shadows of history to become herself a subject of history on whom depends the redemption of many lives and the restoration of peace to a nation. (1994: 149)

This captures succinctly Emecheta's vision for the Nigerian woman, indeed the African woman, in the crisis-ridden and war-devastated countries of the continent – Biafra (Nigeria), Sudan, Angola, Somalia, Rwanda, Liberia and Sierra Leone.

Debbie is in the forefront in the search for peace on behalf of Biafra and Nigeria and in the provision of relief and succour for the brutalized common people. Emecheta's major concern in the novel, therefore, is with social justice and the freedom of people, particularly the freedom of women, who have proved more than a match for men in the fight for peace and human integrity in the society depicted. Although Debbie's attempt to reconcile Biafra and Nigeria does not succeed, she is, at least, able to rehabilitate and care for the children orphaned by the brutal war. Eddie Iroh has also used fiction to probe the issues that led to the Nigerian civil war and those that made it difficult to achieve peace, reconciliation and healing after the war ended. He has distinguished himself as the novelist who has contributed the highest number of works to the body of fiction on the Nigerian crisis and civil war: *Forty-eight Guns for the General* (1976), *Toads of War* (1979) and *The Siren in the Night* (1982). After secessionist Biafra collapsed in 1970, the Federal Military Government announced a period of rehabilitation and reconciliation often described in official and unofficial documents as 'The Three Rs' – Rehabilitation, Reconciliation and Reconstruction. It is this aspect of the post-war experience that Iroh examines in *The Siren in the Night*.

The novel takes a deeper look at the issue of reconciliation and social justice after the war, especially the question of general amnesty declared by the Federal Government, in the wake of Biafra's collapse, as it relates in particular to those who controlled power or held important positions in Biafra. The deprivations suffered by people in the war trigger off a reign of terror in the immediate post-war era in which lawlessness was the order of the day and the crime rate escalated. It was a chaotic and demoralizing period for most people, especially 'Biafrans' who were ruined by the war.

Iroh perceives the suffering that the former 'Biafrans' (Igbos) were put through as not only a consequence of their losing the war, but also a result of ethnic chauvinism on the part of a few tribalistic elements among the high-ranking officers of the Nigerian army. Colonel Mike Kolawole, head of the Federal Security and Intelligence Directorate, embarks upon a vendetta against the former rebel officers, particularly Colonel Ben Udaja and Captain Ulo Amadi. By bringing trumped-up charges against his victims, Colonel Kolawole succeeds in both the physical and psychological destruction of his victims. Iroh is of the opinion that the Federal Government achieved little in reconciling the two sides of the conflict – people of Eastern Nigeria and the rest of Nigeria.

His vision of the post-war declarations of the authorities unmasks the hypocrisy that shrouded the execution of government policy after the war, brought about by the sectional proclivities of the powerful people who controlled the nation. Iroh questions the genuineness of the government's proclaimed reconciliation and rehabilitation for those who suffered defeat. Indeed, many Igbo leaders and thinkers seem to agree with Iroh on this issue. For instance, in a lecture he gave in Enugu, Chukwuemeka Ojukwu (1998) lamented over the fate of the Igbo in Nigeria since the war ended. Most Igbo people felt, and continue to feel, that they have been consistently marginalized in the country and treated as second-class citizens or strangers in their fatherland.

Iroh has also explored, in *The Siren in the Night*, the military dictatorship and terrorism that have attenuated peace in his society and made reconciliation and healing impossible. He does this by graphically depicting the post-war period as having introduced a new kind of terror different from that posed by the war itself. Thus he reveals the activities of the Nigerian secret police and the unjustifiable and brutal victimization of innocent people. The type of mental and physical torture Udaja and Amadi are subjected to recalls vividly the subsequent harrowing experience many Nigerians had in General Abacha's torture chamber. Below is a passage taken from *The Siren in the Night*, depicting the scene of Ulo Amadi's torture by Kolawole:

> He juggled the regulators deftly and the thin blue flame leapt out of the nozzle-like laser beam. Amadi tried to hide his trembling hands by folding them across his stomach. Kolawole raised the hissing nozzle to the centre of the metal plate and pointed it steadily, delicately ... The next day ... the prisoner was a heap on the floor of the narrow cell ... His face was an ugly mosaic of black bruises, burns, blotches of dried blood and tears that would not stop. (1982: 58, 60)

This terrible scene is comparable to the stories one has heard about the victims of Abacha's Special Security Service (SSS) men. The resemblance is uncanny, yet Iroh's novel was written over ten years before Abacha's dictatorship was inflicted on the people of this country. Iroh sees his society as one crying out for justice and reconciliation and, like other writers discussed in the study, he implies that there can be no real re-habilitation, reconciliation and healing without justice.

Soyinka, Achebe, Emecheta and Iroh are writers who explore the issue of social justice in their works and understand the need for equity and peaceful coexistence among people and communities. They project a positive image of women and see them as a catalyst in the task of nation-building, reconciling belligerent groups and regenerating society to wholeness.

Conclusion

From the foregoing, it is quite clear that several forces have contributed to the attenuation of social justice in Africa in general and Nigeria in particular. Some Nigerian creative artists have theorized about these prob-lems and proffered suggestions on how to end them and enthrone social justice, reconciliation and healing in their crisis-ridden nation. Africa must learn from the past and pursue the path of peace and reconciliation. The so-called developed countries had their conflicts and were able to overcome them. African peoples should focus on workable solutions and not sweep problems under the carpet or pretend they do not exist. This will only delay justice and reconciliation. As the saying goes: 'Justice delayed is justice denied.'

In the words of Chief Chukwuemeka Odumegwu Ojukwu, 'There can be no peace without reconciliation and no progress without peace' (1988: 22). For human beings to live together in harmony, there should be justice. The ghost of Biafra continues to haunt Nigeria. Until it is exorcized, there can be no lasting peace. The injustices thrown up by the civil war and the crisis before it have not been addressed. The débâcle that was Biafra deepened ethnicity, nepotism and corruption in Nigeria; the country has not recovered from the evils of that war. Other crisis points in Africa are a replication of Biafra, for the same problems that plague Nigeria also plague the other nations.

One of the problems militating against the entrenchment of social justice in Africa is the reckless use of power by leaders. This has been graphically demonstrated in the works of Soyinka, Achebe, Emecheta and Iroh dis-cussed above. Dictators abound in Africa. The answer to dictatorship is democracy, which operates by the rule of law. To propagate social justice, all the parties involved or the ethnic groups in any nation must have a stake in the nation's destiny and have a sense of belonging. A corollary to this position is the basic fact that nation-building is and should be a collective task to which the two genders are obliged to contribute, to the best of their abilities. Men and women, therefore, should be given equal opportunities to develop their potential to make society better. There is no gainsaying the critical role of women in working towards the achievement of social justice, reconciliation and healing in war-torn communities and nations. It remains to say that African nations should utilize the abundant resources among their womenfolk to create harmonious homes and societies.

Notes

1. Chief Anyaoku's address to members of South Africa's National Assembly has been reproduced in *The Guardian* (Lagos) of Wednesday 3 June 1998, p. 3.

2. The subjective and unreliable nature of people's perspective of reality was originally explored in Plato's Theory of Ideas and Perception. This idea is graphically illustrated in Plato's famous cave image, in which men imprisoned in a cave since birth 'would deem reality to be nothing else than the shadows of the artificial objects which were only reflections of the actual objects cast by the light of a burning fire'. See Plato, *The Republic*, trans. Paul Shorey, London: Heinemann 1963, Vol. III, Book VII.

3. See Armah 1973 and 1995; and Ngugi wa Thiong'o 1977.

4. See particularly Achebe 1983.

5. In a similar development recently, in Indonesia, students were instrumental in the resignation of President Suharto, the head of state, in May 1998.

6. See the back-cover commendations of Achebe 1987.

References

Achebe, Chinua (1975) 'The novelist as teacher', in *Morning Yet on Creation Day*, London: Heinemann.

— (1983) *The Trouble with Nigeria*, Enugu: Fourth Dimension.

— (1987) *Anthills of the Savannah*, London: Heinemann.

Anyaoku, Emeka (1998) 'Address to the South African National Assembly members', *The Guardian* (Lagos), Wednesday 3 June, p. 3.

Armah, Ayi Kwei (1973) *Two Thousand Seasons*, London: Heinemann.

— (1995) *Osiris Rising*, Popenguine, Senegal: Per Ankh.

Boulding, Kenneth E. (1956) *The Image*, Ann Arbor: University of Chicago Press.

Emecheta, Buchi (1982) *Destination Biafra*, London: Allison and Busby.

Ezeigbo, Akachi T. (1991) *Fact and Fiction in the Literature of the Nigerian Civil War*, Lagos: Unity Publishing and Research Company.

Iroh, Eddie (1976) *Forty-eight Guns for the General*, London: Heinemann.

— (1979) *Toads of War*, London: Heinemann.

— (1982) *The Siren in the Night*, London: Heinemann.

Ker, David I. (1998) 'Ends and beginnings: literary views on transition', *The Post Express*, Saturday 5 September, p. 16.

Ngugi wa Thiong'o (1977) *Petals of Blood*, London, Heinemann.

Nnoli, Okwudiba (1972) 'The Nigeria–Biafra conflict: a political analysis', in Joseph Okpaku (ed.), *Nigeria: Dilemma of Nationhood*, New York: Third Press.

Ojukwu, Chukwuemeka (1998) 'No peace without reconciliation', paper presented at the seminar 'Democracy and National Interest', Enugu, *The Post Express* (Lagos), 18 March, p. 18; 20 March, p. 10; 21 March, p. 8; 22 March, p. 18.

Okereke, Grace (1994) 'The Nigerian civil war and the female imagination', in Helen Chukumema (ed.), *Feminism in African Literature*, Enugu, Lagos, Abuja: New Generation Books.

Okonkwo, Juliet (1980) 'The essential unity of Soyinka's *The Interpreters* and *Season of Anomy*', *African Literature Today*, no. 11.

Okri, Ben (1996) *Dangerous Love*, London: Phoenix House.

Plato (1963) *The Republic*, trans. Paul Shorey, London: Heinemann.

Plekhanov, G. V. (1979; first edn 1956) *Art and Social Life*, Moscow: Progress Publishers.

Rutherford, Anna (197) 'Interview with Chinua Achebe', *Kunapipi*, vol. 14, no. 2, pp. 6–7.

Soyinka, Wole (1968) 'The writer in a modern Afrian state', in Per Wastberg (ed.), *The Writer in Modern Africa*, Uppsala: Scandinavian Institute of African Studies, p. 21.

— (1974) *Madmen and Specialists*, in *Collected Plays Vol. 2*, Oxford: Oxford University Press.

— (1977) *A Shuttle in the Crypt*, London: Rex Collings/Methuen.

— (1980) *Season of Anomy*, Surrey: Thomas Nelson.

Social Movements Revisited: Mediation of Contradictory Roles

Abdullahi An-Na'im and Svetlana Peshkova

In this chapter, we are concerned with the nature and dynamics of social movements in relation to issues of social justice, conflict and the role of truth in post-conflict healing and reconstruction. We begin our analysis with an examination of definitions of social movements in relation to the scope and objective of this chapter. To locate an understanding of social movements in African settings, we will also offer some reflections on civil society as the context within which social movements operate. The role of social movement in situations of severe conflict will be examined in the second section, and illustrated with reference to the cases of Rwanda and Sudan. We hope to conclude with suggesting some strategies for promoting the contribution of social movements in achieving sustainable mediation, healing and justice.

The premise of our analysis is that the role of social movements is both necessary and problematic because they are the midwives of the good, the bad and the ugly in human societies everywhere. They are the means people use in exercising their right to self-determination by articulating and realizing their demands for political, economic and social change. Although the right of others to self-determination must be taken into account in exercising one's own right, that does not mean conditioning the right on prior approval of the outcome of its exercise. Rather, as discussed later, the mediation of the outcomes of competing claims to self-determination is a continuing process premised on mutual acceptance of the right in the first place. In relation to the subject of this chapter in particular, social movements are necessary agents of the generation and intensification of conflict and injustice, as well as of sustainable conflict mediation.[1] They can be agents of liberation or of oppression. Accordingly, strategies for the promotion of sustainable mediation and justice should also be founded on a clear understanding of the sources and dynamics of the role of social movements in these processes.

Whither Social Movements?

An initial question is whether and in what sense a definition of social movements is necessary or useful at this stage of the analysis. A major study of social movements and democracy implemented over several years by the Council for the Development of Social Science Research in Africa (CODESRIA) considered this issue, but elected not to confine itself to a single or uniform definition of social movements. As Mahmood Mamdani framed that position: 'The result was a broad perspective on social movements as the crystallisation of group activity autonomous of the state, without succumbing to the variety of added distinctions ... The strength of this outcome lay in that the definition was anchored in our understanding of concrete social processes in the continent, and not *vice versa*' (Mamdani 1995a: 7–8). That approach is not appropriate for our purposes here because this chapter is a theoretical discussion that must define its primary subject.

A definitional dilemma is already indicated in the title of this chapter, namely, that the concept of social movements needs to be 'revisited' because it is too important to overlook as an instrument of comparative analysis, yet its readily available connotations are unlikely to be applicable to African situations. In terms of the usual difficulty of comparative analysis, prevalent definitions and applications of this concept were primarily developed by Western scholars in relation to Western, rather than African, experiences. But this usual difficulty is compounded here by the continuing impact of colonial and post-colonial relations between Western societies, as the primary source of current definitions of the concept, and African societies where we seek to apply those definitions.[2]

This definitional dilemma must be overcome for more important reasons than the obvious utility of comparative analysis in abstract academic terms. As stated in the rationale of the conference resulting in this book, the objective is to redress 'a failure to fully consider the complexities of African issues and a failure to integrate Africa into the construction of theories and models for understanding social processes'.[3] This objective cannot be achieved without balancing an appreciation of African specificities with an integration of African experiences into a multi-disciplinary and comparative framework. Concerned African and Africanist scholars cannot complain about the Balkanization and marginalization of African studies, while claiming that African situations are too different or special to be included in the construction of global theories and models of social processes.

More importantly, we are concerned here with developing a framework for sustainable conflict mediation in order to alleviate the horrendous suffering of millions of people and to support the recovery of their communities and the preservation of the environment that sustains all life on the continent. Given the realities of global security and of economic and other forms of interdependence, the dynamics and consequences of conflict in African settings cannot be isolated or insulated from regional and global actors and factors. This calls for developing analysis of social and political problems in Africa in terms that are understandable to people in other parts of the world if we are to attract their empathy and positive contributions to the mediation of conflict in Africa. To emphasize the African nature and context of these problems is not to say that they are specific to Africa alone. The space to be negotiated in this definitional process is that between the Africa-specific and the general.

In this light, it is necessary to chart a general scope of the concept of social movements in comparative perspectives in order to identify *corresponding* African phenomena that are particularly relevant to our purposes here. What follows, therefore, is neither a comprehensive survey of social movements scholarship in the abstract nor a review of the application of the term to all possible types of African social movements in general. Rather, it is an effort to draw on the most recent comparative reflection in order to develop a working definition of the concept that can be applied to conflict situations and their aftermath in Africa.

Definitional reflections To paraphrase a general definition by Cyrus Zirakzadeh, a social movement is a group of 'non-elite' people from a broad range of social backgrounds who use politically confrontational and socially disruptive tactics in a conscious attempt to build a radically new social order (Zirakzadeh 1997: 4–5). By non-elite he means people who in their daily lives lack substantive political clout, social prestige, or personal wealth, and whose interests are not routinely articulated or represented in the political system. Although desirous of transforming a social situation in dramatic ways, participants in social movements often direct their actions towards visible targets, such as local plant managers or landlords, because of the particular setting in which the particular movement emerged or developed. In their tactics, leaders of social movements balance disruption and confrontation with cooperation, legality and consensus-building. According to Zirakzadeh, the attempt to build a radically new social order, or to bring about change in social structure, does not mean that every person in every social movement wishes to transform the society in its entirety. It is true that most participants want to change the world in significant ways, some with a more radical view of the scope and methods of such change, while others will be primarily seeking immediate gratification and private benefits. Yet all participants would also consciously want to preserve specific institutions in the status quo. What distinguishes a social movement from an interest group or political party is that at least a plurality of its participants intentionally seek far-reaching restructuring of the society.

While this distinction between a social movement and political party is useful, it should not be taken as categorical because movements often assume the structures and operational methods of political parties in pursuit of their objectives. The fact that a social movement 'looks and acts' like a political party does not make it one in every respect. As we shall elaborate later in relation to civil society, definitions and distinctions must be related to specific context and purpose. The notion of a political party is culturally defined, historically conditioned and contextually specific: what constitutes a political party is different in Japan, Scandinavian countries, the United Kingdom or the United States, although all of them can be characterized as politically stable and economically developed countries. The relationship between social movements and political parties in African countries is the product of a combination of such factors as local cultural norms and institutions, colonial and post-independence history, and the impact of the dynamics of political life at any given point in time on the objectives and methods of the movements. But as emphasized in the last section of this chapter, the nature of this relationship should be understood and clarified because of its implications for the role of social movements in the generation and mediation of conflict.

Sidney Tarrow begins his definition of social movements by stating that the 'irreducible act that lies at the base of all social movements and revolutions is *contentious collective action*' by people who lack regular access to institutions, acting in the name of new or unaccepted claims and behaving in ways that fundamentally challenge others. Such action 'produces social movements when social actors concert their actions around common claims in *sustained sequences* of interaction with opponents or authorities' (Tarrow 1994: 2). Leaders can mobilize consensus around shared recognition of common interests in general, but that will not result in the creation of a social movement unless leaders tap more deep-rooted feelings of solidarity or identity. 'This is almost certainly why nationalism and ethnicity – based on real or 'imagined' ties – or religion – based on common devotion – have been more reliable bases of movement organization in the past than social class' (ibid.: 5).

If a social movement is to have significant and lasting effect, it must be able to sustain collective action against better-equipped opponents. How can movements do that despite the realities of personal egotism, social disorganization and state repression? Tarrow argues that changes in the political opportunity structure may create incentives for collective action, but the magnitude and duration of such action depend on mobilizing people through social networks and around identifiable symbols that are drawn from cultural frames of meaning. Social movements combine cultural, ideological as well as organizational strategies in mounting, coordinating and sustaining collective action among participants who lack more conventional resources and explicit programmatic goals.

According to another study that reviews a wide range of sources (McAdam et al. 1996), earlier work in the United States sought to explain the emergence of a particular social movement on the basis of changes in the institutionalized structure or informal power relations of a given national political system. European scholars, on the other hand, focused on accounting for cross-national differences in the structure, extent and success of comparable movements on the basis of differences in the political characteristics of their respective nation-states. Both approaches are guided by the underlying belief that social movements are shaped by the broader set of political constraints and opportunities unique to the national context in which they are embedded.

For example, initial mobilization for the American civil rights movement centred largely on the black church. Consequently, the initial 'framings' (shared meanings and definitions) that came out of the movement had a distinctly religious cast to them. The influence of that mobilizing structure was also reflected in such features as reliance on the mass meeting as a mobilizing device, and the disproportionate number of ministers among the early leaders of the movement.

Civil society as context To qualify these definitional reflections for our purposes here, we suggest consideration of the nature and role of 'civil society' in present-day Africa as the context within which social movements operate. Mahmood Mamdani questions the universalistic pretensions of a civil society-governed perspective by asking whether this notion is not simply a restatement of the earlier perspective of the unilinear evolutionism of 'modernization' theory, with its notion of the 'traditional' as the problem and the 'modern' as its solution (Mamdani 1995b: 613). In his view, whatever their differences may be, Western Africanists 'are agreed that African reality has meaning only in so far as it can be seen to reflect a particular stage in the development of European history. The central tendency of such a methodological orientation is to lift a phenomenon out of context and process. The resulting bias lends itself more to description and speculation than to concrete analysis' (ibid.: 608). Without necessarily accepting Mamdani's characterization of Western Africanist scholarship, one can appreciate the point that it is seriously misleading to insist on translating African experiences into European history.

This does not mean, however, that the concept of civil society as developed and applied in relation to other parts of the world has no relevance to the African context. As already emphasized in relation to the definition of social movements, African settings cannot be excluded from analyses that are applicable to other human societies. Rather, the point here is that civil society in Africa should be taken for what it actually is in its own setting, without assuming that it must fit certain preconceived notions of what it should be. It is in this sense that civil society is the essential context within which all social movements operate, whether in Africa or elsewhere. In acting as agents or proxy for their civil societies because they are the more organized and active elements of the general population, social movements reflect the distinguishing characteristics of their own societies.

Civil society is transformed by the changing social order as represented by the state, and the latter is transformed by the changing objectives of civil society. These complementary and dialectical relations are realized through existing social structures, including social movements. A useful distinction to note here is that between 'civic community' and 'civil society'. Civic community is marked by an active, public-spirited citizenry, egalitarian political relations, trust and cooperation, where the public domain is more than a battleground for pursuing personal interests. In contrast, civil society is traversed by class interests, ethnic particularisms, individual egotism and all types of religious and secular fundamentalism (Fatton 1995: 71). Since civic community in this sense is clearly more conducive to the realization of social justice and conflict mediation, the question is how can this quality be promoted in the civil society of various African situations, especially those that have experienced, or are still experiencing, violent conflict.

It is necessary to reflect on the state–civil society dynamics in African countries in terms of the specific features of each side of the relationship, namely, the post-colonial state, on the one hand, and civil society in the same setting, on the other. Regarding the post-colonial state, we should note that:

> Their borders were usually defined not by African political facts or geography, but rather by international rules of continental partition and occupation established for that purpose. Their governments were organized according to European colonial theory and practice (tempered by expediency), and were staffed almost entirely by Europeans at decision-making levels. Their economies were managed with imperial and/or local colonial considerations primarily in mind. Their laws and policies reflected the interests and values of European imperial power, and these usually included strategic military uses, economic advantage, Christianization, European settlement, and so

forth. Although the populations of the colonies were overwhelmingly African, the vast majority of the inhabitants had little or no constitutional standing in them. (Jackson and Rosberg 1986: 5–6)

In addition to those antecedents, the timing and manner of independence were determined more by international moral and political pressures within the framework of the United Nations for juridical statehood than by internal political cohesion and maturity as state societies. Consequently, the sovereignty and stability of African states are constantly contested in regional conflicts and internal civil wars,[4] as well as by the forces of diminishing sovereignty over vital national economic and social policy under current structural adjustment programmes imposed by the International Monetary Fund, and unfavourable global trade relations in general.

In response, African states tend to be more concerned with their territorial integrity and political stability at almost any cost. In the vast majority of cases, independence signified the transfer of control over authoritarian power structures and processes of government from colonial masters to local elites, with neither experience or prospects of popular participation in governance and the diffusion of authority and power at the national level. Unable to govern effectively and humanely, post-colonial governments tended to compensate by using oppressive and authoritarian methods, usually employing the same colonial legal and institutional mechanisms maintained by several cycles of 'native' governments since independence.

African civil society can only be expected to reflect the demographic and sociological features of the region (Seligman 1992: 202–3). Accounting for the dialectical interaction between the state and civil society, the expressions of African social movements are in the same equation with the performance of the authoritarian regimes. To say that state and society are interdependent is not to say that their relationship is productive for either side. The mechanisms that are supposed to play a mediating role between state and civil society are non-existent or inadequate; social movements are in disarray and political structures are articulated unclearly, if at all. Far from being homogeneous or unitary, African civil society is fragmented by the contradictory historical alternatives of competing social actors, institutions and beliefs.

This evaluation of African civil society is not intended to suggest the possibility or even desirability of cultural, social or political homogeneity in any society. In our view, a degree of heterogeneity in civil society is both unavoidable and desirable in any part of the world, especially in Africa, where deeply entrenched ethnic, religious and other forms of diversity will probably continue for the foreseeable future. Rather, it is a question of degree and balance between two unsustainable extremes of oppressive homogeneity and destructive fragmentation. The question to be addressed in the next section is how social movements can contribute to achieving the best possible mediation of competing claims and conflicting interests.

Towards Sustainable Mediation of Conflict

By definition, the objectives and forms of collective action by social movements are bound to be in conflict with those set or sanctioned by the existing order or pursued by other social movements in the same context. This indicates to us the need for mediation between conflicting roles of different social movements and other actors, especially in view of the possibilities of reformulation of objectives and re-selection of forms of collective action *within* the framework of each social movement at any given time. As noted by Mamdani, 'neither social forces [entrepreneurs, workers, students, women, peasants] nor social movements [ethnic, religious, communist, national liberation] can be presumed to have an internal consistency and coherence, or be the agent of realising a trans-historical agenda' (Mamdani 1995a: 9–10). Exposing the tension internal to these forces and movements is important not only for understanding the circumstances and confrontations that shape outcomes, but also for appreciating the contingent element in each historical instance.

All human beings live by the moral and pragmatic choices they make, whether as participants in social movements or within the wider society. It is true that choices are often made in response or reaction to choices made by others. But we also believe that there are always possibilities for new initiatives, even when responding or reacting to choices made by others. In relation to our subject here in particular, every time people respond or react to a violent or hostile act, they can choose to do so in a spirit of conciliation and healing, or one of confrontation and acceleration of reciprocal violence. To explore the possibilities of positive new initiatives at this stage of analysis, we shall first offer a theoretical framework for the transformation and mediation of conflict, and then attempt to apply this framework to the current situation in Rwanda and Sudan.

Conflict transformation The concept of 'conflict transformation', as distinct from 'conflict resolution' and 'conflict management', is a relatively new approach to understanding and constructively dealing with conflict. Conflict resolution implies that conflict is potentially negative and should be ended. Focusing on the immediate issues, this approach implies the short-term nature of conflict, which can be resolved permanently through such intervention tools as mediation, negotiation and position bargaining.

On the other hand, conflict management assumes the long-term nature of a conflict, and seeks to apply the notion of 'management' to control and direct its scope and dynamics. This approach also assumes that the core of the conflict is in its immediate expression, thus avoiding addressing what might be seen as its underlying causes or sources.

In contrast to these two approaches, the idea of conflict transformation suggests a holistic approach and an understanding of the dialectical nature of conflict. It approaches conflict as a natural phenomenon, which 'transforms events, the relationships with which conflict occurs, and indeed its very creators' (Lederach 1995: 17). This notion acknowledges that, without conflict, social, personal and communal transformations and growth would not be possible. Recognizing the dynamic nature of conflict, the idea of transformation relies on a certain degree of predictability of its development. By seeking to change people's attitudes or the behaviour of the social organizations involved, this approach seeks to transform the very context and relationships defined by different perceptions of conflict in a given situation. Conflict transformation is about modifying perceptions of the Self and the Other, and the relationships between them. But precisely because of its dialectical nature, the conflict itself gets modified and transformed, as well as the people, context and relationships involved.

Methodologically, the notion of transformation suggests a prescriptive as well as a descriptive direction. 'Transformation ... is a generalized learning from historical experience' (Vayrynen 1991: 129). Since conflict has the potential to take on a destructive expression, its energy should be 'channeled toward constructive expression' (Lederach 1995: 18). That is, this approach seeks to use the energy of the conflict itself in transforming its course, system, structure and the relationships that lie at the core of the conflict; thereby seeing conflict 'as a transforming agent for systematic change' (ibid.: 18).

The above-noted internal inconsistency of social movements should be seen as a resource for conflict transformation. The nature and degree of such internal transformation would of course depend on a variety of factors, applying both to the society at large and to the specific social movement, such as economic and political development of the country, cultural trends in the society, social stratification or differentiation, and gender relations. On a more particular level, conflict transformation draws on the emotional and spiritual dynamics of individual actors, such as reaction to the denial of certain freedoms and status, fear of the loss or betrayal of certain values, contingency of trust, and potential miscommunication or misunderstanding of the objectives and behaviour of others.

It is also important to take into account the ambiguity of the internal inconsistency within social movements because it can contribute to the transformation of the existing order, as well as repair tense or strained relations within the movement itself. As shown by Francis Deng in the case of the internal division in the SPLM–SPLA of Southern Sudan to be discussed below (Deng 1995: 232–4), the ambiguity of internal inconsistency opens up issues of internal organization and possibilities of questioning the legitimacy of the leadership, raising the issues of broader-based participation in the decision-making process, (re)examination of the goals and assumptions, recognition of limitations and priorities. All these factors and processes might be helpful for conflict transformation in a given situation.

The issue of violence needs to be addressed in a broader context of the economic, social, political and cultural background of the country. But for the purposes of our analysis here, we hold that the use of violence can be justified only as a last resort in self-defence. Even then, we suggest, it must be seen as a temporary emergency measure, and must always be coupled with the pursuit of non-violent alternatives. From an instrumentalist point of view, violence is sometimes seen as the way in which political groups defend or expand their interests in a given social structure, a reflection of the underlying social reality (Vayrynen 1991: 3). When non-violent methods are believed to have failed to address the issue, violence is used for breaking the isolation. But as repeatedly shown in African cases, desired outcomes of violence may satisfy the needs of the powerful groups, while producing untold human suffering and material destruction for the powerless, while also being a channel to express grievances.

The major difficulty facing possibilities of mediation of conflict is the atmosphere of distrust and misunderstanding that is often heightened by memories of historical or recent atrocities, like the events of April–July 1994 in Rwanda. With charges and counter-charges about past events, there seems to be no constructive space in the history of the conflict for effective negotiations to take place. Creating that opening, or point of entry into the conflict, would therefore be a high priority in the conflict mediation process. Somehow conducive or favourable conditions need to be established for the process to take place. Ideally, a dialogical framework should be elaborated to ensure the effective participation of all relevant actors (social movements, other civil society organizations, governments, etc.), to enable them to communicate and negotiate about their perspectives, grievances, demands and so forth.

The creation of a favourable conducive mediation environment must also deal with many other difficulties: opposition from elites, backlash from 'rejectionists', persistence of incompatible goals and lack of political progress, re-politicization of peace-building initiatives, lack of human and material resources of implementation of various strategies and programmes. Finally, there is the question of how to make the whole process sustainable, moving from initial processes of creating a favourable or conducive environment to maintaining human relationships, and generally building on the momentum of the conflict transformation process. In our view, this theoretical framework can be better understood if its application is illustrated by reference to some concrete situations in Africa today, such as Rwanda and Sudan.

Social Movements in the Mediation Process: Rwanda and Sudan

Rwanda Rwanda is an 'ethnically' diverse country with the Hutu constituting an overwhelming majority, about 80 per cent, and the Tutsi and Twa being the two main minorities.[5] It is commonly accepted that the pre-colonial identity of the peoples of the region was based on clan, rather than ethnic affiliation. Gradually, ethnic affiliations partially based on local history and indigenous mythology were emphasized, especially during the colonial period, as indicated below. Although the people were united into one country during the second part of the nineteenth century, the rigid political boundaries demarcating the central African region into European-style 'nation-states' was the result of colonial intrusion.

The Berlin Conference of 1874–76 for the partition of Africa among various European colonial powers had two major consequences for the central African region as a whole. First, the traditional kingdoms of Rwanda and 'Urundi' (now known as Burundi) were reduced in size and left without sufficient resources for healthy economic development. This is clearly reflected in economic problems facing Rwanda today – food shortages and frequent economic crises. Second, substantial numbers of Tutsi and Hutu were left by arbitrary colonial boundary demarcations as minorities within Uganda, Tanzania and Congo–Zaire. This resulted in internal destabilization of the region, as reflected in the role of Uganda in the overthrow of the Hutu-dominated government in 1994, or the 1996 effort of Zaire to 'repatriate' ethnic Tutsi to Rwanda despite their centuries-old ancestry in Zaire.

In 1916 Belgium occupied Rwanda, and in 1946 the country became Belgian trust territory under the United Nations. The Belgian colonial administration emphasized ethnic divisions by relying on Tutsi elites in the administration of the country. The Belgians ruled through the traditional Tutsi kings and retained the traditional feudal structure, thus allowing the Tutsi to hold on to their dominant position in the society. Gradually, however, the Belgians sought to establish a more democratic atmosphere, and this encouraged the rise of the Hutu lower classes. The colonial borders that may have served the plans of the colonial powers left Rwanda a landlocked country with little mineral wealth, and mistreatment of the soil resuted in a lack of sufficient land to produce food. It can be argued that much of the ethnic conflict in the region is reflective of the hope of gaining land, whether by territorial expansion, genocide or expelling certain ethnic groups.

By the mid-1950s, political demands were formulated in ethnic terms, leading to the Hutu violent revolt of 1959, which forced several hundred thousand Tutsi into exile, mainly in Uganda. In the process of decolonization, the general elections of 1961 resulted in a crushing victory of the Hutu-led parties, thereby entrenching the exile of those who had already left and the exclusion of Tutsi from the government of the country. Large numbers of Tutsi were forced to leave the country after independence. A raid launched from Burundi by Tutsi exiles in 1963 brought severe reprisals against Tutsi within Rwanda. A military coup, led by Juvénal Habyarimana, took place in 1973. Although the new government pledged to put an end to tribal hostility, the Hutu monopoly of power continued. A new constitution was introduced in 1978. Elections held in 1981 brought Rwanda its first elected legislature since the military coup of 1973. In the late 1980s Rwanda's economy deteriorated sharply as world coffee prices fell and a serious drought caused crops to fail. In October of 1990 the Rwandese Patriotic Front/Army (RPF/A) invaded Rwanda from Uganda. RPF troops were mostly Tutsi who had fled from ethnic violence during the 1960s and in 1973. The peace negotiations of 1993–94, known as the Arusha process, resulted in an agreement that would have given the Tutsi a greater role in the government of the country and allowed the return of those living in exile.

To break the stalemate in the implementation of that agreement produced by strong resistance among the Hutu majority, further talks were under way during the early months of 1994. President Habyarimana of Rwanda was returning from Arusha, apparently with a renewed commitment to facilitate and accelerate the implementation of the peace agreement, when the aeroplane carrying him (and the prime minister of Burundi) was shot down as it was about to land at Kigali airport on 6 April 1994. This event triggered the wide-scale indiscriminate killing of Tutsi and those Hutu who supported the peace process, and who for that reason were seen by Hutu extremists as 'traitors' to the cause of Hutu control of the country. During the next three months, close to a million Rwandese, mainly Tutsi, were killed. The genocide was finally stopped by the military victory of the RPF, which took over Kigali in July. Most observers agree that the massacres were planned in advance by high-ranking officials in the local and national government, the army and the Presidential

Guard. Although preceded and followed by many other outbreaks of mass violence, the genocide of 1994 was clearly planned and executed by Hutu extremists as a 'final solution' to problems of ethnic tensions in the country by eliminating 'the enemy' altogether.

Sudan The territory in northeast Africa known as the Republic of Sudan was united for the first time through the Turko-Egyptian conquest of 1821, but that unification process was both slow and nominal, especially for the southern parts of the country. For most of the Turko-Egyptian period of colonial rule, southern Sudan was primarily seen as a source of slaves and ivory, rather than an integral part of the country that is entitled to the minimal degree of economic and social development enjoyed by the northern parts of the country. Turko-Egyptian control was terminated in 1884 by a native revolt led by Mohamed Ahmed, a northern Sudanese Muslim Sufi who claimed to be al-Mahdi, the divinely-guided saviour. Upon al-Mahdi's death a few months after the capture of Khartoum, the capital, al-Khalifa Abdullahi (Caliph or successor in Islamic religio-political terms) ruled the country until 1898, when the Anglo-Egyptian conquest established a new colonial administration known as the Anglo-Egyptian Condominium (joint control). But as Britain was occupying Egypt itself at the time (as a 'protectorate'), British army officers and civilian administrators held all senior positions throughout this second colonial administration, which lasted until independence was declared on 1 January 1956.

Since independence, Sudan has been politically unstable under both civilian and military governments, and embroiled in intermittent civil war in the south. The first phase of civilian government ended with the country's first military coup of 17 November 1958, and the military government ruled the country by decree until it was overthrown by a combined civilian and military effort in October 1964. After less than five years of civilian government, however, the army seized power for the second time on 25 May 1969. By 1973, this second military phase established a single-party state and enacted a new constitution under which it ruled the country until it was overthrown by another combined civilian and military effort in April 1985. The third civilian government was once again overthrown by the army on 30 June 1989. Unlike the previous military governments, however, the third military coup was staged by the National Islamic Front (NIF), which is determined to transform the country into an Islamic state and apply more strictly the Islamic Shari'a law that was introduced for the first time by presidential decree in 1983, during the single-party state of former President Numeiri.

The first stage of civil war in southern Sudan started on the eve of independence and continued intermittently until it was settled through the

Addis Ababa Agreement of 1972. In accordance with that agreement, the southern region enjoyed regional autonomy for nearly ten years. By the late 1970s and early 1980s, however, former President Numeiri of the Sudan started gradually to abrogate the Addis Ababa Agreement and undermine the autonomous status of the southern region. The culmination of that abrogation by the imposition of Islamic Shari'a law throughout the country in 1983 triggered the current phase of the civil war. The objectives and strategies of the southern rebel movement this time are quite different from those of earlier phases.

According to the Sudanese People's Liberation Movement and Army (SPLM/SPLA), the grievances of the southern Sudanese are part and parcel of those of all marginalized and disadvantaged peoples of Sudan and must be redressed as such. The SPLM/SPLA is therefore seeking a radical structural transformation of political power and economic relations throughout the country and not simply in north–south terms. Since the NIF coup of 1989, however, the SPLM/SPLA appears to be willing to cooperate with the northern political parties it strongly criticized in the past, at least for the limited objective of ridding the country of the Islamic fundamentalist military rule of the NIF. Several cycles of negotiations between the NIF government in Khartoum and the SPLM since 1992 have failed to achieve a permanent ceasefire, let alone settle the underlying issues of the civil war in Sudan.

The causes of the civil war in Sudan are too complex and controversial to be examined in detail here, except to mention three general considerations that are useful for the purposes of this chapter. First, like most African countries, Sudan reflects the basic paradox of artificial political unity in a situation of intense diversity without a clear consensus on the bases of national identity (Deng 1995). The root causes of that paradox should be traced to the nature of north–south relations since the Turko-Egyptian conquest of the 1820s, especially the role of northern Sudanese in the slave trade against peoples of the south, and their own practice of slavery until the early twentieth century. That history is clearly reflected in the social and political attitudes of northern towards southern Sudanese that prevail to the present day, whereby the assumptions of equal citizenship in political participation and economic development are repudiated by pretensions of racial and cultural superiority of the Arabized Muslim northerners over southerners in general.

Second, historical divisions between the two parts of the country have been intensified by the British colonial policy of severely restricting all interactions between the north and south from the early 1920s to the middle 1940s. Through what is known as the 'closed districts policy', the north was encouraged to develop its identification with the Arab Islamic

Middle East, while the south was opened to European Christianity and missionary education, probably with a view to unite it eventually with British East Africa (now Kenya and Uganda). When that policy was reversed, the British colonial administration 'had neither the time nor the political will to put in place constitutional arrangements that would ensure protection of the South in a united Sudan' (Deng 1995: 11).

Third, as northern Sudanese continued to marginalize and manipulate the south under both civilian and military governments since independence, resistance by southern Sudanese began to be reflected in the desire for radical change in the political, social, economic, cultural, legal and other aspects of the north–south relationship. This desire is now effectively articulated by the educated leaders of the south, who not only strongly resent the subordination and exploitation of their people but also appreciate the possibilities of better alternatives, through either internal restructuring of power and economic relations or complete separation from the north.

Contradictory roles of social movements in these crises Despite significant differences, the violent conflicts in Rwanda and Sudan are instructive for our purposes here because they are both internal conflicts with strong regional and international dimensions and implications. In each of the two countries, a profound crisis of national identity is severely undermining individual and communal life and personal security, as well as obstructing possibilities of peaceful mediation of conflict, prospects of political participation and economic development. Both conflicts are multi-dimensional and protracted, characterized by increasing militarization and the establishment of a self-perpetuating war machine. They are also propelled and intensified by heightened ethnocentrism, decline in moderation, physical separation, residential segregation and/or sharpening of the territorial boundaries. Other typical symptoms of severe and protracted conflict to be found in these two situations include psychological distancing of the Other through scapegoating, stereotyping and dehumanization.

The situations in these two countries present particular difficulty for both inside and outside mediators because of the tendency to extend the same negative characterizations to them: insiders are perceived as traitors, as shown by the killing of Hutu moderates during the genocide in Rwanda, while outsiders are deemed to be biased agents of the other side or pursuing their own hidden agenda. To overcome these obstacles, there must first be a clear appreciation of the realities of the conflict (Vayrynen 1991: 9).

This is not to say that all issues of concern to each side can simply be bargained away, or that it is easy for the parties to a conflict to be well organized and recognize each other, with sufficiently legitimate leadership and genuine sustainable representation of all concerned. Moreover, as indicated earlier, efforts to control or eliminate violence will be futile unless social context is taken into consideration. As is generally true of other parts of Africa, the cases of Rwanda and Sudan involve violence at the micro as well as the macro level, from the local village level to genocide and terror on a national scale. The primary actors in these conflicts operate not alone, but in the context of social movements or other forms of civil society organizations whose interests and preferences are hard to define in fixed durable terms. Institutionalized mechanisms for conflict transformation are unlikely to be readily available and accessible to those whose contributions are most needed.

Without attempting a comprehensive discussion of all types or forms of social movements in Rwanda and Sudan, we wish to identify two main movements in each case for their contradictory roles in these countries. To the extent that the violent conflict in Rwanda is defined in terms of ethnicity, the ex-FAR (the former Hutu-dominated Rwandan Army) and NLF (National Liberation Front) and RPF/RPA[6] are apparently the primary protagonists. Similarly, to the extent that the conflict in Sudan is defined in terms of religio-cultural identity, the NIF and SPLM are the primary protagonists. In each case, the contribution of other actors to both the generation and mediation of conflict must be considered in broader analysis, but we are simply focusing on the above-mentioned movements for the purpose of illustrating our argument. We take the role of these sets of actors to be particularly significant for understanding and working with the contradictory role of social movements in Rwanda and Sudan today.

We also wish to emphasize the need to keep in mind the ramifications of regional and international trends and developments. For example, Western countries have strongly encouraged and pressed for the process of democratization in the African countries, especially since the end of the Cold War in the early 1990s (Purvis 1996). While some positive developments in this regard can clearly be seen in different parts of Africa, democratization has come to be associated with getting international economic and humanitarian aid. Even where a degree of multi-party democracy has been achieved, ongoing rivalry for political power has not been accompanied by the necessary respect for the diversity of the opinions and tolerance of political opposition. In the case of Rwanda in particular, the application of democratic principles as an 'all or nothing' game ended with the genocide and military take-over that followed. The NIF military regime in Sudan is also pursuing a superficial approach to democratization in order to achieve international legitimacy, without any serious effort to accommodate the genuine political, cultural and religious diversity of the country. In this light, we emphasize that sustainable peace, stability and democratic governance can be achieved only when there is due regard for the historical experiences and local, regional and international context of each country. Moreover, entrenched long-term problems, such as export dependency, land reform and lack of regional cooperation, should also be addressed if the mediation is to succeed.

Before turning to our proposed approach to mediation, we should note a number of suggested structural alternatives, like establishing a Protectorate Administration for Rwanda, the partition of the country into Hutu Land and Tutsi Land or the establishment of a Confederation of Central Africa (for greater autonomy of the units, as opposed to federation). Different forms of federation or confederation have also been suggested for Sudan, in addition to exploring the possibility of complete separation for the southern part of the country. Whether it is any of these alternative approaches, or the one we are proposing, there will be need for addressing the issues of centralized political power in state-directed violence, as in the case of Rwanda in 1994; the role of regional considerations; how to keep the transformation flexible enough to reflect changing circumstances of the local, regional and international context; how to encourage the participation of the general public, especially particularly affected communities.

Conflict mediation and transformation in these cases In this light, we shall now consider how to apply our general thesis to the practical mediation of the competing claims of the following social movements: ex-FAR/NLF and RPF/RPA in Rwanda, and the NIF and SPLA/SPLM in Sudan. In particular, in working towards a framework for comprehensive regional peace-building as a proactive attempt to address the problems of the particular sub-region of Africa, we propose the deployment of two sets of strategies:

1. Strategies for mediation of the competing claims internally within the respective movements, be it the NLF or RPF in Rwanda, or NIF, SPLM in Sudan.
2. Strategies for mediation of the competing claims between the opposing sides in each country, that is to say, ex-FAR, NLF vs. RPF and NIF vs. SPLM.

It should be emphasized, however, that these two sets of strategies should not be understood and applied in isolation from each other or to the exclusion of other types of initiatives. On the contrary, as indicated earlier and elaborated below, there is a strong dialectical and reciprocal relationship between these two sets of strategies, as well as between them and other types of initiatives. Otherwise, there would be little prospect of initiating and sustaining internal mediation or of external mediation having access to and influence on the relevant actors.

The dynamic relationship between all these processes is enhanced by their concurrence in time, although some elements of one may apparently presuppose a certain degree of another. In other words, a degree of internal mediation is necessary for opening wider possibilities of external mediation, but the initiation of some external mediation efforts is also necessary for internal mediation to play its role. Realistically speaking, since there is always a history to every internal or external initiative, often in reciprocal relation to each other, it is difficult and artificial to think of any of them in isolation from the other, whether in the nature of the activities, the people involved or the time sequence.

The basic framework for these two types of mediation of competing claims is the relationship between the articulated objectives and the actual methods of a social movement, on the one hand, and those of the wider civil society in whose name it claims to act. For example, to what extent do the objectives and methods of the NIF address the needs of the Sudanese population as whole? In particular, since the primary objective of the NIF is to establish an Islamic state to apply Islamic Shari'a law in Sudan, is that consistent with the fundamental requirements of national unity and peaceful coexistence among all the peoples of Sudan? Is the discourse of cultural/religious superiority represented by the NIF compatible with essential national objectives of peace, stability and development in a highly diverse and multicultural, multi-religious country like Sudan?

It is true that part of the causes of conflict and civil war in Rwanda and Sudan is precisely the lack of national consensus on matters of national identity, principles of governance and international relations, strategies and methods of economic development, and so forth. But since this is the subject of political disagreement everywhere, the real issue is the underlying agreement about how to mediate competing claims about these matters in a peaceful and orderly manner. The question of minimum national consensus should therefore be expressed in terms of the prerequisites of coexistence and continuous peaceful mediation of conflict and disagreement, rather than an imposition of an allegedly final and permanent 'resolution'. In the case of Rwanda, for example, there is certainly serious disagreement about many issues of national policy, but what is necessary for credible mediation of conflict over such issues is to establish a clear consensus that territorial expansion, genocide or expelling of one ethnic group or another can never be the way to bring about desirable results in that country. The question is therefore how to hold all social movements in the country (such as the FAR, NLF and RPF in Rwanda or NIF and SPLA/SPLM in Sudan) accountable to the rationale of their legitimate objectives.

To begin with, since the emergence of these movements was itself the result of the conscious strategic efforts of groups of people in order to fashion and legitimize collective action, there should be similar conscious strategic efforts continually to evaluate the rationale and methods of the social movement in relation to its objectives. More broadly, this continuous evaluation should also be undertaken regarding the relationship between the rationale, methods and objectives of a social movement as a whole, and those of the wider civil society within which it is operating. That is, to what extent are the FAR, NLF or RPF in Rwanda, or NIF and SPLA/SPLM in Sudan, representatives of the civil society in whose name they claim to speak? For example, the alliance of the ex-FAR with the Hutu militia from Burundi inflamed the tense situation inside Burundi and threatened to regionalize the conflict. How can that be good for the Hutu in particular, or the people of Rwanda in general? Raising these and similar questions is important for the membership of the social movement as well as the wider civil society. Each side needs to act on the fact that the sustainability and future success of any social movement depends on the support of the civil society on holding the leadership of any movement accountable. In other words, a social movement or its leadership either have to adjust their objectives and methods or perish.

Why not, one may ask, create new social movements or counter-movements, if the existing ones betrayed their goals? In our view, this would be neither necessary nor sufficient for the mediation of the conflicts in Rwanda and Sudan. First, the problem with any one of the social movements under discussion is in its nature, structure, ideology and methods, rather than in its name or superficial characteristics. Second, there is no guarantee that a new movement would be any different or more constructive in the most relevant aspects of its characteristics. Third, it would be more practical and productive to work with the existing movements because they are the present significant actors on the ground in Rwandan and Sudanese societies. Regardless of what one may think of any of these social movements, their roles in the generation as well as mediation of the conflict cannot be denied or ignored. That is precisely why it is so important for the civil societies of Rwanda and Sudan, and for their regional neighbours and the rest of the world, to hold the leadership of these movements accountable for their actions and omissions.

Conclusion

The real question, therefore, is who is going to hold these leaderships accountable, and how? In our view, this can and must be done by *whatever* forms of civil society organizations exist in each society. This includes community-based councils of elders, market women's groups, farmers' associations, and people's committees organized for administrative or other purposes. It is vitally important to motivate and encourage such organizations to act in this way for two reasons. First, such organizations are immediately concerned with questions of the survival and security of the population at large, and they are the best judge of the practical and sustainable utility of the objectives and methods of a social movement for the well-being of their own society. Second, because of their ability to reach and influence the same wider communities on which social movements rely for support and legitimacy, such community-based organizations will be effective in influencing the leadership of those movements.

Expectation of such action, of course, assumes considerable concern and motivation to act, both within social movements and the wider society. If it is reasonable to assume, as we do, that human beings are always concerned about and motivated to act on matters that directly affect the immediate survival and security of themselves and their facilities, how does one explain the fact that there is little indication of concern and action on the ground? The reasons for this apparent apathy and inaction include a sense of powerlessness and of the futility of organized action, a belief in the lack of effective means of participation, and the ability of those in control of the state or leadership of the social movement to terrorize and intimidate their opponents. In this light, it is not enough simply to urge people to hold social movements accountable without addressing the underlying causes of inaction or inefficacy of the action taken. In our view, this can be done through an examination of the structural and operational nature of the movement in question, and of the relationship between internal and external mediation.

Regarding the first point, we recall what we said earlier about the nature and role of political parties in relation to social movements. As indicated in the first section of this chapter, the nature and consequences of this relationship in African countries like Rwanda and Sudan is the product of a combination of such factors as local cultural norms and institutions, colonial and post-independence history, and the impact of the dynamics of political life at any given point in time on the objectives and methods of the movements. We would therefore emphasize the need to understand and clarify the nature of this relationship for each of the movements under discussion in order to develop more effective strategies for the degree and quality of participation and accountability that we are proposing here. In other words, granted the overlap between the social movement and political party in question, the issue is how can participation and accountability be achieved in a manner that is conducive to a positive role for the movement in the mediation of conflict?

As to external mediation, we would first recall its dialectic relationship to internal mediation, as emphasized earlier. On the one hand, it can be argued that the failure of many attempts to achieve peaceful settlements of the violent conflicts in Rwanda and Sudan (the Arusha process since 1992 for Rwanda, the several cycles of negotiations between NIF and SPLM since 1992) is the result of the lack of internal mediation. Conversely, the latter can be seen as the result of the failure of external mediation. Instead of accepting such deadlocks or frustrations as enduring or unavoidable, we would emphasize the interdependence between the two realms of mediation. External mediators certainly have specific opportunities to act in ways unavailable to internal actors, as well as their own strong incentives for mediation because of the external (regional and international) consequences of violent conflicts. For example, while violent conflicts threaten the security and stability of neighbouring countries, their control of access for warring parties to sources of arms and funding can give those countries significant advantage in pressing for the mediation of the conflict.

As already emphasized, the continuity of all these interdependent mediation efforts should be accepted and utilized. For Rwanda, external mediation efforts include the International Conference on National Dialogue held in Bujumbura (Burundi) in May 1994, and the National Convention in September of the same year. In the case of Sudan, there is the IGADD framework of the East African countries that sponsored several rounds of peace negotiations between the NIF and SPLM. The OAU and the UN can also provide useful frameworks for external mediation of conflict in Rwanda and Sudan. But the point we wish to emphasize is the interdependence and mutual influence between all possible external and internal mediation initiatives.

Notes

1. As discussed below, since conflict is a permanent feature of all human societies, it is misleading to speak of its resolution because that implies permanence of purported 'solutions'. Accordingly, we prefer to speak of 'sustainable mediation' of conflict.

2. This is reflected in several of the CODESRIA studies. See, for example, Admadiume 1995.

3. See 'Introduction' in Dartmouth College, *Reconceptualizing African Social Movements: Gender, Religion, Culture, Politics and Cross-Cultural Interactions*, June 1997, p. 1.

4. Regional conflicts have ranged from Tanzania's invasion of Uganda to overthrow Idi Amin in 1978–79, Morocco's forcible occupation of large areas of the western Sahara since 1976, the Ethiopian/Somali wars of the 1970s and 1980s, and invasions and destabilization tactics by apartheid South Africa against neighbouring countries until the early 1990s, to the current conflicts in the Great Lakes region of central Africa. Many African countries have also suffered devastating civil wars, some continuing for many decades, as in Sudan, or in several cycles, as in Chad.

5. The following review of the situation in Rwanda is based on two sources: first,

Richard Griggs, 'Geostrategies on the great lakes conflict and spatial designs for peace', Center for World Indigenous Studies, 1997, http://www.halcyon.com/fwdp/hutu3-1.html; second, Steering Committee of the Joint Evaluation of Emergency Assistance to Rwanda, 'The international response to conflict and genocide: lessons from the Rwandan experiences', *Journal of Humanitarian Assistance*, April 1996.

6. There are several Hutu armed forces and militia operating within the Great Lakes Area, such as: FDD (a Burundi-based party); Interahamwe (the militia alleged to have organized the 1994 genocide); ADF (Allied Democratic Forces); and FNL. The RPA – Rwandese Patriotic Army – is the military wing of the Rwandese Patriotic Front.

Bibliography

Amadiume, I. (1995) 'Gender, political systems and social movements: a west African experience', in M. Mamdani and E. Wamba-di-Wamba (eds), *African Studies in Social Movements and Democracy*, Dakar: CODESRIA, pp. 35–68.

Deng, F. (1995) *War of Visions: Conflict of Identities in Sudan*, Washington, DC: Brookings Institution.

Fatton, R. Jr (1995) 'Africa in the age of democratization: the civic limitations of civil society', *African Studies Review*, vol. 38, no. 2: 67–99.

Jackson, R. H. and C. G. Rosberg (1986) 'Sovereignty and underdevelopment: juridical statehood in the African crisis', *Journal of Modern African Studies*, no. 24: 1–31.

Lederach, J. P. (1995) *Preparing for Peace: Conflict Transformation Across Cultures*, Syracuse, NY: Syracuse University Press.

Mamdani, M. (1995a) 'Introduction', in M. Mamdani and E. Wamba-di-Wamba (eds), *African Studies in Social Movements and Democracy*, Dakar: CODESRIA.

— (1995b) 'A critique of the state and civil society paradigm in Africanist studies', in M. Mamdani and E. Wamba-di-Wamba (eds), *African Studies in Social Movements and Democracy*, pp. 602–16.

McAdam, D., J. D. McCarthy and M. N. Zald (eds) (1996) 'Introduction: opportunities, mobilizing structures, and framing processes – toward a synthetic, comparative perspective on social movements', in D. McAdam, J. D. McCarthy and M. N. Zald (eds), *Comparative Perspectives on Social Movements: Political Opportunities, Mobilizing Structures, and Cultural Framings*, Cambridge: Cambridge University Press, pp. 1–20.

Purvis, Andrew (1996) 'Revenge of the big man', *Time Magazine*, 1 April, p. 36–7.

Seligman, Adam B. (1992) *The Idea of Civil Society*, New York: Free Press.

Tarrow, S. (1994) *Power in Movement: Social Movements, Collective Action and Politics*, Cambridge: Cambridge University Press.

Vayrynen, R. (ed.) (1991) *New Directions in Conflict Theory: Conflict Resolution and Conflict Transformation*, London: Sage.

Zirakzadeh, C. E. (1997) *Social Movements in Politics: A Comparative Study*, London and New York: Longman.

Post-Biafran Marginalization of the Igbo in Nigeria

Nnaemeka Ikpeze

Marginalization is defined in this chapter as the deliberate disempowerment of a people politically, economically, socially and militarily by a group or groups that – during a relevant time-frame – wield political power and control the allocation of material and other resources at the centre. The phenomenon is endemic in societies whose constituent groups are bedevilled by unequal and antagonistic relationships. Relatedly, the national question in Nigeria is a product of tensions engendered by the dynamics of such adversarial inter-ethnic relations. Marginalization has been used as a strategy for the exploitation of these relationships in post-colonial Nigeria, especially since the collapse of Biafra in 1970. In particular, the Igbo have been victims of marginalization since the end of the Nigerian civil war.

As a people the Igbo have been systematically disempowered politically, economically, militarily and socially by the Hausa/Fulani and Yoruba groups. This is the subject of a poorly circulated essay 'Marginalisation in Nigerian polity: a diagnosis of the "Igbo problem" and the national question', published by the *Nsukka Analyst* in 1994. The present effort derives significantly from my contribution to that essay. Underscoring the fact that the question of the marginalization of the Igbo is still an issue, a lobby document titled 'Military dictatorship and the marginalisation of the Igbo in Nigeria', and attributed to one Mr Onyekwere, has recently described the 'economic, political, military and social marginalisation of Igbos' as a 'nagging' issue that ought to be resolved (*The Guardian* – Nigeria – 29 April 1998, p. 4). Curiously, however, it has also been claimed by some writers, within the same time-frame, that both the Hausa/Fulani and the Yoruba groups are marginalized. The Hausa/Fulani case has been made, for example, in two anonymous articles, 'Who's marginalised?' and 'Revenue allocation: the winners, losers', which appeared respectively in *The Sentinel* of 19 and 26 September 1994. More recently, the Yoruba case has been stated by Professor Adedeji in a lecture titled 'The Yoruba in the

Nigerian political economy'. Professor Adedeji is reported to have deplored what he described as 'the marginalization of the Yoruba in national affairs', citing as examples the states creation ratio between the North and the South and the annulled 12 June 1993 election (*The Guardian* – Nigeria – 7 May 1998).

The procedure employed in this chapter to arrive at the 'truth', in the face of these claims and counter-claims of marginalization by various ethnic groups in Nigeria, consists in distinguishing clearly between the marginalized and the marginalizer, indicating the implications of the problem for the resolution of the national question. Also in the search for 'truth', the chapter draws lessons from history and, in particular, from the experiences of such conflict-ridden countries as Rwanda and Burundi.

Due attention is given to two aspects of the Igbo response to economic marginalization: the strategies of the economically distressed Igbo woman, and adjustments by the men via the informal sector of the Nigerian economy.

In its conclusion the chapter proffers proposals for removing the obstacles that marginalization of the Igbo – or of any other group – poses for the attainment of truth, healing and social justice in post-Biafran Nigeria.

The Marginalized and the Marginalizer

Contexts in which the term marginalization easily advances to the forefront of public discussion are those that are characterized by at least one of the unequal or antagonistic relationships classified by Adedeji (1993: 1) as 'fast-track/slow-track (or on-track/off-track); centre/periphery, majority/minority, possession/dispossession, independence/dependence, superiority/inferiority, and dominance/subordination. The context in which the term is used – and sometimes abused – in Nigeria is one in which the national question looms so large as to dwarf all other questions. It is a context in which ethnically heterogeneous peoples, involuntarily thrown together as a mere 'geographical expression' (Awolowo 1947) and utterly lacking in the 'basis for unity' (as claimed by General Gowon in a radio broadcast in 1967), have laboured for about nine decades under the yoke of unequal and antagonistic relationships and are grappling with the imperative of autonomously negotiating the fundamentals of a corporate existence as a nation-state in which no group is marginalized. The gravity of the national question underscores the need for rigour in the definition of marginalization and the essential distinction between the marginalized and the marginalizer – a distinction that is at the root of the national question and is, therefore, crucial to its resolution.

The two terms are liable to be innocently, but dangerously, treated as though they were interchangeable. Marginality has been defined in the literature as 'the relative or absolute lack of power to influence a defined social entity while being a recipient of the exercise of power by other parts of that entity' (Adedeji 1993: 1). Marginality, so defined, simply and neutrally refers to the state of being peripheral without attributing blame to any particular factor or marginalizer. Thus a group that, for instance, by systematically insulating itself from the forces of modernization (e.g. Western education), becomes peripheral in terms of such indices of social development as enrolment in educational institutions (primary, secondary and tertiary) and the supply of high-level manpower is adequately described as marginal if it is outstripped, in terms of those parameters, by other groups that happen to have embraced modernity. Such a group will be hard put to identify an exogenous marginalizer. The first step out of marginality is for the group to recognize that its status derives from its relative or, perhaps, absolute backwardness. Unlike marginality, marginalization necessarily presupposes the existence of a group or groups that possess the capacity to disempower others.

Marginalization, being an emotion-laden term, is highly susceptible to abuse, especially in the hands of ethnic chauvinists and political charlatans. A classic case of such abuse has been serialized in *The Sentinel* by – usually faceless and nameless – 'concerned citizens of Nigeria'. The first and second articles in the series ('Who's marginalised?' and 'Revenue allocation: the winners, losers'), which appeared in the 19 September and 26 September 1994 issues respectively are examples of statistical misrepresentation of marginalization through the devious selection, and partial analysis, of data to demonstrate that northern Nigeria is educationally marginalized with reference to the number of northerners admitted into the nation's tertiary institutions. The authors, however, conveniently neglect to display (a) the regional distribution of the candidates who presented themselves for the entrance examinations, (b) the regional distribution of passes and failures in terms of the numbers scoring below and above the statutory minimum mark, (c) the distribution, by region, of admissions as a percentage of number of candidates, (d) the relative capacities of the regions, based on their secondary school enrolments, to produce candidates for entrance examinations, etc. Further statistical analysis along these lines should have buttressed the simple fact that more southerners gain admission into tertiary institutions because the north is, by far, less enthusiastic than the south about Western education. In the article in question educational marginality has either been grossly mistaken for, or mischievously misrepresented as, marginalization. Clearly, the south would be guilty of confusing marginality for marginalization if it complained of being marginalized in admissions into schools of Arabic studies.

The Origins of Marginalization in the Country

The history of marginalization in Nigeria divides conveniently into two periods: the period up to 1960 and the period since 1970. In the former, marginalization was perpetrated against all Nigerians irrespective of ethnic or regional affiliation by the colonial master, Britain. In the latter, the Igbo people have been jointly marginalized by the Hausa-Fulani and the Yoruba. It took the intervening period (1960–67) for the forces of ethnic particularism, which had been artificially repressed by the colonial regime, to burst forth, gather momentum, and culminate in a civil war (1967–70). By the end of the civil war in January 1970 the control of political power and the disposition of economic resources at the centre had fallen squarely into the hands of the Hausa-Fulani and Yoruba ethnic groups. For the first time in the history of Nigeria some groups acquired the capacity to marginalize others. In spite of protestations to the contrary, the Igbo people became a 'vanquished' group and have since then been systematically marginalized as such by the 'victorious' coalition, the 'No victor, no vanquished' declaration by General Gowon notwithstanding.

The Mohammed/Obasanjo regime, which ousted General Gowon, was at pains to abort Gowon's programme of 'reconciliation, rehabilitation and reconstruction'. Both generals, unlike Gowon, had personally commanded troops on Biafran soil in the bid to subdue the Igbo militarily and had, therefore, experienced first-hand the indomitable spirit of the Igbo people. In what must be reckoned the bitterest battle of his military career, Mohammed narrowly escaped death or capture and suffered colossal losses in men and equipment at Abagana in February 1968 during the ill-fated attempt of Nigeria's Second Division to take Onitsha by land. Colonel Obasanjo, as he was then known, took over the command of the Third Marine Commandos when that force, under Colonel Adekunle, was seriously dented by the Biafran army in the Owerri/Port Harcourt sector. After slugging it out for eight long months, Obasanjo also had to oversee the formal surrender of Biafra in January 1970. These personal experiences translated into a tremendous personal stake for both generals in the post-war marginalization of the Igbo. It was, understandably, important to them that the Igbo were not only conquered but were also seen thereafter to be a vanquished people.

In the pre-independence era (before 1960), power was exercised and allocated by the colonial master in favour of metropolitan interests and to the detriment of Nigeria as a whole. The entire country was marginalized into being a source of cheap raw materials for British industry and a captive market for British manufacturers. It is by no means trivial to stress the point that during the colonial period no group of Nigerians was marginalized by any other group, for the simple reason that none possessed the capacity to do so. All that happened was that, within the common constraint of colonial marginalization, the various ethnic groups competed among themselves for such goodies as admission into the higher educational institutions, entry into the intermediate and higher echelons of the public service and the military, and the rewards of enterprise in the private sector of the economy.

Although the Yoruba had given the rest of the country a head-start in terms of early exposure to Western education and business contacts, the Igbo, unlike the Hausa-Fulani, moved rapidly to make good their educational and other deficits. In a very short time, the Igbo produced a solid corps of high-level manpower and were able to secure a respectable share of the public service and military positions relinquished by British officers under the policy of Nigerianization. They were also able to field a respectable number of high-calibre persons in the various professions – medicine, engineering, law, university teaching. To dramatize what the Igbo man was able to achieve on merit within a short time we draw attention to the following: the first indigenous general officer commanding (GOC) of the Nigerian army was an Igbo; the first indigenous vice-chancellor of the nation's first university was an Igbo; the first indigenous economic adviser to the Nigerian government was an Igbo. These achievements were all recorded before the outbreak of the 1967–70 civil war.

It was, however, in the economic sphere that the Igbo were at their best in the game of competition. In industry, commerce, transportation and other services Igbo businessmen exercised unparalleled initiative and were exceptionally sensitive to the opportunities presented by the Nigerian economy. To be able to exploit such opportunities, they quickly learned the new, even if alien, ways of doing business. Many took advantage of the expansive business horizon to amass great fortunes. Such successes inspired many enterprising and risk-taking Igbo people to venture forth. In this quest for economic achievement Igbo businessmen became rather ubiquitous in Nigeria. They sniffed out market opportunities even in the remotest corners of the country. They were no respecters of ethnic, regional or state boundaries. Naturally, the Igbo businessman encountered competition in other parts of the country. But always and everywhere, he has been able to hold his own. Unfortunately, however, beyond normal business competition – which he relishes – the Igbo man has also had to cope with sheer resentment on account of his drive, which is often misperceived by his fellow competitors as unwarranted aggressiveness. Thus, in his study of the Hausa–Igbo conflicts in Kano between 1953 and 1991, Albert identifies 'the economic assertiveness of the Igbo' as one of the major factors that set the Igbo immigrants in Kano and their Hausa hosts at variance. The Igbo businessman's competitive prowess led the Kanawa before Nigerian independence to complain of Igbo dominance, in both the formal and informal economy of Kano. This eventually led to conflict between the Igbo immigrants and their Hausa hosts (Albert 1993).

At the end of the Nigerian civil war, the Hausa-Fulani and the Yoruba, who had cornered and shared political, military and economic power to the exclusion of the Igbo people, cast overboard the priceless colonial heritage of meritocracy in an insidious bid to stem the tide of competition and thus emasculate the enterprising, competitive and geographically mobile Igbo man. The progressive principles of merit and competition were now supplanted by such nebulous and retrogressive policies as 'federal character', 'quota system' and 'state of origin'. It is, of course, quite easy to see through the unholy design to use the policies of 'federal character' and 'quota system' to impose upper limits on the rewards that can naturally accrue to the Igbo man from sheer enterprise and free competition. It is also easy to see that the rationale for the new-found emphasis on the disclosure of 'state of origin' is to facilitate the conservation, by the dominant groups, of opportunities in their home states for 'sons of the soil' and the exclusion, from their homesteads, of the ubiquitous and highly adaptable Igbo, who respect no ethnic or state boundaries in their search for opportunities.

As will be seen in the next section of this chapter, these retrogressive principles underpin most of the instruments that have been effectively used to marginalize the Igbo politically, economically, militarily and socially. This will be shown to be invariably true, whether their mode of application is discriminatory or differential. Their application is discriminatory, albeit in reverse, if in deference to, for instance, 'federal character', highly qualified and competent Igbo persons yield positions in the public service to less qualified and mediocre persons from other groups. The application may be called differential if, where the Hausa-Fulani, Yoruba or any other group enjoys more than its fair quota of top military, bureaucratic and other positions, the quota of the Igbo or any other group, for that matter, is grossly underfilled. It is partly through the manipulation of such nebulous and retrogressive principles that a deliberate programme of marginalization can be executed.

Instruments of Marginalization

The arsenal that has been used for the marginalization of Igbo people since the end of the civil war boasts a motley assortment of deadly peace-time weapons. We attempt here a classification of these instruments according to the various dimensions of marginalization: economic strangulation, politico-bureaucratic emasculation, military neutralization and ostracism.

Economic strangulation   There are two good reasons for beginning our review of the instruments of marginalization with economic strangulation. The first is that it was both the earliest and the most pernicious instrument employed to undermine the very existence of all Igbo men, women and children who had survived the civil war. The second is that it is the instrument that easily underscores the fact that the Yoruba involvement in the marginalization of the Igbo people dates all the way back to the beginnings of post-colonial marginalization in Nigeria, thanks to the role of the champion of the Yoruba ethnic group – Chief Obafemi Awolowo – in his capacity as Nigeria's minister of finance during and after the civil war.

Chief Awolowo had masterminded the economic blockade of Biafra and rationalized the use of hunger, raising it to the status of a legitimate instrument of war. Little wonder that he had no qualms about super-intending over the application of various peacetime variants of that weapon against the Igbo immediately the shooting war ended. Three examples are particularly noteworthy:

1. Immediately after the war, Awolowo put a ceiling of 20 pounds on all bank accounts that had been operated in Biafra during the hostilities. This was deliberately calculated to neutralize the savings and, therefore, the capacity of Igbo people to rehabilitate themselves and to re-enter (and, indeed, regain their share of) the Nigerian economy, which he was intent on reserving for the Yoruba people.

2. Seeing that the effective demand of the federal troops for goods and services in Igboland was beginning to put some money back into the ever-enterprising Igbo hands, the federal government quickly effected a massive withdrawal of troops from that territory. The measure was clearly designed to deny the Igbo economy the stimulus it badly needed for recovery.

3. Only two years or so after the war, when the Igbo were still in the economic doldrums, Chief Awolowo contrived to auction off the Nigerian economy to the Yoruba through the so-called Enterprises Promotion (otherwise known as the Indigenization) Decree. The timing of this policy ensured the effective exclusion of Igbo people from ownership in Nigeria's industrial sector.

In addition to these early measures to disempower the Igbo people economically other strangulatory policies that have, to date, been operated against the Igbo people include the manipulation of the revenue-sharing arrangements and federal economic presence.

With respect to revenue-sharing: between the Phillipson Commission Report (1946) and the Dina Committee Report (1968) the principle of derivation had always enjoyed pride of place among the criteria for revenue allocation in Nigeria. During this period agricultural produce was the major source of revenue, and it was very convenient for the west (mainly Yoruba) and the north (mainly Hausa-Fulani), whose cocoa and groundnuts were respectively bigger revenue-earners than the east's (mainly Igbo) palm produce, to insist that priority be accorded to the principle of derivation. But since the late 1960s, when it was clear that petroleum, located mainly in the east, was going to replace agriculture as the major revenue source, the west and the north have, in a dramatic *volte face* and to the embarrassment of the east, ensured the downgrading of the principle of derivation to the point where today it has all but completely vanished as a criterion for revenue-sharing. It is significant that in the same year that the war ended the principle received its death-blow through Decree No. 13, 1970, which recognized only two equally weighted principles – population and equality of states. Of course, the principle of derivation has, since, been revived to appease the oil-producing areas (which now happen to be some of the minority states) but in a grossly attenuated form. Originally directed against the Igbo, prior to the dismemberment of the east in the name of state-creation, the persistent downgrading of the principle of derivation is today ironically taking its heaviest toll on the oil-producing minority peoples of the east. Ironically, because these minority peoples have been – and are still being – pressed into the service of aiding and abetting the marginalization of the Igbo people (*vide* Section 4b).

Concerning the manipulation of federal presence, it is an understatement to observe that 'federal economic presence' is conspicuously absent in Igboland. We draw attention to three principal aspects of lowly federal economic presence in Igboland:

1. There is an inordinately high incidence of infrastructural destitution, which has been brought about by the abysmally low level of federal provision and maintenance since the end of the war of roads, bridges, telecommunications, medical, educational and other facilities. Only lip-service was paid to the post-war slogan of 'reconciliation, rehabilitation and reconstruction'. There has, of course, been an occasional token donation – especially to educational institutions – towards infrastructural provision or upkeep or an equally occasional adoption of a sick and infrastructurally deficient educational institution. These, however, pale into insignificance when put side by side with the massive injections of federal funds into infrastructural projects located in the Yoruba and Hausa-Fulani zones of the country.

2. In terms of industrial location, Igboland has, so far, been cheated out of at least two basic industries that should, ideally, have been located in that zone – an iron and steel complex and the petrochemical industry.

Studies have already shown that Igboland satisfies the raw materials, transportation, market and other requirements for the successful establishment of these industries. The choice of artificial locations, usually in the north and the west, for these industries has been calculated to deny Igboland the usual linkage and other possibilities.

3. There has been a negligible federal concern for the major ecological problem of Igboland – soil erosion – as compared to the impressive desertification, locust and flood relief programmes sponsored by the federal government in the north.

Political emasculation Although reasons have been advanced for presenting the instrument of economic strangulation before that of political emasculation, it must be borne in mind that the latter is, by far, the most fundamental of all instruments of marginalization. It is the instrument that has set the stage for, and facilitates the operation of, all other instruments. It is the instrument with which the Hausa-Fulani and the Yoruba have excluded the Igbo effectively from participation in the exercise of political power at the centre. To be thus politically emasculated is to be fundamentally rendered vulnerable and marginalizable on all other fronts.

From a pre-war position of strength in the political configuration known as the Big Three (Hausa-Fulani, Yoruba and Igbo) and pre-eminence in the presidency (the only pre-war president that the country ever had was an Igbo) the Igbo people have been systematically relegated to a marginal status in terms of power-sharing arrangements in the country. The Yoruba and the Hausa-Fulani, who cornered the political and bureaucratic positions vacated at the centre in 1966/67 by the fleeing Igbo, have not yet seen fit to use their new-fangled principles of 'federal character' and 'quota system' either to restore the pre-war balance or, at the very least, to ensure that the Igbo are otherwise adequately represented in the power-sharing structures at the centre. They have instead employed these nebulous principles, albeit discriminatorily and differentially, to exclude the Igbo effectively from the political-cum-administrative scheme of things. Whether or not an Igbo can ever again be the president of Nigeria has become an issue that is to be settled – or so it seems – not by open and free political competition. Since the end of the civil war all that the Igbo have enjoyed in terms of federal cabinet posts are token appointments to strategically insignificant positions. The key cabinet posts have now become the special preserves of the Yoruba and Hausa-Fulani. The same has been true of Igbo presence in the administrative structure and headship of ministerial and extra-ministerial departments as well as parastatals.

To seal the political fate of the Igbo and put their marginalization on all fronts on a permanent footing the Hausa-Fulani and the Yoruba have conspired to distort the geopolitical structure of the country to the point where it is decidedly and permanently skewed against the Igbo, to revamp boundary adjustments against Igbo interests, and to exploit the fragility of the relations between the Igbo and their minority neighbours.

The cumulative outcome of the distribution of states and local government areas (LGAs) during the Gowon, Mohammed/Obasanjo and Babangida regimes is shown in Table 5.1 below:

TABLE 5.1 Distribution of states and local government areas (LGAs) in Nigeria

Ethnic group	No. of states	No. of LGAs
Hausa/Fulani	15	334
Yoruba	6	133
Igbo	5	95

Given the country's vertical and horizontal revenue-sharing arrangements, it is clear that the ethnic distribution of states and LGAs has been consistently calculated to give the Hausa-Fulani and the Yoruba an in-built advantage over the Igbo in the sharing of the federation account.

Boundary adjustments

- The anti-Igbo boundary adjustment that Obasanjo used the Irikefe Panel to accomplish in the former Rivers State. The boundary adjustment amounted to an addition to that state of some Ijaw communities, previously located in what is now called Delta State; and the objective of the manoeuvre was, of course, to marginalize the Igbo, who had been in the majority in that area, into a minority group.
- Sporadic boundary disputes between the Igbo and their Akwa Ibom and Cross River neighbours, particularly in the Azumini, Ngwa, Isu-Arochukwu and Itumbauzo areas. It is significant that these disputes were unknown before the civil war and that the Federal Government has, up to now, taken little definitive action to settle them equitably.

The exploitation of the fragility of relations between the Igbo and their minority neighbours is vividly exemplified by the 'abandoned property' syndrome in post-war Port Harcourt. At the end of the civil war, the Igbo were denied access to the properties they had built in the city before 1967. These properties were brazenly seized by the non-Igbo elements of Rivers State. Indigenes became instant landlords and acquired the power to eject and terrorize the legitimate owners of the properties which they were usurping. That the federal and state authorities have maintained their indifference to this injustice and failed to uphold the constitutionally inviolable national residency and citizenship rights of the original Igbo owners of the properties is indisputable evidence of official exploitation of the fragility of relations.

Military neutralization In the logic of the victorious coalition, military neutralization is bound to be the final solution to the possibility of Igbo military resurgence. To neutralize the Igbo militarily the policy of according them only a token presence in the Nigerian army was accordingly adopted. The lowly presence of the Igbo in the military has been brought about over the past quarter of a century through the re-absorption of only a negligible number of the Nigerian army officers of Igbo origin who had fought on the Biafran side; a post-war recruitment policy that was aimed against Igbo presence in the military; a promotion policy that ensured both a slow rate of upward mobility for Igbo officers and the virtual exclusion of Igbo officers from the highest military positions; and a retirement policy calculated to ensure that the few Igbo officers who get anywhere near the top do not stay there for any reasonable length of time.

A critical consequence of this state of affairs is, at worst, a total absence and – at best – a token military representation of Igbos in the country's military ruling councils over the years. This has effectively ensured that political, economic and other decisions taken at the highest level do not necessarily take Igbo interests into account. Similarly, Igbo officers have not been adequately represented in the running of strategic military locations. Furthermore, Igbo land is virtually bereft of such military facilities. Igbo officers have received high-level assignments mainly in non-combatant positions (usually in the navy and the air force) and, of course, away from Igboland. Important installations such as the mechanized divisions and armouries are sited in the north and the west and are officered by northerners and westerners.

The under-representation of the Igbo in the military – complemented by a similar situation in the police, state security service, directorate of military intelligence, immigration, customs, etc. – is a clear case of the deliberate violation of the post-war principles of 'federal character' and 'quota system' by the victorious coalition. In the logic of the vanquished these principles have been discriminatorily and differentially employed to marginalize the Igbo militarily.

Ostracism Since the end of the civil war, the Igbo have continued in their characteristic way to venture to other parts of the federation in search of business and other opportunities. They do so in the belief that their citizenship and residency rights are sacrosanct under the law and the

Nigerian constitution. However, widespread resentment of their drive and competitiveness has combined with post-war derision and snobbery – typically reserved for a conquered people – to produce an emphatic negation of these rights in non-Igbo parts of the country. Both federal and state authorities have signalled their approval of the ostracism of the Igbo by looking the other way and not enforcing the relevant legal and constitutional provisions on national citizenship and residency. Particularly in the north and the west the retrogressive principle of 'state of origin' has been notoriously used to exclude the Igbo from social acceptance in matters of employment and business. The Igbo have also been routinely discriminated against in school enrolment and taxation.

As if these indirect and subtle means of social marginalization do not go far enough, they have been bolstered, from time to time, with direct physical attacks in both the north and the west. These attacks have usually resulted in the death and maiming of Igbo people as well as the destruction and looting of their property. Whether called religious or political, the assaults have usually been sponsored by the protagonists of Igbo marginalization in both camps of the 'victorious' coalition. The Kano and Bauchi attacks in the North and the 'June 12' disturbances in the west are recent and vivid cases in point.

In whatever form the social rejection of the Igbo manifests itself – direct or indirect, covert or overt – it is part of the grand design of the 'victorious' coalition to destroy the Igbo psyche and induce the ubiquitous and competitive Igbo to withdraw into their shell, thus imprisoning themselves within a circle of marginalization that is viciously closed politically, economically, militarily and socially.

The Response of the Igbo to Economic Marginalization

In terms of social movements the Igbo have responded to economic marginalization in two major ways: the survival strategies adopted by the economically distressed Igbo woman, and the adjustments made by the Igbo man via the informal sector of the Nigerian economy. As indicated by the ensuing analysis, the two movements are not unconnected. Indeed, the former is reinforced by the latter. But our first order of business is to delineate the responses.

Strategies of the economically distressed Igbo woman The gravity of the socio-economic destabilization of Igbo women, within the context of the economic marginalization of the Igbo, and their adjustments to the distress cannot be adequately appreciated unless they are presented against the background of an analysis of the linkage between the economic role of women and their status in the traditional Igbo society. The socio-economic equilibrium enjoyed by Igbo women in the traditional political economy framework had served them well in both the pre-colonial and colonial periods but has been significantly upset in the post-colonial era by the post-war marginalization of the Igbo.

The economic role of women in Igboland should ideally be discussed under the following categories: sectoral/occupational distribution, labour force participation, and contribution to the national income or product. Unfortunately the extant literature has generally not followed any such scheme. Investigators, mainly historians and anthropologists, have concentrated on the description of their sectoral/occupational distribution. Economists who are better equipped to cover all three categories have, so far, been frustrated by certain conceptual and statistical difficulties that bedevil the measurement of women's work but are beyond the scope of this chapter.

Basden (1966), Ottenberg and Ottenberg (1962), Uchendu (1965) and Ezumah (1988) have portrayed Igbo women as traditionally pursuing occupations in three main sectors of economic activity – agriculture, manufacturing and trading. Although usable data are not available, casual evidence suggests that, in terms of the number of women involved, their level of responsibility in decision-making and execution, and the amount of time allocated, Igbo women fill a substantial role in agricultural production and associated food-processing activities. By comparison, the men have, traditionally, been concerned mainly with clearing and preparing the land for cultivation, planting yams – the king of all crops – and harvesting oil-palm produce. All other crops – maize, cassava, coco-yam, beans, tomatoes, vegetables, pumpkins, okra – are women's. All pre-harvest weeding on the farm has also been the responsibility of women. In the manufacturing sector certain activities have been reserved for women: cotton-spinning and weaving, mat-making, basket-weaving, pottery (cooking and water pots) and soap-making. Regarding the third sector, trading, the marketplace has been the domain of the women in traditional Igbo society. It is the forum for selling their agricultural output and their handicrafts and other manufactured goods. Women have traditionally dominated trade, especially of the retail and local varieties.

An important concern of the political economy approach to the study of Igbo women is the analysis of the relationship between their economic role and their status in society. Feminists typically lament that it is the lot of women everywhere to be placed in an inferior status relative to men. Brunsden writes: 'Defined primarily through our destinies as wives and mothers – to be somebody else's private life – women are principally placed politically, ideologically and economically, in the private sphere of the family' (Brunsden 1978: 23). Like Marxists, feminists see the pre-eminence of the man in the family as being at the root of the subjugation of women. It is indeed the case that in most cultures men are considered to have the birthright to rule women. Everywhere women are patronizingly lumped together with children as a 'vulnerable' group.

But, following Gallagher (1981), women must be analysed in connection with the socio-economic structure of society. In Igboland the economic roles filled by women in agriculture, manufacturing and trading are considered to be only of secondary importance. For example women's crops, even though more numerous than the man's, follow the man's crop, yam. Again, long-distance trade – a man's domain – is the pre-eminent form of commerce. Not only are the men's economic activities considered more prestigious, they supposedly are also more lucrative. Men, therefore, tend to exercise greater command over economic resources. Other important factors that contribute to the superiority of the man's status in Igboland are patrilineage and the associated male control over land.

It has, however, been argued by Leacock (1978) that wherever women have been able to maintain their economic autonomy as traders, their status has remained unimpaired and they have usually been able to organize to keep their rights intact. Leacock cites West Africa as a region that boasts exceptions to Engels's thesis that women are universally oppressed and subjugated. Indeed, within that region, Igboland has traditionally been a veritable exception. In indicating the limits to the possibility of oppression in Igboland, Achebe (1988) argues that one 'important' and 'concrete' limit in the traditional Igbo society was the 'role of women in the economic domain', pointing out their important role in the economy. Igbo women have traditionally managed to maintain considerable economic integrity. We must also hasten to add that, more significantly, there have been no institutionalized restrictions on women's political power. For both sexes, status is achieved, not ascribed, and leaders in Igboland have been men and women who (combined) wealth and generosity with 'mouth', i.e. oratory (Allen 1972).

This traditional state of affairs remained basically unchanged by the colonial incursion. Indeed, status-wise colonialism cut against, as well as in favour of, the Igbo woman. In terms of the Western impact on the Igbo status system, Uchendu has shown that 'the old and the new coexist', modifying each other. The church, the school, urbanization and modern politics – all products of the colonial experience – have opened up new statuses from which women are not barred. In politics, especially, women can, and do, hold high public office at the federal, state and local government levels.

The socio-economic equilibrium depicted above, in terms of the link between economic role and social status, was dynamic in the sense that it served Igbo women well during both the pre-colonial and colonial periods. It was, however, significantly disturbed, notably by the economic marginalization of the Igbo as a result of the civil war.

Although agricultural tasks and crops had been delineated according to gender (Basden 1966; Uchendu 1965) the literature has in more recent times reported a major breakdown in the gender division of labour. It has been observed that Igbo women are now increasingly involved in male tasks such as land clearing and the cultivation of yams, the male crop (Okorji 1985; Ezumah 1990; Ezumah and Di Domenico 1995; Ezumah 1997). Greater male involvement in rural–urban migration in search of economic opportunities has contributed to female dominance in food production in Igboland and other parts of eastern Nigeria and creates greater work burdens for women who are left behind (Ezumah 1990; Ezumah 1997). Although women constitute the majority of farmers they have inadequate access to improved farm technologies, capital/credit, land, wage labour and other production inputs. Owing to this marginalization, women are liable to achieve low yields at farm level and to suffer from chronic food insecurity and poverty (Ezumah 1997). Post-war public policy has so far failed to address the need to ensure women's empowerment.

Although the literature has begun to document these facets of the economic destabilization and marginalization of the Igbo woman it has remained silent on the origins of these negative shifts. It is my hypothesis that both the breakdown in the gender division of work and the preponderance of women in agricultural work assumed significance for the first time in Igboland during the Biafran revolution (1967–70), when all able-bodied men were involved in some aspect or other of the war effort.

The movement that has been described as the 'flight' of men from agriculture in response to the attractions of city life and urban wage employment (Ezumah 1997) is significantly, in the case of Igbo men, a rational response to their post-Biafran exclusion from the mainstream of the Nigerian economy. The 'flight' was not necessarily into urban wage employment but mostly into self-employment in the urban informal sector.

Adjustment via the informal sector of the economy By the late 1960s, it had become clear that the failure of industrialization in Nigeria to yield the expected 'trickle-down' effects (a downward diffusion of economic opportunities) was largely responsible for the crystallization of two interrelated sectors – formal and informal – of the economy. The major function of the informal sector has, therefore, understandably been informally to distribute 'survival chances for all those who are denied access to the formal sector' (Herrle 1982).

Activities that make the least demands in terms of capital, skills and technology, such as street-trading, hawking, personal services, casual labour and petty services, have formed the easiest ports of entry. Ease of entry into the informal sector has also been promoted by the virtual absence of laws, contracts, registration and licensing requirements in that sector. But the sector also embraces more sophisticated small-scale manufacturing, service, commercial and transport activities.

There has been in every part of Nigeria a more or less substantial informal sector, operating outside the framework of state laws, where free entry and wage flexibility have combined to enlarge the scope for the employment of economically marginalized or socially ostracized persons. Free entry has, of course, not always implied a total absence of inter-ethnic conflict in this sector. As noted above, at various times before Nigerian independence the Kanawa had one reason or another to complain that the Igbo dominated the formal and informal sectors of the Kano economy (Albert 1993).

A recent study (Obadan et al. 1996) has reported that employment in the Nigerian informal sector between 1970 (when the civil war ended) and 1989 amounted to 33.0 per cent of employment. The share of informal sector employment in total employment grew from 27.3 per cent in 1970 to 38.2 per cent in 1989. Wage employment, as distinct from self-employment, grew from 17 per cent in 1970 to 30 per cent of the total workforce in the informal sector in 1989. Nigeria's informal sector may therefore be described as a labour sponge. In addition to accommodating large numbers of persons in varying states of disguised unemployment and underemployment, it serves as a cushion against the open unemployment that should have resulted from the various dislocations of workers arising from such major upheavals as the 1967–70 civil war (in the case of Igbos) and the massive retrenchments and rationalizations that have accompanied the Structural Adjustment Programme from 1986 to date (in the case of all ethnic groups).

Igbo men responded to their post-war economic marginalization by moving quickly into the informal sector. This response was understandably massive for a people who had fled from other parts of the country in 1966–67, leaving behind their jobs, businesses and property. There was a dire and urgent need for economic rehabilitation. In the face of economic strangulation, as the official attitude, the informal sector appeared to be the easiest – and perhaps the only feasible – port of re-entry into the Nigerian economy at the end of the shooting war.

To recapitulate and indicate the connection between the two movements delineated above, the response of the economically distressed Igbo women is epitomized in the breakdown of gender roles and a greater work burden for women, both of which assumed significance for the first time during the Biafran revolution, when able-bodied men were not available for agricultural and other work. The response of the Igbo men to economic marginalization in the post-war era has been to migrate in large numbers to other parts of Nigeria in search of economic opportunities in the informal sector as a strategy for re-entering the mainstream of the Nigerian economy.

Implications of Marginalization for the Resolution of the National Question

The marginalization of the Igbo or any other group must not only be condemned as an atrocity but must also be understood to be inextricably bound up with the national question. It is idle to seek a resolution of the national question while doing nothing to stop the marginalization of a group or groups within the country. As cautioned by Achebe in his book *The Trouble with Nigeria*: 'The policy of overt and covert exclusion and discrimination beginning with Awolowo's banking regulations at the end of the civil war and pursued relentlessly by the Mohammed/Obasanjo administration has had its day and must now end in the interest of stability and progress' (Achebe 1983). History is replete with the lessons that the marginalization of peoples is, in the final analysis, unsustainable. The transatlantic trade in slaves could not endure beyond a certain point. The vast colonial empires of the European powers have had to be liquidated. The problems of the minorities in the United States are eventually being addressed through 'affirmative action'. Ian Smith's Rhodesia yielded place to present-day Zimbabwe. Apartheid, finally unable to cope with the reactions it elicited, has had to be terminated, at least officially. Marginalization, if allowed to fester, is bound to resolve itself autonomously in the fullness of time, but not without unleashing explosive and cataclysmic reactions. For ignoring this lesson of history, Rwanda, Burundi, Somalia, Sudan and a number of other African countries have paid dearly with the blood of their citizens.

The cases of Burundi and Rwanda are particularly instructive. The genesis of the catastrophic situation in Burundi is neatly summed up by the following quotation from Lemarchand and Martin (1974: 18): 'a new society has in fact emerged in which only Tutsi elements are qualified to gain access to power, influence and wealth; what is left of Hutu society is now systematically excluded from the army, the civil service, the university and secondary school. Hutu status has become synonymous with an inferior category of beings; only Tutsi are fit to rule.' In Rwanda, the Hutu have, since their pre-independence uprising against the erstwhile Tutsi domination, been able – more or less – to wield power to their political and economic advantage. Unequal and antagonistic relationships have in each case engendered the marginalization of one ethnic group by another. In both cases the failure to redress imbalances has precipitated genocide on a horrifying scale and has been responsible for persistent fear, tension and conflict. The prospect of such a catastrophe is not far-fetched for a country like Nigeria, whose volatility has already been made manifest by a full-blown civil war.

Conclusion

I have attempted in this chapter to contribute towards the unveiling of the truth in the face of claims and obscurantist counter-claims of marginalization in Nigeria. I have shown that the Igbo have been victims of marginalization since the end of the Nigerian civil war: that, as a people, they have been systematically disempowered politically, economically, militarily and socially by the Hausa-Fulani and Yoruba groups.

A basic agreement on this truth is a *sine qua non* for the achievement of healing and social justice. As long as the various ethnic groups continue to engage in an endless game of claims and counter-claims, rather than direct their energies towards redressing the offending imbalances and inequities, truth, healing and social justice will be delayed. The marginalization of the Igbo proves that Nigeria's post-war declaration of 'no victor, no vanquished' and the related policy of 'reconciliation, rehabilitation and reconstruction' were not founded on truth. In the absence of a genuine commitment, truth is typically elusive in these matters even when a special commission is set up, as in post-apartheid South Africa, to pin it down.

Based on this contribution towards establishing the truth in the case of post-Biafran marginalization of the Igbo, I proffer the following proposal for a two-pronged attack on marginalization in Nigeria. First, the fundamental cure is to eradicate the capacity to marginalize. The second cure is an emergency measure to demarginalize the Igbo and any other group(s) that pass the litmus test provided by our definition of marginalization.

The capacity for marginalization will surely evaporate if:

- we devise a federal structure in which the centre is not all-powerful;
- no ethnic group or coalition of groups can monopolize political-cum-bureaucratic power and the nation's economic resources;
- no group or coalition can corner the military and use it either to stultify or to nullify (e.g. with a coup) the arrangements worked out under the first two points; and
- no Nigerian can officially be socially discriminated against anywhere in the country on account of his or her ethnic or state/regional origin.

The proposals have obvious implications respectively for:

- structural geopolitics (e.g. regrouping of states into regions);
- power-sharing and resource-allocation arrangements (e.g. adequate representation and equity);
- restructuring of the armed forces (decentralization); and
- enforcement of national citizenship and residency rights.

Demarginalization involves an immediate alleviation of the most glaring cases of marginalization, pending a full redress to be based on the arrangements that will materialize from the proposals for eradication of the capacity to marginalize.

Bibliography

Achebe, C. (1983) *The Trouble With Nigeria*, Enugu: Fourth Dimension.

— (1988) 'Myth and power: The hidden power of Igbo women', lecture delivered at Umea University, Sweden, reprinted in R. Granqvist (ed.) (1990), *Travelling: Chinua Achebe in Scandinavia*, Umea University, Umea, Sweden.

Adedeji, A. (1993) 'Marginalisation and marginality: context, issues and viewpoints', in A. Adedeji, *Africa within the World*, London: Zed Books.

Albert, I. O. (1993) 'Inter-ethnic relations in a Nigerian city: a historical perspective of the Hausa–Igbo conflicts in Kano 1953–1991', Ibadan: IFRA, University of Ibadan.

Allen, J. (1972) 'Sitting on a man: colonialism and lost political institutions of Igbo women', *Canadian Journal of African Studies*, vol. 6, no. 2: 165–82.

Awolowo, O. (1947) *Path to Nigerian Freedom*, London: Faber and Faber.

Basden, G. T. (1966) *Niger Ibos* (first published 1938), London: Frank Cass.

Brunsdon, C. (1978) 'It is well-known that by nature women are inclined to be rather personal', in Women's Studies Group (eds), *Women Take Issue: Aspects of Women's Subordination*, London: Hutchinson and University of Birmingham.

Dina Committee (1968) *Report of the Interim Revenue Allocation Committee*, Lagos: Government Printer.

Ezumah, N. N. (1988) 'Women in agriculture: neglect of women's role', *African Notes*, no. 3, pp. 9–15.

— (1990) 'Women in development: the role of Igbo rural women in agricultural production', unpublished PhD dissertation, Ibadan: University of Ibadan.

— (1997) 'Gender and environment: Dissemination of agricultural technologies to women farmers: cases in Nigeria and Cameroon', paper presented at the Conference on Environment and Sustainable Development in Nigeria by Social Science Council of Nigeria at Women's Development Centre, Abuja, 30 June–3 July 1997.

Ezumah, N. N. and C. M. Di Domenico (1995) 'Enhancing the role of women in crop production. A case study of Igbo women in Nigeria', *World Development*, vol. 23, no. 10: 1731–44.

Gallagher, M. (1981) *Unequal Opportunities: The Case of Women in the Media*, Paris: UNESCO.

Guardian, The (Nigeria) (1998) 'Igbo group urges tougher US action against military', 29 April, p. 4.

Guardian, The (Nigeria) (1988) 'Adedeji decries marginalisation of Yoruba', 7 May, p. 55.

Herrle, P. (1982) 'The informal sector: survival economy in Third World metropolitan cities', *Economics*, vol. 26: 109–26.

Leacock, E. (1978) "Women's status in egalitarian society: implications for social evolution', *Current Anthropology*, vol. 19, no. 2: 247–75.

Lemarchand, R. and D. Martin (1974) *Selective Genocide in Burundi*, London: Minority Rights Group.

Nsukka Analyst (1994) *Marginalisation in Nigerian Policy: A Diagnosis of the Igbo Problem and the National Question*, Nsukka: Nsukka Analyst.

Obadan, M. I. et al. (1996) 'Strategies for revitalising the Nigerian economy: the role of the informal sector', paper presented at the one-day seminar of the Nigerian Economic Society, 16 January.

Okorji, E. C. (1985) 'The role of women in arable cropping enterprises in farming communities of south-eastern Nigeria: a case study', *Development and Peace*, vol. 6, no. 2: 165–73.

Ottenberg, S. and P. Ottenberg (1962) 'Afikpo markets 1900–1960', in P. Bohannan and G. Dalton (eds), *Markets in Africa*, Evanstown, IL: Northwestern University Press.

Phillipson Commission (1946) *Report of the Phillipson Commission*, Lagos: Government Printer.

Sentinel, The (1994) 'Who's marginalised?', 19 September.

Sentinel, The (1994) 'Revenue allocation: the winners, losers', 26 September.

Uchendu, V. C. (1965) *The Igbo of South-East Nigeria*, New York: Holt, Rinehart and Winston.

6

Towards a Social History of Warfare and Reconstruction: The Nigerian/Biafran Case

Axel Harneit-Sievers and Sydney Emezue

Most studies of armed conflict in post-colonial Africa focus on the *origins of war* – they analyse factors causing wars, be they ethnic politics, conflict group dynamics, the arms trade or international competition. Often enough, studies of armed conflict terminate at the very point in time when hostilities break out. Studies about African *societies at war* are rather rare. While the news media report about the human and social consequences of – at least some – wars in Africa, many academic works seem to be content with summing up such reports, possibly for want of better sources, possibly also for lack of theoretical interest.

However, knowledge about what happened during a war is surely not only of academic interest. It is important in order to understand the needs and preconditions for post-war socio–economic reconstruction; furthermore, it is important in order to comprehend how people who have gone through a war experience remember it and rebuild their lives and their societies. To heal the wounds of war may involve some degree of forgetting, but it is also necessary to deal with individual and collective memories, some of them conscious, some less so. There are numerous forms of how societies deal with such memories in an institutionalized, public way, aiming at establishing 'truth' about the past in order to reach 'justice': judicial procedures – from war-crime tribunals to truth commissions – are one possibility; another, somewhat less formalized one, is the writing of history.

The aim of this chapter is two-fold. First, we want to consider a number of studies of war in post-colonial African societies conducted by historians and social scientists in recent years, providing various approaches to the theme. Second, we want to introduce some results of a research project on the social history of the Nigerian civil/Biafran war that we conducted ourselves. This not only serves as an example of one particular approach to the study of war, its possibilities and its limitations, but it also provides insights into the forms of remembrance of the civil war experience in Nigeria today.

Studies about African Societies at War: Some Observations

Much of our knowledge about African societies under conditions of war derives from 'disaster studies' and 'refugee studies', which have emerged as fully fledged sub-disciplines[1] of the social sciences, supporting and (sometimes quite self-critically) reflecting the work of the 'humanitarian international' (de Waal 1997: 3–4). Besides such pragmatically oriented research, 'war and society in Africa' has been studied, in a more comprehensive way, in a number of regional case studies, conducted mostly by anthropologists. They frequently concentrate on the theme of *violence*: its exertion and experience, its role in creating social 'anomie' and popular reactions to it. Among these works are some of the most impressive analyses of the 'inside' of African wars. For example, Christian Geffray (1990) showed for the Nampula province in northeastern Mozambique how the local dynamics of the civil war of the 1980s was much more influenced by popular reactions to violence exerted from both sides than by the 'official' political dimension of the war. Norma Kriger (1992) studied the social effects of violence in Zimbabwe, its role in mobilizing for the guerrilla force, but also its divisive effects on rural society. Other studies have focused on the relationship between violence and religious beliefs – their role in mobilizing for violent political movements, by offering political legitimacy and magical protection (Lan 1985 for Zimbabwe; Wilson 1992 for Mozambique; Behrend 1993 for Northern Uganda).

There is no doubt that violence constitutes a wartime core experience and deserves primary attention of researchers. Violence can be studied as an irregular, sometimes outrageous experience, or even as something irregular that, in wartime, attains to a status of 'normality' and becomes embedded in everyday life. However, warfare involves aspects that are less spectacular than manifest acts of violence, but nevertheless have a profound impact on everyday life. Societies at war undergo a large-scale process of mobilization of material (arms, food, transport, etc.) and social (from recruitment of soldiers to attempts to gain popular legitimacy) resources. Efficient resource mobilization is decisive for the outcome of a war: its concrete forms strongly impact on the society at war as a whole, affecting relations between state, combat forces and the population as a whole. Forms of mobilization may involve different degrees of pressure, force or even physical violence; the spectrum reaches from 'regular' taxation to military conscription, food supply enforced from villages, outright looting by military units in their operating areas ('living off the land') and even their employing of slave labour. Besides direct violence, such forms of mobilization decisively shape a population's wartime experience.

The need to take account of dimensions of the war experience beyond

destruction and violence becomes even more obvious when trying to understand processes of post-war reconstruction. Literature on the ending of
wars and conflict settlement (Licklider 1993; Matthies 1995) again focuses
mainly on the *politics* of peace and reconciliation, and on certain issues
(like refugee repatriation, demobilization and the land-mine problem) that
have attracted the attention of international agencies. In contrast, the
potentials and capabilities that African societies *themselves* have to recover
from the ravages of war receive little attention. Such capabilities arise from
what was not destroyed in war: human and social resources; experiences
and know-how in agriculture, crafts and trade; networks and institutions
of cooperation and self-help. Programmes of aid and reconstruction have
to take account of these capabilities and identify and relate to them if they
want to be successful and efficient.

What this argument amounts to is a call for taking seriously the issue
of human *agency* in studies of war in Africa (as elsewhere), rather than
studying people purely as objects of violence. Few studies of contemporary
war and society in Africa have seriously looked at war-affected populations
not only as victims, but also as human beings who actively manage their
survival and develop perspectives for their lives under adverse and even
disastrous conditions. One such example is Paul Richards's (1996) study of
Sierra Leone, which highlights the role of the youth – the concepts they
have for their own lives, and their dreams – in a war that some earlier
analyses took only as a prototype of senseless fighting and meaningless
'new Barbarism'. A different example is Mark Chingono's (1994, 1996)
work about Manica province, Mozambique. It looks at the potentials of
individual and collective capabilities developed during wartime (for example,
in the commercial sector) for post-war development perspectives. Chingono's analysis, informed by a political economy approach, at times seems
to interpret the various dimensions of human behaviour (for example,
small-scale commercial accumulation, marital relationships, religious conversion) all too unilaterally in terms of their political implications and class
formation. However, the perspective is important in reminding us that
even the victims of war remain human beings seeking to maintain active
control of their lives.

Studying the Social History of the Nigerian Civil War

The Nigerian civil war (1967–70) – resulting from the secession of
Nigeria's Eastern Region, with its Igbo ethnic majority, as Biafra in June
1967 – was one of the first armed conflicts in post-colonial Africa, and one
of the bloodiest. It stood at the beginning of a series of crises – crises
resulting from drought, hunger, displacement and war – that created the

pervasive Western image of Africa as a continent of disasters. Biafra became, as Ifi Amadiume (see Chapter 2) has argued, a metaphor for conflict in Africa; photos of starving African children that were first seen during the war still dominate media images of Africa today.

The civil war continues to be a 'national trauma', though in different ways for different parts of the population (cf. Harneit-Sievers 1998). The Federal Government's declared post-war policy of reconciliation did not encourage remembering, and what official commemoration there is restricts itself mostly to military and political issues, focusing on the need for future national unity. For about two decades, the war played little part in public discourse in those parts of the country not directly affected by the war; this has changed since 1993, in the political crisis after the cancellation of the presidential election results when 'secession' once again became a formidable topic in public debate. In the formerly war-affected areas of Nigeria's southeastern states, of course, collective memory of the war is intense and multi-faceted. There are numerous literary accounts of the war experience, and a number of (auto)biographies mostly by leading military and political personnel (for an overview of this literature see Osuntokun 1989). However, besides writing the 'high-level' political and military history, academics have rarely approached the war experience itself. Political considerations may be one reason for this neglect; furthermore, there are methodological difficulties involved in this kind of research.

This situation formed the background to a research project conducted in the first half of the 1990s by the authors, in cooperation with Jones Ahazuem and history students of universities of Nsukka, Uturu and Port Harcourt, into the social history of the civil war and its aftermath. The project looked at the war experiences of 'ordinary' people – people who do not normally write books about their war experience. In the meantime, results of the study have been published (Harneit-Sievers et al. 1997).[2] In the following, we want to outline the research design, discuss a few methodological issues and summarize some of the results. The study documents aspects of the experience and memory of the Nigerian civil war, and we also hope it may encourage others to conduct further studies on these issues, in Nigeria and elsewhere.

The aim of the project on the social history of the Nigerian civil war was to write a 'history from below'. Many people approached to participate, co-researchers and interviewees alike, regarded this as a legitimate and useful enterprise. Further factors conducive to the research were that more than two decades had passed since the end of the war; that the post-war settlement, though often perceived to have led to the 'marginalization of the Igbo', has nevertheless gained a solid amount of acceptance; and that Nigerian public discourse generally allows the expression of a considerable measure of criticism and dissent. Without doubt, there were limits as to the extent to which people were prepared to speak about their experiences and views; some did not want to talk at all. However, we encountered no general reluctance or fear of reprisals when asking people to talk about the war, even when political issues were touched. In a similarly designed project about the civil war in Mozambique, conducted in 1994–95 only about 18 months after the ceasefire, the neglect of directly political issues proved important to ensure the readiness of people to speak to the researchers (Liesegang 1995).

In the Nigerian project, much of the interviewing was done by students who worked in selected communities, in many cases in their own home areas. An open questionnaire was used, allowing for a certain degree of standardization of questioning as well as openness for the collection of individual life histories. A 'representative' survey in a strict sense was not aimed at. The topics mentioned in the questionnaire included the local history of the war; civil–military relations; survival strategies; the experiences of specific vulnerable groups like refugees or women; inter-communal conflicts; the experience of the post-war situation and reconstruction; and finally, the long-term effects of the war.

The research design proved feasible, even under the constraints of infrastructure and finance prevailing in Nigeria in the first half of the 1990s. The project documented views and experiences of the civil war period from a wide array of strata of society and localities, much beyond the classical case study approach, and it provided the researchers with a sense for the differences of life and experience in various parts of the war area. A broad spectrum of experiences and views was recorded, allowing for statements about (regionalized) 'common patterns' as well as about more or less exceptional individual cases. The regional diversity of the war experience became clear. Numerous aspects of life under war conditions were documented – aspects about which little, if any, research has been done before, and about which people who did not experience the war themselves could know only from fictional literary accounts. At the same time, individual life stories were recorded only as far as interviewees were prepared to speak about themselves – no attempt was made at an in-depth study of those dimensions of the war experience that interviewees tended to 'hide', or did not dare or were unable to speak about explicitly. The research design could not be expected to document individual trauma resulting from the war experience.

One of the problems encountered was a certain heterogeneity of the interview material, resulting from differences among the interviewers' qualifications, questioning strategies and general interest. While the interviews held in one locality in sum provided an outline of a wartime and post-war history of this locality, no in-depth case study emerged.[3] In hindsight it would have been advisable to let the interviewers write, in addition to their interview transcripts, a summary of their research experience and results in the form of a short local case study. The choice of students doing research in their respective home communities proved ambivalent: while it facilitated easier access and solved the language problem in ethnic minority areas, students turned out sometimes to be too close to their community to ask seemingly 'self-evident' questions that outsiders would find important.

Similar differences of interest and perspective between the Nigerian and foreign co-authors sometimes arose in the process of writing up the research results. At times, there were different views about how to deal with events, behaviour and views that seemed 'self-evident' from a Nigerian perspective, but needed documentary evidence and explanation from an outsider's perspective. Lengthy discussions resulted, especially regarding the analytical difference to be made between what interviewees described as *facts*, and what the authors described as interviewees' *perceptions* of these facts.

Problems of this kind are not new, but are characteristic of oral history research. Interviews were conducted about a quarter of a century after the events and experiences they describe. Thus, their status as primary evidence for events and perceptions in the period they speak about is problematic; strictly speaking, the interviews do constitute sources only for the time when they were conducted, i.e. the 1990s. This, of course, is a general problem historians encounter when doing oral *history*; individual narratives, centred around a person's biography and his or her experiences, are different from the oral *tradition* (in Vansina's [1985] sense) well known to historians of Africa; particular traditions are frequently narrated in a much more formalized way, showing less variation depending on the individual narrator. In oral history, in effect, every individual evidence has to be scrutinized, because the forms in which individual persons narrate vary so widely. For example, a distinction has to be made between narratives of individual experience understood as 'life history' proper, and forms of 'hearsay' that reflect common perceptions of events, rather than their individual experience. Another common problem is the emergence of certain clichés – i.e. common patterns of narration emerging from the fact that the events and experiences have been narrated before frequently, and have already become topics of a more widespread discourse in society. In her study of nineteenth- and twentieth-century oral history in the Transvaal region, Isabel Hofmeyr (1993: 13) has differentiated between 'core clichés' that come up in narratives again and again, 'less stable elements' with some coherence, and 'unstable', highly diverse and individual elements of the narrative. In practice these elements can be found side by side in the same interview. Besides analysis of the individual interview, comparison between a number of them helps to identify the different elements and levels.

In the following, we summarize some findings of the project. From among the many issues touched upon, we focus on three issues: the experiences of women and their perceptions during and immediately after the war; individual experiences of post-war opportunities for re-establishment and reconstruction; and a particular myth explaining the end of the war.

Women's Experiences of the Nigerian Civil War

The problem of cliché-building mentioned above was particularly obvious when studying the experiences of Igbo women during the war. A good proportion (about 30 per cent) of interviews were conducted with women, many of them by female interviewers. In the following, we focus on two issues: the changes in female roles – in the domestic and the public spheres – resulting from the war situation, and the relationship between women and soldiers during and in the aftermath of the war. In both cases, preconceptions and clichés[4] became apparent during the study and had to be put into context.

The role of women Igbo women play important and visible public roles in society. Even if their public status, and especially their political institutions, have been considerably diminished in the course of the twentieth century by colonial policies and the introduction of missionary Christian norms (Amadiume 1987), their role, especially in commerce, remains important. Our research showed that the civil war situation was perceived by both men and women to have strengthened female positions within the domestic and the public realms. However, the research also showed that neither men nor all women viewed this change in positive terms.

In the public arena, women directly and indirectly contributed to the war effort, although they were not enlisted as soldiers into the Biafran army (which remained a rather conventional one; see Peters 1997: 119–28). Younger women, particularly in the early phases of the war, served in paramilitary forces ('civil defence'). Women of all age groups played important roles in securing the food supply of the Biafran army, both as individual food-sellers and in community-based organizations (such as the 'Women's Front').

To some extent, women even replaced men in the public sphere. After an initial phase when many young men volunteered to enter the Biafran army, forced recruitment became common in 1968. While conscription at some places was organized by communities, it frequently took the form of indiscriminate conscription of men 'caught' anywhere by army units, while desertions were common. As a result, it became dangerous for men to be seen in public. Instead, women increasingly took over jobs requiring public visibility, especially in the markets. This happened in a situation when income from (petty) trading became more important than ever for many households, especially for those who had become refugees and needed to supplement the food rations supplied by relief organizations.

Women formed the majority among those involved in the so-called 'attack trade' (*ahia attack*). By this trade conducted through the frontline, high-priced low-weight goods like salt and cigarettes were imported from Federal into Biafran territory. According to one of its participants, the attack trade was 'a very risky venture; risky both physically and morally' (Cecilia Achiugo, in Harneit-Sievers et al. 1997: 146). Participating women could be accused as spies or 'saboteurs', or had to enter into relationships with soldiers in order to be able to conduct the trade.

The increased participation of women in trade significantly strengthened their role as earners of household income, resulting in an increased domestic weight *vis-à-vis* their husbands. This affected established domestic roles, which men found difficult to cope with. Clichés (especially male ones) have it that women refused to care for their husbands, or were even leaving them. This is perceived to have happened in polygynous families where women were used to act more independently from their husbands for themselves and their children. While it is, of course, nearly impossible to find out to what extent such clichés represented wartime realities, they certainly indicate widespread male fears arising from role reversals resulting from war conditions.

The women interviewed in the course of the research project generally confirmed the picture of an increased female role in income generation and domestic affairs. However, they looked at this development in a rather ambivalent manner. Female accounts of the war experience generally lay less weight on the strength women gained, but rather emphasize the stress put on them by the war situation, especially the need to cope with the food crisis. According to many women's accounts, increased strength went along with increased responsibility and stress. Contrary to male clichés, women today do not remember the war period as a time of gained influence, status or prestige, but primarily as a period of hardship and suffering.

Sexual violence against women While sexual violence of soldiers against women of a conquered area did not, in Nigeria, amount to a comprehensive attack on the ethnic and cultural identity of the enemy side (as happened in Rwanda or Bosnia), sexual violence against women was a widespread experience there, too. However, it also became clear in our study on the Nigerian civil war that the category of 'violence' does not sufficiently describe the variety of relationships between women and soldiers. Rather than perceiving women principally as victims of (male and war-related) violence, we may describe many aspects of their relationship with soldiers as forms of (proactive or reactive) negotiation for chances to survive under extreme circumstances.

In the Nigerian case, it became clear that the relationship between women and soldiers cannot be analytically isolated, but should be viewed in the context of the more general state of relationships between the military and the civilian population. Relationships between Biafran soldiers and women were usually described (by both men and women) as friendly and largely unproblematic for most Igbo-speaking core areas, where support for the Biafran cause was strong. Exceptions were cases of conflicts between women and soldiers desperately searching for food. In contrast, many accounts from at least some of the southeastern Nigerian minority areas, whose loyalty towards Biafra was often in doubt, speak of violence and assaults by Biafran soldiers. On the other side of the frontline, Federal soldiers were frequently described to have committed rape in occupied territories, in minority areas as well as in Igboland, especially in the immediate aftermath of the war. When describing experiences with violent soldiers, male and female interviewees alike usually did not single out cases of sexual violence against women as a particular act of aggression. Rather, they frequently mentioned cases of murder, robbery and rape together as indicators of a bad general relationship between civilians and army units.

Common male descriptions of the situation of Igbo women in the immediate post-war setting oscillate between their being perceived as victims of sexual assault and being seen as wilful profiteers from the opportunities opened up by the presence of soldiers. Women engaging in relationships with Federal soldiers were very critically looked at, while their families were seen as profiting from such relationships. A similar image, though less politically loaded, already existed with regard to such relationships within Biafra. Obviously, much cliché-building (not only by men) is involved in such perceptions, and strong moral judgements go along with them, as has happened in similar circumstances in other wars throughout the world. Igbo women who were perceived to have voluntarily engaged with Federal soldiers in the immediate post-war period carried a social stigma that seems to persist today.

While general descriptions of soldiers committing violence against civilians frequently include rapes, very few individual cases of rape could be documented in the course of the research; reluctance to give details about this sensitive and traumatic issue was obvious. Clearly, the research design reached some limits at this point.

Instead of 'rape', the category 'war marriage' was frequently used by interviewees to describe the relationship between women and soldiers. The term 'war marriage' carries a variety of meanings. It includes connotations of 'force', physical violence, but also the pressure exerted by conditions of life, and necessities of survival. It also connotes a certain degree of voluntariness to engage on the woman's side. This broad spectrum of meaning may indeed reflect more correctly the constraints as well as options experienced by women during and after the war.

Strategies of Post-war Survival and Reconstruction

When the Nigerian civil war ended in January 1970, few people would have expected that a process of recovery and reconstruction – in terms of socio-economic development as well as politically – would be possible within few years. Until today, judgements about the success of socio-economic reconstruction and political reintegration of the Igbo population group in Nigeria remain highly controversial (for a discussion of these issues see Ekwe-Ekwe 1990; various contributions in Oyeweso 1992; Glauke 1995).

On the one hand, data on economic and infrastructural development in southeastern Nigeria, as well as official statements of the time, suggest that the overall pre-war level of economic activity in most sectors was reached again within three or four years after the end of the war; the same is true for infrastructural facilities like education or health services. On the other hand, dissatisfaction with actual achievements remained widespread. Criticism of the marginalization and relative under-development of Igboland *vis-à-vis* other regions of Nigeria increased in the 1990s, a period of severe economic and political crisis.

Reconstruction did not primarily result from large-scale financial transfers of the Nigerian state into the war-affected area. Nor can reconstruction be simply described as a 'trickle-down' effect of the oil boom, the major impact of which was felt later, in 1973–74. Rather, reconstruction in southeastern Nigeria seems to have taken place largely by means of self-help, combined with certain strategic inputs like agricultural seeds and tools, provided by the government or relief organizations. Self-help involved making use of the generally positive economic conditions Nigeria experienced during the early 1970s. The return of refugees and displaced people, the re-establishment of agricultural production and small-scale businesses, and the resettling of urban centres were achieved within relatively short periods of time, mainly by the initiatives of the people concerned, or of whole communities who engaged in the rebuilding of roads, bridges and schools. The re-establishment of a money economy was helped by fast re-employment of former Igbo civil servants and by the ingenious reactivation of commercial know-how and connections available among the numerous traders in Igboland. The state and international relief agencies came in only in certain aspects, for example by providing seeds and agricultural tools in 1970, and in the rebuilding of large-scale infrastructures and industries (Harneit-Sievers 1992).

Our study of the Nigerian civil war largely confirmed the picture of a post-war reconstruction process based on individual and communal self-help, rather than on external agencies, like government or international relief organizations. It documented a variety of individual strategies of survival and improvisation during the immediate post-war period, and of more long-term strategies employed in order to find a place for oneself in post-war Nigeria (Harneit-Sievers et al. 1997: 172–90). While the first months of 1970 still were characterized by widespread disease and hunger, local agriculture proved remarkably resilient. Farmers returned to their land and found a minimum of security and inputs to restart. Numerous small-scale services and businesses evolved around the Federal army units stationed in southeastern Nigeria whose comparatively large purchasing power created demand on the market. Businessmen and businesswomen re-established commercial connections still available from the pre-war period; by means of the commercial credit system (a financial as well as a social institution), many of those who had lost 'everything' in the course of the war were able to restart trade. Igbo traders returned to other parts of the country from where they had fled during and after the 1966 pogroms. Overall, the Igbo business class soon recovered and seems to have lost remarkably little commercial terrain, compared with the pre-war situation, although a number of frequently mentioned factors operated against them. There were restrictions of access experienced in Port Harcourt and Rivers State. There also was the 'abandoned property' issue that caused many Igbo house-owners to lose their property in non-Igbo states. Finally, there was the lack of capital, resulting not only from wartime destruction but also from the official exchange of Biafran into Nigerian currency in mid-1970, instituted by the Federal Government. Pre-war savings and cash accumulated within the wartime Biafran economy were rendered almost worthless. As has already been mentioned, few of these strategies of survival and reconstruction depended on external support, be it from governments on the state or Federal levels, or from international agencies. Many of the strategies were based on the mobilization of social and intellectual resources within the former war area – human resources that had survived the destruction of the war – using opportunities created by the expanding oil economy of the early 1970s. Accordingly, and with much justification, many Igbo today view post-war development as having been achieved without support by the government, or even *against* official policies.

Of course, not all individual accounts of post-war events documented in the course of our research project were success stories. In order to find out more about individual perceptions of the post-war reconstruction process, interviewees were asked to state when 'normalcy' returned for them, or whether and when they re-established their pre-war standard of life. The results (Harneit-Sievers et al. 1997: 191–5) were revealing, not the least because the category 'normalcy' carries a variety of connotations, allowing some insight into what people believe their life and society *should* look like. While for some of the farmers interviewed, 'return to normalcy' just meant being able to return to the land and restart farming in 1970, a majority of those who gave any particular year or period for their personal – or, in some cases, their community's – 'return to normalcy' dated it somewhere between 1971 and 1975. This confirms the validity of the overall picture of a comparatively fast reconstruction process, as sketched above.

However, there also were some interviewees who dated their 'return to normalcy' later than that, and even more of them think that 'normalcy' has not reappeared even today. Some among this latter group meant that statement to express their dissatisfaction with the current state of affairs in Nigeria; others felt that the war had changed society so strongly that the concept of a 'return to normalcy' was meaningless to them. In other cases, again, such statements referred to serious problems of individuals to re-establish themselves after the end of the civil war. Thus, some of the most vulnerable groups of people can be identified. Among them were: the woman who lost children and husband during the war and remained isolated afterwards; the rural household that became poor due to wartime losses of family members who would otherwise have worked the farm (see Uzozie 1981); the ex-soldier who found it psychologically difficult to come to terms with the post-war situation; and the elderly businessman who had lost his capital in the war and did not feel strong enough to start all over again.

The war cut into the life chances especially of persons of higher age, although a 'critical age' line is difficult to identify. Younger people able to enter into education or business were much better placed to re-establish themselves in post-civil war Nigeria. Employees in the public sector formed an exceptional group, as a good number of them were re-employed after the war, though some faced limitations to their careers. In any case, besides certain careers in business, it was the factor of education that seems to have constituted the most promising way of individual reconstruction, and socially upward mobility, in pre- and post-war Nigeria alike.

Myth-making about the End of the War

A rather unexpected discovery made during the research is the fact that many people in the former war-affected area hold the view that the Nigerian civil war ended not through an outright military defeat of Biafra by the Nigerian Federal army, but through the intervention of some outside force. Usually, the intervention force is believed to have come from the OAU, but there are variations to this: further questioning shows that the mentioning of 'OAU' may as well refer to troops of the United Nations, or from Chad and Niger, Nigeria's immediate northern neighbours. Some people insist that 'OAU' supplied special troops fighting Biafra into submission; others believe that the organization gave special weapons, hitherto unknown in the war; another variant of the story has it that specially trained pilots joined the services of the Nigerian air force some time in late 1969, introducing a new dimension of precision bombing which ensured Nigeria's victory. While such versions of the story stress the aggressive character of the intervention, others describe a display of overwhelming force that in effect ended the violence because further resistance by Biafrans seemed useless, or illegitimate. As one former captain of the Biafran army put it: 'At Umuna Okigwe we really saw several OAU country flags at the head of an advancing Nigerian army formation. We did not fight them because of the OAU flags' (Harneit-Sievers et al. 1997: 164). There is also the belief that Nnamdi Azikiwe, the grand old man of Igbo politics who had left Biafra in 1969, called in the intervention. Most people speaking about this issue said that they heard about the intervention; a few claim to have actually seen 'OAU' soldiers, or to have had direct contact with them. To one Biafran soldier, the soldiers of the intervention force looked more disciplined, better trained and equipped than the Nigerian soldiers with whom he had contact soon after the war ended.[5]

The myth – for this is what it is – of an outside intervention that ended the war is believed not only by illiterate people, but also by fairly well-educated ones. A foreign intervention to end the war never took place, and was not even seriously discussed internationally; the myth, however, combines elements of wartime diplomacy and propaganda with actual experiences undergone during and at the end of the war.

The OAU was involved in the international diplomacy around the Nigerian civil war. In contrast to some of its member states, which supported Biafra, the organization took an anti-secessionist stand. The attitude of the United Nations to the conflict, again, was largely determined by that of the OAU; Biafra's efficient propaganda frequently attacked both international bodies for their taking sides for Nigeria. Another common topic in Biafra's propaganda was that of foreign mercenaries, from European and African countries alike, who in fact played some part (though hardly decisive) on both sides. Thus the emergence of the OAU intervention myth can, to a large extent, be explained as a lingering effect of Biafran war-time propaganda, however distorted.

Certain popular experiences and perceptions seem to have further contributed to the emergence and shaping of the myth. After a reorganization in 1969, the Nigerian Federal army was indeed a better equipped and disciplined force than before, impressing Igbo observers. Even more important might have been the fact that the end of the war, despite the lawlessness and violence encountered in many places, did not result in the mass killing of Igbo people that was widely feared because of the 1966 pogroms; Biafran propaganda had done much to keep this memory alive. Compared to the worst expectations about what would happen if Biafra was defeated, Nigerian soldiers behaved in a comparatively restricted way, and the Federal Government did not embark upon large-scale violent revenge on the Igbo. The myth of some external intervention helps to explain this contradiction between expectations and actual experience, by supplying an argument that it was *not really* the Nigerians, or at least not the Nigerians acting on their own and unobserved, whom one encountered at the end of the war.

The mythological explanation of the end of the civil war carries another, more long-lasting and self-justifying message: that it was *not really* the Nigerians who defeated Biafra. This, again, may be related to wartime propaganda, which had pertinently claimed that Nigeria could never subdue Biafra; the myth thus helps to keep past and present beliefs consistent. However, it also helps to raise the self-consciousness of the Igbo, as the ethnic group that lost the war, in competition for power in post-war Nigeria.

We have not been able to trace the history and development of the intervention myth and do not know whether it emerged in the immediate post-war period, or constitutes a later phenomenon. It is clear, however, that the belief was widespread in Igbo-speaking areas during the first half of the 1990s.

Overall, the intervention myth constitutes counterfactual collective memory – a way of keeping past and present fears and beliefs consistent, and a way of raising the self-consciousness of a people defeated in civil war. The myth points to the fallacies of collective memory, which does not necessarily need 'truth' in order to gain 'justice' – rather the contrary might be the case. The myth also shows the difficulties of oral historical research. In this particular case, we were able to identify the counterfactual character of an aspect of collective memory because it encompasses a dimension of international politics that is well studied. But in other cases – especially those of more localized myths – we may have little chance to do so.

Conclusion

Many studies on war in Africa analyse the politics or the large-scale socio-economic structures that led to war, rather than the experiences of the people affected by it. This chapter has discussed a research project on the social history of the Nigerian civil war, which has focused on individual and collective experiences of the war and post-war periods. The research was conducted by means of oral history, with the support of students of local universities, mostly originating from the respective localities, using a comparatively simple research design.

The chapter has discussed issues in the fields of gender relations during the war, post-war strategies of reconstruction, and the construction of a popular myth about the end of a war. Roles of women in the public sphere were strengthened during the war, although this hardly went along with an increased self-awareness of female strength, and sexual exploitation and violence remained permanent threats. Reconstruction in the post-war years was largely based on individual and communal self-help, and the mobil-ization of social resources locally available, rather than on external agencies (like the Federal Government or international relief). Today, numerous Igbo people believe that the end of the war was brought about not by Biafra's defeat through the Nigerian Federal forces, but by some foreign intervention. We have analysed this as a process of reshaping of collective memory which (though factually wrong) not only helps to keep consistent past beliefs (influenced by wartime propaganda), experiences at the end of the war, and present convictions, but also supports a specific form of self-consciousness among a vanquished people.

The chapter has tried to show some possibilities of research on the social history of war in Africa, allowing us to identify popular perceptions, patterns of behaviour, and even individual experiences and coping strat-egies. Thus, more prominence can be given to the role of *individual* and *collective agency* in times of war – an issue overlooked by much of the existing literature on war in Africa, which focuses largely on states or armies and sees the civilian population simply as victims of warfare.

Notes

1. The development of the field is documented by the journals *Disasters* (established in 1977) and the *Journal of Refugee Studies* (established in 1988).

2. We wish to thank the German Research Council, Bonn, and the German Agency for Technical Cooperation, Eschborn, for their financial support, without which the project would have been impossible.

3. However, some students used the material collected as sources for BA dissertations about the local history of the war.

4. Remarkably, the two clichés pointedly contradict each other, as the widely-perceived more 'active' role of women in domestic and public affairs contrasts with their perceived role as 'passive' victims of violent assaults by soldiers.

5. Interview with John Nwagwu by Sydney Emezue. Nwagwu was aged 21 in 1967.

Bibliography

Amadiume, I. (1987) *Male Daughters, Female Husbands: Gender and Sex in an African Society*, London and New Jersey: Zed Books.

Behrend, H. (1993) *Alice und die Geister. Krieg im Norden Ugandas*, Munich: Trickster.

Chingono, M. (1994) 'War, social change and development in Mozambique: catastrophe or creation of a new society?', PhD thesis, Cambridge: Faculty of Social and Political Sciences, Cambridge University.

— (1996) *The State, Violence and Development: The Political Economy of War in Mozambique 1975–92*, Aldershot: Avebury.

de Waal, A. (1997) *Famine Crimes: Politics and the Disaster Relief Industry in Africa*, London: James Currey and Bloomington, IN: Indiana University Press.

Ekwe-Ekwe, H. (1990) *The Biafra War: Nigeria and the Aftermath*, Lewiston, NY: Edwin Mellen Press.

Geffray, C. (1990) *La cause des armes au Mozambique. Anthropologie d'une guerre civile*, Paris and Nairobi: Éditions Karthala/Credu.

Glauke, C. O. (1995) *Die Integration der Ibos nach dem Bürgerkrieg in Nigeria*, Berlin: Verlag Wissenschaft und Technik.

Harneit-Sievers, A. (1992) 'Nigeria: Der Sezessionskrieg um Biafra. "Keine Sieger, keine Besiegten" – eine afrikanische Erfolgsgeschichte?', in R. Hofmeier and V. Matthie (eds), *Vergessene Kriege in Afrika*, Göttingen: Lamuv, pp. 277–318.

— (1998) 'Beyond Biafra: the civil war in Nigeria's political debates', *Bulletin of the Association of Concerned Africa Scholars*, no. 52, Fall.

Harneit-Sievers, A., J. O. Ahazuem and S. Emezue (1997) *A Social History of the Nigerian Civil War: Perspectives from Below*, Enugu: Jemezie and Hamburg: LIT.

Hofmeyr, I. (1993) *'We Spend Our Years as a Tale that is Told': Oral Historical Narrative in a South African Kingdom*, Johannesburg: Witwatersrand University Press.

Kriger, N. (1992) *Zimbabwe's Guerrilla War: Peasant Voices*, Cambridge: Cambridge University Press.

Lan, D. (1985) *Guns and Rain: Guerrillas and Spirit Mediums in Zimbabwe*, London: James Currey and Berkeley: University of California Press.

Licklider, R. (ed.) *Stopping the Killing: How Civil Wars End*, New York: New York University Press.

Liesegang, G. (1995) 'Ablauf und Auswirkungen des Bürgerkriegs in Mosambik aus lokaler, regionaler und struktureller Sicht. Bericht über ein 1994 mit mosambikanischen Studenten durchgeführte[s] Projekt über die Sozialgeschichte des Bürgerkriegs ca. 1980–1992', unpublished manuscript, Maputo: Universidade Eduardo Mondlane, 1 December.

Matthies, V. (1995) *Vom Krieg zum Frieden. Kriegsbeendigung und Friedenskonsolidierung*, Bremen: Edition Temmen.

Osuntokun, A. (1989) 'Review of literature on the civil war', in T. N. Tamuno and S. C. Ukpabi (eds), *The Civil War Years*, vol. VI of *Nigeria Since Independence: The First 25 Years*, Ibadan: Heinemann, pp. 85–105.

Oyeweso, S. (ed.) (1992) *Perspectives on the Nigerian Civil War*, Apapa: OAP Publications.

Peters, J. (1997) *The Nigerian Military and the State*, London and New York: Tauris Academic Publishers.

Richards, P. (1996) *Fighting for the Rain Forest: War, Youth and Resources in Sierra Leone*, London: James Currey and Portsmouth, NH: Heinemann.

Uzozie, L. C. (1981) 'The changing context of land use decisions: three family farms in the yam cultivation zone of eastern Nigeria, 1964–1977', *Africa*, vol. 51, no. 2: 678–93.

Vansina, J. (1985) *Oral Tradition as History*, London: James Currey.

Wilson, K. (1992) 'Cults of violence and counter-violence in Mozambique', *Journal of Southern African Studies*, vol. 18, no. 3: 527–83.

7

Latin American Experiences of Accountability

Juan E. Méndez

The transition from dictatorship to democracy in most of the western hemisphere in the 1980s and 1990s was remarkable for many reasons. One of them was that, for the most part, the military establishments that had had the reins of government retreated in a more or less orderly way and were, for that reason, generally able to set some conditions and limitations on the range of policy options available to successor governments. The area in which they were most interested in setting limits was that of accountability for the crimes of the recent past. This was so because another salient feature of the transitions was the tragic legacy of human rights violations these governments left behind. Although Latin America had witnessed repressive governments for a long time, the cycles of revolution and repression in the 1970s and 1980s had exceeded – in number of victims and quality of the atrocities committed – everything the region had experienced before.[1]

Victims, their families and human rights organizations set out, in each country, to make the most of the window of opportunity they had to see justice done, to obtain respect and recognition for the plight of lost loved ones, and to learn about the fate and whereabouts of the *desaparecidos* (disappeared). It is a tribute to their commitment and courage that, gradually, larger and larger circles of society came to embrace and champion their demands. In fact, although there were certainly other burning issues as well, the struggle for truth and justice and against impunity, silence and oblivion eventually shaped the character of this latest transition to democracy and contributed ideas and principles to a fast-developing area of international human rights law.

Based on those and other experiences, there are now emerging principles in international law to the effect that the victims of certain types of crimes, and the societies they belong to, are entitled to certain affirmative actions on the part of their governments, and that those obligations remain in force even with regard to a successor government that is not guilty of the crimes.

Not every type of human rights violation gives rise to this heightened responsibility: it is only when the nature and scope of the abuses reach the level of war crimes or crimes against humanity that these obligations are triggered. Extra-judicial executions, torture, disappearances and prolonged arbitrary detention acquire such a character when they are committed as part and parcel of a deliberate, massive, systematic pattern.

In those cases, governments are faced with four related but distinct obligations (Méndez 1997). In the first place, the victims have the right to see justice done via a regular process with full guarantees for a fair trial. It follows that blanket amnesties and pardons designed to 'create an atmosphere of impunity' (in the words of the UN Human Rights Committee)[2] violate this principle and are contrary to international law. Second, the victims and society have a 'right to truth', meaning that the government must do all in its power to investigate each case, establish all that can be reliably known about the circumstances, and disclose that information to the victims and to the public. Third, the victims and their families are entitled to just reparations, in both material and moral terms, that respect the inherent dignity of each person. Finally, societies have a right to see that the armed and security forces of the newly democratic state are free of the elements within them that planned, executed or supervised egregious crimes.

Each of these obligations is an 'obligation of means' and not 'of results', meaning that a government will be in general compliance as long as it attempts to live up to them and even if in the end it obtains only partial results. It is unreasonable to expect that *all* perpetrators will be prosecuted and convicted, or even that *every* detail of what happened in each case will be uncovered. It is sufficient to make an affort in good faith to comply with each one of the four obligations. At the same time, although all four rights are related, they lend themselves to separate actions by the government. In that sense, the fact that one of those obligations is rendered impossible because of legal or *de facto* obstacles does not relieve the government of its duty to implement the other three. More importantly, these four obligations cannot be seen as a menu of options for a government to choose from in devising a policy on accountability; governments are not free to choose truth over justice, for example, or reparations over both of them.

An Overview of Latin American Experiences

In Argentina, the military retreat was accelerated by the defeat in the Falklands/Malvinas war, and a very discredited junta was unable to impose conditions on the new democracy, although it certainly tried. For that reason, it was in Argentina that democratic sectors were able to push for a wide array of measures against impunity for the crimes of the 'dirty war', and set in motion a process that was later reproduced, with some changes, in several other Latin American transitions. In 1983, President Raul Alfonsin's first act in office was to ask Congress to declare that a self-amnesty law dictated by the junta only a few days before the election was null and void (by then, and even before the change of government, courts had refused to apply it). At the same time, Alfonsin announced his policy on accountability: he created a National Commission on the Disappeared (CONADEP), chaired by writer Ernesto Sabato; he ordered the prosecution of the members of the three juntas that had ruled the country since 1976, for the thousands of disappearances, extrajudicial executions and cases of torture of the 'dirty war', as well as the prosecution of some well-known guerrilla leaders. As for the executors of the 'dirty war', he proposed to amend the Code of Military Justice so that those who obeyed orders would be exempt from punishment unless they exceeded those orders or committed egregious crimes. Military courts would retain jurisdiction over these criminal cases. In the parliamentary debates, civil society was able to push for a stronger policy: 'due obedience' was allowed as a defence only if the defendant was unaware of the illegality of the order (thus bringing Argentine law closer in line with international law on the matter). Military courts had six months to show due diligence and, if not, federal courts of appeal would take over from them.

The report of the Sabato Commission was published in late 1984.[3] It stands even today as an example of how to conduct this type of inquiry. It describes the pattern and practice of 'disappearances' and demonstrates that it was a carefully conceived master plan, executed by zealous intelligence and operations task forces, but closely supervised by their superiors. On the basis of testimony of survivors and other evidentiary means, the report identified more than 200 clandestine detention centres operated by the three armed forces. Under pressure from the government, the Sabato Commission declined to name the names of some 400 officials it had identified, but the list was soon leaked to the human rights community.

The report set the stage for the trial of the junta members, which took place before the Federal Court of Appeals of Buenos Aires in 1985, and it was closely followed by a mesmerized public. In the end, the court sentenced General Jorge R. Videla and Admiral Emilio Massera to life in prison on dozens of counts of murder; other defendants were given lesser terms, and the members of the third junta were acquitted because the court found that the relevant crimes had stopped at the time they had been in charge of the government (although they could still be tried for crimes attributed to them while in previous postings). Significantly, the court ordered the prosecution of other high-ranking officers for crimes committed in regions and sub-regions. By early 1987, literally dozens of cases were under prosecution, and at least one other significant case resulted in convictions and jail sentences. At the same time, unrest in the ranks of army officers produced an uprising in Easter of that year, and the Alfonsin government retreated and forced through two bills (Punto Final and Obediencia Debida) that effectively put an end to all prosecutions except for those of 25 or 30 high-ranking officers. In 1989 and 1990, Carlos Menem, who succeeded Alfonsin as president, issued two pardon decrees that prevented those prosecutions and eventually released Videla, Massera and all others who were serving sentences at the time.

The matter seemed to have come around full circle to impunity again. Significantly, however, the issue has never died down. In the 1990s, Menem instituted reparations schemes for those who had been held in administrative detention without trial or had been tried by military courts during the dictatorship, as well as for the families of the disappeared. There has not been a systematic purge of bad elements in the armed forces, but the better-known culprits have been forced into retirement because the pressure of public opinion forced Congress to withhold consent to their promotion to higher ranks, or simply because the armed forces have had to shrink their ranks considerably in the democratic era. Meanwhile, the human rights groups have been able to keep the issue of impunity alive. In 1995, the confessions of a 'dirty warrior' (Verbitsky 1996) prompted the present chief of the army to apologize publicly to the nation for those crimes. In 1998, General Videla was again arrested and he is currently under prosecution for crimes that were deliberately left out of the pseudo-amnesty laws and the pardons, involving the taking of newborn babies from pregnant prisoners who were later executed, and giving those babies into irregular adoption. Although 15 years have gone by since the advent of democracy, accountability for the crimes of the dictatorship remains a high-visibility issue, and one in which a great majority of Argentines agree on its importance for the quality of democracy.

In Chile, General Augusto Pinochet was able to exert much more control over the pace and character of the transition, to the point of remaining as commander-in-chief of the army well after the elections of 1990 (in 1998 he stepped down and, under the Constitution he imposed in the 1980s, became an unelected life senator). Most of the human rights crimes had been committed in the early years of the dictatorship (1973–78) and they were covered by a 1978 self-amnesty law that had been repeatedly applied by the courts. In addition, although democratic forces had a strong majority, a conservative minority with strong bonds to the army commanded a respectable percentage of the electorate, and controlled key parliamentary processes via 'appointed' senators and slanted vote-counting.

For all of these reasons, the government of Patricio Aylwin and his democratic coalition opted for a solution that, compared to Argentina, relied much less on prosecutions and much more on the need to uncover the truth about human rights crimes (Zalaquett 1998). There were no further amnesties or pardons, so that a few criminal cases did indeed make their way through courts, involving cases that had happened after 1978 and the one case that had been exempted from the amnesty because of its international repercussions: the murder of Orlando Letelier and Ronnie Moffitt in the streets of Washington in 1976. Two key figures in the Pinochet repressive machinery were eventually convicted for it. But the emphasis was placed on truth-telling. Aylwin appointed a Commission on Truth and Reconciliation, headed by Jorge Rettig and composed of respected figures from different political camps, including the right (Aylwin 1996). The Rettig Commission produced a powerful report, which included many facts and episodes not previously known to the Chilean public. More importantly, it also set the tone for what the process of truth-telling should be, by making a point of holding hearings and listening to the voice of the victims, and by carefully gathering evidence.

The report is distinctive because it is a painstaking effort to document each case and to give each family an 'individualized truth' rather than a picture of the structure of repression.[4] It made reconciliation its ultimate objective, but rightly insisted that true reconciliation had to start with full knowledge and disclosure of the facts and a recognition of the dignity of the victims and of their plight. In presenting the report to the public on national television, President Aylwin apologized to the victims in the name of the nation. The files and archives of the commission were then turned over to a publicly funded corporation that devised a scheme for reparations. Except for the handful of officers convicted at trials, the perpetrators have remained in the armed and security forces, controlled as they are by General Pinochet and his loyal subordinates.

With these two models as precedent, the next exercises occurred in Central America, in the context of attempts by the international community to put an end to bloody internal conflicts in El Salvador, Nicaragua and Guatemala. The need to bring insurgents back to politics and away from military action meant that they had to be assured of immunity from prosecution; this in turn was a powerful incentive towards blanket amnesties to favour all sides under the guise of reconciliation. That was the result in Nicaragua: after the Sandinistas surprisingly lost the 1990 elections and before they handed over power, they rammed through a blanket amnesty law to which no significant sector objected. In El Salvador instead, the United Nations took over a sputtering peace process and brokered negotiations that culminated in 1992 with a final settlement. In the meantime, however, and before a ceasefire had been arranged, the UN was allowed to deploy a resident mission to verify compliance with the parties' pledges to respect human rights.

These partial accords also produced a truth commission, the first one sponsored and financed by the United Nations (Hayner 1994; Buergenthal 1996). Its three members were prominent international figures, and significantly all three were non-Salvadorans. The staff was also recruited abroad. Though its mandate was very broad, the TC had only six months to gather its facts (later extended to eight). Even with these limitations, the TC produced a strong report that had a powerful impact in El Salvador and abroad. It was the first to 'name names' of perpetrators that were known to it. The report did not call for prosecutions, but did issue a powerful indictment of the Salvadoran judiciary for its complicity in the crimes. As soon as the report was out, the conservative ARENA government pushed through Congress a blanket amnesty law, which the commissioners criticized. There have been no reparations in El Salvador but, significantly, an important purge of officers involved in atrocities did take place. As part of the UN-sponsored accords, a separate commission (this time formed by three Salvadorans) investigated individual records and called for the dismissal of more than 100 officers, many of them of very high rank. The issue created great unrest, and the three commissioners had to leave the country for a while due to threats, but the purge was actually conducted.

At the time of writing, a similar model of a UN verification mission and a UN truth commission is currently under way for Guatemala. The TC's report was expected in the second half of 1998, but in the meantime it seems to have conducted a thorough and professional job, especially reaching out to rural and indigenous communities in the countryside. According to the peace accords, the mandate is limited: the word 'truth' is not even mentioned in the title.[5] The commission, chaired by a non-Guatemalan but composed of two other Guatemalan members, is supposed to produce a 'historical interpretation of the reality' of the 37-year conflict, and is not expected to name names. In the meantime, some prosecutions have started, though obviously handicapped by the sad state of the Guatemalan judiciary. The human rights organizations won a significant victory in December 1996, when they successfully lobbied for a limited amnesty. The amnesty law was required by the peace accords, so that the leadership of the guerrilla movement could safely return to sign the final settlement and rejoin political life. Nevertheless, the final act became the first amnesty law in Latin America that distinguishes the offence of rebellion and sedition, as well as relatively minor offences committed by all sides, from atrocities that reach the level of crimes against humanity and are exempt from the amnesty.

This short description of Latin American experiences must end here for lack of space. Nevertheless, it is important to note that the matter is by no means restricted to these four countries. Bolivia produced the conviction and life sentence of General Garcia Meza, a former president. Paraguayan judges discovered secret archives of the Stroessner-era crimes. In Uruguay, successive democratic governments have refused to reopen the issue, but the human rights community forced the matter into a national plebiscite to overturn a blanket amnesty law and narrowly lost it (Michelini 1996). In Brazil, after years of similar refusal, President Fernando Henrique Cardoso passed a law of reparations for a number of named victims of army atrocities; the law also created a commission to produce a truth report on the episode and a scheme for reparations for other victims as well. Surinam has just decreed that a truth commission will be created and civil society organizations are preparing themselves for it. In Haiti, the UN partially financed a truth commission set up by the restored Aristide government to look into crimes of the previous military regimes (a largely failed exercise that would well merit some additional comment). In Honduras, the human rights ombudsman produced an important report on the policy of disappearances practised in the early 1980s. Although there is no similar process in Mexico, the office of the human rights ombudsman created in 1990 routinely produces and publishes reports of its findings of fact and of law in the thousands of cases that are brought to its attention. In Peru, just when some important investigations resulted in the discovery of secret murder squads within the army, the government of Alberto Fujimori issued a shameful blanket amnesty that buried both justice and truth.

Comparisons with Other Regions

The Latin American experience of the 1980s and 1990s has elicited comparisons with other historical experiments in accountability. The most obvious reference is to Nuremberg and Tokyo, although a more relevant comparison would be to the domestic prosecutions in several European countries for war crimes and crimes against humanity that followed them up until the present. Nuremberg and its aftermath are relevant for the notion of crimes against humanity and its attendant legal consequences; for the principle that obedience to orders is no defence; and for the theory of 'command responsibility', that establishes criminal liability on those who had effective control of the actions of others, even if they were not direct perpetrators. But otherwise, Latin Americans reject the comparison because Nuremberg and Tokyo are 'victors' justice', whereas prosecutions in Latin America are not in any way controlled by the military's former enemies. If former guerrillas participate at all, they do so as witnesses; the impulse comes from organizations of civil society, prosecutors and magistrates who were and are *neutral* as regards the previous violent conflict.

In other settings, comparison is made with the transitions from communism to democracy in Eastern European countries. At the risk of generalization – and in stark contrast with Latin America – truly democratic sectors in Eastern Europe embrace a policy of 'forgive and forget', the 'thick line' approach of Poland's Thadeusz Mazowiecki and Adam Michnik. In the interest of reconciliation, they object not only to trials for the crimes of communism, but also to truth-telling exercises. In fact, some of the efforts at settling accounts that have taken place in Eastern Europe are truly damaging to the cause of human rights, for instance, the Czech 'lustration' laws and some clumsy German prosecutions of well-known figures in the East, for crimes committed when they resisted the Nazis before the war (McAdams 1996; see also Méndez 1996). Not all attempts at accountability in Europe are so misguided, however.

The crimes of communism and those of the military dictatorships are different, although both flow from unbridled abuse of authority. Pervasive spying and intrusions on private life, the use of *confidants* and the promotion of betrayal of family loyalties are serious enough offences against human dignity, and they deserve condemnation. But they don't lend themselves to a treatment based on prosecution under the criminal law of the state, both because they were not clearly illegal acts at the time they were committed and because they have left behind a large web of complicity for which it is hard to draw clear lines and avoid the stigmatization of large numbers of persons. In contrast, murder, indiscriminate attacks on the civilian population, torture and disappearances are clearly discernible as illegal under any laws and at any time, and it is far easier to establish levels of criminal authorship and responsibility for them. Neither Europeans nor Latin Americans should want to use the criminal process to indict the sycophants, cheerleaders and opportunists who gave political support to the enemies of democracy; the present and future generations should penalize them by other means, like exposing them via public opinion and letting history judge them. But even Adam Michnik agrees that 'murder is murder' and it must be punished, so the difference in approach is much less profound than it appears.[6]

The South African experiment draws the greatest attention in our day. The emphasis is on truth-telling, but prosecutions are not out of the question. An important novelty is the incorporation of a conditional amnesty, which does not apply automatically but for which potential defendants must make a formal application. The benefit is granted only in exchange for full and truthful confession. The Truth and Reconciliation

Commission (TRC) was expected to complete its task by late 1998. It has been a controversial and sometimes rocky road, and the debate about how much truth and how much justice South African victims are entitled to will probably continue. Nevertheless, the process deserves admiration and support for the openness of the debate that preceded it, for the transparency of the proceedings, for the regard and consideration shown to all victims, and for the earnest attempt by Archbishop Tutu and his colleagues to engage the old defenders of apartheid in a profound dialogue about ethics and responsibility.[7]

Finally, comparisons are inevitable with the recent attempts by the United Nations to establish practical forms to implement the principle of universal jurisdiction for the most serious crimes against the human person, in the creation of two *ad hoc* courts for the former Yugoslavia and Rwanda (Meron 1995) and in the just concluded Rome conference that gives birth to a permanent International Criminal Court. Latin American governments and NGOs have actively participated in the long debates about the shape that such an ICC should have, and not surprisingly they have taken consistent and unified positions in favour of an independent, impartial, fair and effective court, one that can actually help in breaking the cycle of impunity for the most egregious crimes.

The Case for Truth and Justice

Against trials and truth commissions, it is often said that fragile democracies need to be stabilized and not put at risk by provoking still-powerful elements in the armed forces that can strike if they feel threatened and stage a coup. This argument is not persuasive because it amounts to allowing the enemies of democracy to blackmail legitimate leaders and condition the way they rule. The political argument in favour of accountability proceeds from a conception of the nature of the new democratic order: it must be based, from the start, on an affirmation of the rule of law and on the simple notion that in a democracy there are no privileges – much less in criminal cases – for those who wear uniform or happen to be powerful. Those principles are the key to actual stability, because they will make the new order attractive to future generations. Even if a majority favours a 'thick line' approach, in a truly democratic society the will of the majority cannot be imposed against the right of minorities to see justice done and to have their plight as victims recognized.

An ethical argument against accountability states that the most important task of the transition is to seek reconciliation between factions whose recent battles brought so much suffering. In this light, trials and truth-telling exercises are seen as attempts at retribution that will inevitably prolong the factionalism and not allow the wounds to heal. This argument presupposes that oblivion and the passage of time will have the effect of reconciliation, a proposition that is far from proven, especially if the crimes are tragic enough and they remain clouded in secrecy. It is important, nevertheless, to recognize that the ultimate objective of any effort is to obtain national reconciliation. The problem is that reconciliation cannot be decreed, nor should it be demanded only from the victims. Reconciliation must be preceded by some act of contrition by the victimizers. The victims will some day be ready to forgive, but they rightly do not want state authorities to forgive in their name. And they insist that they have to know all the facts before they can forgive, including the identity of those who caused them harm.

The legal arguments in favour of truth and justice are much more straightforward: no one can deny that murder and torture are criminal offences for which the institutions of a democratic state are there to act to provide a remedy. The validity of blanket amnesty laws, when passed by democratic parliaments and through open and free debate, is a harder issue, but international law principles are evolving in the direction of requiring that they are not so broad as to leave crimes against humanity unpunished, or to create an atmosphere of impunity and silence about them.

As it happens, there are now few arguments in favour of a policy of oblivion. By and large, all commentators recognize that tragic legacies require some affirmative action on the part of newly democratic states. The more important debates are now about whether to promote account-ability *and* reconciliation by means of truth-telling or by means of criminal trials. In that sense, in some camps there is a dangerous tendency to consider truth as an alternative to justice (Krauthammer 1994; Forsyth 1995; Pastor 1995). When conceived that way, the exercises in truth-telling can quickly degenerate into tokenism, as if the rights of victims could be satisfied with a relatively cursory report on what they already know, and a demand that we all move on to other things. This is a serious misunder-standing of the nature of truth-telling experiments. They function best when they are conceived as a step in the process of overall accountability, and worst when they are conceived as the final stop along that road. In fact, truth commissions do a lot of good by assembling evidence that can later be used at trial, and by sorting out those cases where prosecutions can proceed with an economy of resources and with good prospects of success.

A prejudice against trials is generally based on the assumption that a trial is the prolongation of conflict by other means, reflecting a war mental-ity of sorts. Conflict is of course inherent to the whole nature of a judicial setting, but it must be noted that it is conflict with clear rules, with equality of arms and where the parties specifically renounce any resort to violence. For that reason, trials are a good way to settle conflict in a law-abiding society, even if they should not be expected to solve all types of conflict. Specifically, it would be a mistake to expect that trials for past human rights crimes will settle disputes about the historical interpretation of recent events. History cannot be 'settled' in this sense, for it is in the nature of historical interpretation that such debates should go on. Trials, however, can go a long way in settling the factual basis of some events, so that discussions can then proceed over a shared understanding of what actually happened (Osiel 1995). Truth commissions and trials have their own advantages, but it is by no means clear that the truth reached by a commission is automatically superior to the truth that can be obtained at trial, assuming that both exercises respect their own basic rules and conditions of legitimacy.

Conditions of Legitimacy

The benefits of trials are meaningless unless their inherent conditions of legitimacy are rigorously applied. This means, first and foremost, that due process and fair trial guarantees as spelled out in universal standards must be afforded to any and all defendants without exception. Second, some discretion as to what cases to bring is acceptable, but the decisions in this regard must be transparent and not discriminatory on illegitimate grounds. It may be hard to draw the line in the abstract, but trials conceived as scapegoating or vendetta are unacceptable. The defendants are at all times entitled to guarantees of a fair trial, including the presumption of innocence, the right to counsel of their own choosing, the right to confront evidence, and so on, and most especially the right to be tried by an impartial and independent judiciary pre-established by law. This means that trials under military courts will not do, either because they will tend unduly to protect the defendant if he is a military officer, or because they will be prejudiced against him if he is an adversary.

Other conditions of legitimacy include the need to disclose the truth and let it be known, both by the families and by society. A trial that proceeds on the basis of suppression of some facts, either because the proceedings are confidential or because convictions are a result of plea-bargaining, will not satisfy this condition, at least when it comes to crimes against humanity (Méndez 1996; see also Zalaquett 1992). A final condition of legitimacy is that the policy regarding trials and clemency must be transparent and arrived at through democratic debate, rather than in closed circles. Of course, this does not mean that any policy is acceptable as long as it enjoys the support of the majority of the population. The majority cannot *choose* to take away rights of a discrete minority, not even of a minority of one, and not even if that decision is arrived at after open and democratic debate (Neier 1998). But in order to succeed in achieving all its objectives, a policy of accountability must be clearly presented to the public and openly debated by all concerned; where legitimate choices have to be made (for example, with regards to time limitations or objective standards for the use of discretion in bringing charges) they must be made in the open and allowing for meaningful participation by all concerned in the process of policy formulation.

Of course, the object must be to arrive at national reconciliation, and to achieve it in ways that are meaningful and lasting. In fact, the primary condition of legitimacy is that this objective must be kept closely in mind (Zalaquett 1992). If under the circumstances it is clear that a prosecution would be detrimental to that purpose, it should not proceed. Nevertheless, it is important not to see trials as *prima facie* not conducive to reconciliation; on the contrary, they may well contribute to reconciliation by settling old scores and by removing the stigma attached to individuals who are seen as culpable although they have never been tried, as well as the stigma attached to their comrades-in-arms or the members of an ethnic group, for the sake of their belonging to the same force or ethnicity as those who indeed committed terrible deeds (Weschler 1995; see also Roth 1996).

If trials require these stringent conditions, it must be noted that a policy that leans more towards truth-telling than to prosecutions is not exempt from its own conditions of legitimacy. Due process and fair trial standards are undoubtedly different when the result is a report and not a criminal conviction and a jail term. Nevertheless, it would be a mistake to conceive of a truth commission without some minimal fairness, because it would be easily and rightly attacked as biased and its report therefore unpersuasive. A truth commission's primary goal is to establish an *official version* of the facts over which there is considerable disagreement. In the words of Professor Thomas Nagel, that version achieves the status of *acknowledgment* and not simply knowledge, by virtue of the official nature of the endeavour (see Weschler 1989). But government sanction is not by itself what confers that status on the facts thus disclosed; unless that version is supported by rigorous methodology and a fair hearing to all sides of the story, it will become just another report to be soon forgotten.

Conclusion

Many will argue that the conditions of legitimacy mentioned above rule out the applicability of either trials or truth commissions to many situations in the world today. In many countries that have recently lived though a human rights tragedy, the judiciary is simply not up to the task of hearing and adjudicating these cases and may not even meet the most basic requirement of impartiality and independence. Even a fair and objective truth commission, with the attendant financial costs of proceeding in the proper way, may be unattainable for some countries destroyed by war and poor to begin with.

In those cases, it would be a mistake to soften the conditions of legitimacy for the sake of doing something about accountability. In this sense, a clear example is the domestic prosecutions for the genocide in Rwanda: the international community must withhold support and indeed condemn them as human rights violations, unless the appalling conditions of detention are improved and unless each defendant gets a fair trial according to international standards. The fact that the genocidal acts that are being tried were much worse violations of human rights is no excuse.

On the other hand, it is not immediately clear that nothing can be done unless a country has already in place the whole machinery of institutions of justice. This argument was widely debated in Haiti at the time of Aristide's restoration to power, and it must be noted that, with obvious differences of degree, all countries coming out of dictatorships have to do something to bring their judiciaries up to international standards. If countries are going to need independent judiciaries in any event (if they truly profess to be guided by democratic principles), then why not force the issue and proceed to assert that independence by tackling the hard case of the legacy of human rights violations? In such a situation, a policy that combines truth and justice in sequential order and with separate assignation of duties may serve both the immediate interests of accountability and the longer-term needs of a truly democratic order. For example, a truth commission could gather evidence and hear the victims while the judiciary is under reconstruction as an independent and impartial body; when the task of the TC is done, the material thus gathered can be used by courts and prosecutors to conduct trials under conditions of fairness, and with the benefit of having the evidence sorted out beforehand.

In the end, universal standards are not minimum common denominators: as the Universal Declaration of Human Rights puts it, they are 'common standards of achievement' for all nations. Therefore, the fact that some countries are not up to them at any given moment does not deprive them of their universality. At the same time, societies must be free to find their own ways towards reconciliation through truth and justice. What the preceding thoughts are meant to convey is not that all countries must follow a standard prescription, but that each society should devise its own path bearing in mind some universal principles. Cultures differ and each one of them contributes to the richness of the human experience. But there is nothing culturally relative about notions of human dignity, especially the inherent dignity of the victims of human rights abuse, and the desire to know the truth and to see justice done is common to us all.

Notes

1. *Nunca Más*, Buenos Aires, Eudeba, 1984; *Informe de la Comisión Nacional de la Verdad y Reconciliación*, Santiago de Chile, 1991 (English version University of Notre Dame Press, 1992); *Guatemala Nunca Más*, ODHA, Guatemala, 1998.

2. CCPR/C/79/Add. 46, adopted at Meeting No. 1411, 53d. Session, 5 April 1995, Item 10.

3. *Nunca Más*, Buenos Aires, Edudeba, 1984.

4. *Informe de la Comisión Nacional de la Verdad y Reconciliación.*

5. Acuerdo sobre la Creación de la Comisión de Esclarecimiento Histórico de las Violaciones a los Derechos Humanos y los Hechos de Violencia que han Causado Sufrimiento a la Población Guatemalteca, 23 June 1994.

6. Statement made in the course of a discussion at a conference in Cape Town, South Africa, February 1994.

7. Republic of South Africa, 'Promotion of National Unity and Reconciliation Bill, 1995'; see also Méndez 1997.

Bibliography

Aylwin, P. (1996) 'La Comisión chilena sobre la verdad y reconciliación', *Estudios Básicos de Derechos Humanos*, vol. vii, San José: IIDH.

Buergenthal, T. (1996) 'La Comisión de la Verdad para El Salvador', *Estudios Especializados de Derechos Humanos*, San José: IIDH.

Forsyth, D. (1995) 'The UN and human rights at fifty: an incremental but incomplete revolution', *Global Governance*, 1: 297–318.

Hayner, P. B. (1994) 'Fifteen truth commissions – 1974 to 1994', *Human Rights Quarterly*, November.

Krauthammer, C. (1994) 'Truth, not trials', *Washington Post*, 9 September.

McAdams, J. (1996) 'The Honecker trial: the East German past and the German future', Working Paper 216, January, Paris: Kellogg Institute, University of Notre Dame.

Méndez, J. E. (1996) 'Accountability for past abuses', Working Paper 223, Kellogg Institute, University of Notre Dame, repr. *Human Rights Quarterly*, vol. 19, no. 2, May 1997.

— (1997) 'Derecho a la verdad frente a las graves violaciones a los derechos humanos', *La aplicación de los tratados sobre derechos humanos por los tribunales locales*, Buenos Aires: Ed. Del Puerto-CELS.

Meron, T. (1995) 'International criminalization of internal atrocities', *American Journal of International Law*, vol. 89, no. 3, July.

Michelini, F. (1996) 'El largo camino a la verdad', *Revista IIDH*, no. 24, San José: IIDH.

Neier, A. (1998) *War Crimes*, New York: Times Books, Random House.

Osiel, M. J. (1995) 'Ever again: legal remembrance of administrative massacre', *U. Penn. L. Rev.*, vol. 144, no. 2, December.

Pastor, R. (1995) cited in 'The nation: Nuremberg isn't repeating itself', *New York Times*, 19 November.

Roth, K. (1996) introductory essay to Human Rights Watch, *World Report 1996*, New York: Human Rights Watch, December, p. xv.

Verbitsky, H. (1996) *The Flight: Confessions of an Argentine Dirty Warrior*, New York: The New Press.

Weschler, L. (1989) 'Epilogue', *State Crimes: Punishment and Pardon*, New York: Aspen Institute.

— (1995) 'Inventing peace', *The New Yorker*, 20 November.

Zalaquett, J. (1992) 'Balancing ethical imperatives and political constraints: the dilemma of new democracies confronting past human rights violations', *Hastings Law Journal*, vol. 43, no. 6.

— (1998) 'Procesos de transición a la democracia y políticas de derechos humanos en América Latina', in L. González (ed.), *Presente y Futuro de los Derechos Humanos*, San José: IIDH.

8

Truth in a Box: The Limits of Justice through Judicial Mechanisms

Julie Mertus

The problem with the war crimes tribunals for the former Yugoslavia and Rwanda is that they are war crimes tribunals. The stuff of law – the elements of the crimes, the rules of procedure, the dance of witness, lawyer, judge – can only do so much. And the closer one is to the crime, the less likely it is that 'so much' is enough.

Tribunal justice may be meaningful to lawyers drafting pleonastic legal documents in The Hague, diplomats declaring success at stabilizing conflicts, and local politicians staking their claims to power amid the smouldering embers of destroyed communities. But little satisfaction will come to survivors. Genocide, mass murder, rape, torture and other crimes may be tried, and a small percentage of the perpetrators may be convicted. International principles will triumph or fail; respect for international law will expand or diminish. The new governments arising out of conflict will be legitimized or de-legitimized. In any case, the voices of survivors will remain largely unheard and unaddressed.

For survivors, storytelling is not a luxury. War serves to strip survivors of control over their lives and to erase all sense of a volitional past and future. As Elaine Scarry observes in *The Body in Pain*, the discourse of torture, rape, murder and other forms of violence teach their targets that they are nothing but objects (Scarry 1985). The process of telling and observing one's story being heard allows survivors to become subjects again, to retrieve and resurrect their individual and group identities. From voice comes hope.

In August 1994, tucked away in a refugee camp in Pakistan, a dozen Bosnian Muslim refugees sat in a circle on the cement floor and, taking turns, wrote the following poem:

> I used to believe that the world was full of many colors,
> now I know it's just black.

I used to believe that all people are kind,
now I know only some of them are.

I used to believe that my friends would be with me all of my life,
now I know that none of them would give any part of their body for me.

I used to believe that I could trust people,
now I know that I should be careful.

I used to believe that I would have a good life with my neighbors,
but now I know it is easy for them to kill in war.

I used to believe that no one could force me away from my homeland,
but now I know this isn't a dream.

I couldn't believe that my generation could be worse than the older
    generation,
but now I know they are.

I used to believe in everything,
but now I believe in nothing.

I used to believe in happiness,
but now I cannot even believe my eyes.

I used to believe that I would live by my wishes,
but now I know I will live by other people's wishes.

What I couldn't believe, I now believe.

(A 'Group Poem', one line each told by Adisa, Nasir, Hajra, Muriz, Mirsada, Remzija, Melisa, Senid, Aziz, Uzeir, Mevlida, Sahza, aged 13 to about 54, refugees from Sarajevo, Jajce and Donji Vakuf in Islamabad, Pakistan, August 1994. Reprinted from *The Suitcase: Refugees' Voices from Bosnia and Croatia* (University of California Press 1997).

When first asked to contribute to the poem, many had difficulties in answering, not because they did not have ideas, but because, in the words of one man who participated: 'No one has asked us what we think in such a long time.' They had been treated as mere objects, first by their tormentors, then by the refugee camp handlers, government spokespeople, asylum officers, visiting journalists. They had been denied their complex selves and stamped with unitary identities: enemy, victim, refugee, the 'ethnically cleansed', asylum-seeker, spectacle. The telling of the poem helped many of the Bosnians in Pakistan to reclaim a part of their identity. The war crimes tribunal, however, threatens to retard or even reverse this process.

For the war crimes tribunal, survivors of war wear the stamp of potential witness; they become conduits through which investigators and prosecutors can make their case. Despite their good intentions, investigators and prosecutors – the agents of law – must focus on piecing together facts to prove the crime. Even if they avoid putting the personal suffering of survivors on trial, they cannot return the survivors' rightful claim to subject-hood. The legal process is inherently counter-narrative; it opens and closes, letting in only enough information to prove the issue at hand.

Victims can testify about the hand that beat them, confirm the size of the room, the colour of the door, the width of the wooden table on which bodies were broken. But they cannot talk about how their child's face looked when the paramilitary troops dragged her away, they cannot remember what they ate for dinner on the last day the entire family was alive and together, they cannot cry about their dog who was left behind or reminisce about their long walks through their old town square. No one will see the stories, poems, pictures, jokes, coffees, gossip, walks around the refugee camp yard – no one will know the little things that helped them survive. A war crimes tribunal is, after all, only a war crimes tribunal. That a tribunal holds great utility for lawyers and history writers is unquestionable. That it alone can address the concerns of survivors is questionable.

The refugee woman who listened to the asylum officer calmly inform her that her application was rejected because she was *only* threatened with rape and was not *actually* raped or tortured in a concentration camp; the newly-wed doctors who escaped Bosnia by paying the aid convoy 4,000 Deutschmarks each and who somehow made it across borders to Germany where they disappeared into the ranks of the shadow labour force; the teenage girl who carries in her rucksack the poetry of her dead soldier boyfriend; the four-year-old boy who wants to become a plane so he can fly his family back home; the elderly couple who lived four months in their basement before a sympathetic *enemy* neighbour found them and arranged for their safe exit. The tribunal may fulfil many functions, but it cannot serve the needs of these and other survivors.

We do not yet know all of the mechanisms necessary to promote in war-torn socities truth, healing and transformative social change. Witness the deep division within Chile over the appropriate response to bringing General Pinochet to justice for violations of human rights during his dictatorship. We do know, however, that formal tribunals serve only limited functions. This chapter outlines these functions and suggests additional alternatives that may address more fully the interests of survivors.

A Paradigm of Functions and Interests

Like cases before domestic criminal courts, even-handed investigations and fair prosecutions before a war crimes tribunal can fulfil certain discrete functions. Six of the main functions are as follows:

1. *naming* crimes;
2. *blaming* individual perpetrators;
3. *punishing* the guilty and *deterring* potential perpetrators;
4. *delivering reparations* to survivors;
5. *reforming* lawless societies; and
6. *recording* what happened for history. (For alternative distillations of goals of tribunals, see ASIL 1994.)

The problem is not that the war crimes tribunals will utterly fail to address these functions. It is rather that their success in doing so will be measured differently according to one's particular interest. To be sure, everyone has some interest in 'justice' being served. Justice, however, is frequently related to *position*. We can locate four elements of position:

1. *location and placement*: relative proximity to the crimes, the conflict, the region and the issues;
2. *attitude and disposition*: assessment of the origins of conflict, the account-ability of various actors for crimes and their continuation and the need to remember or the desire to forget;
3. *job*: role and responsibility as an international, regional, national, com-munity or family leader, and;
4. *Status C* position inside or outside international, regional, national and community power structures, and worth accorded to one's existence according to that position.

When measured by these attributes, most survivors, close to the crime, are far from achieving their vision of justice.

Table 8.1 below illustrates some of the intersections between *functions* and *position*. It lists the interests served by each function for three main groups of actors: the epistemic 'international community' (see Roht–Arraiza 1995) – international and regional institutions and organizations, states and individual actors outside Rwanda and the former Yugoslavia; local power-brokers, including both *de facto* and *de jure* leaders and the states, territories and communities arising out of the conflicts and their opposition; and individual survivors, victims and bystanders including both those who stayed in the area in conflict and those who fled for safer ground (but excluding those who previously or presently held positions of power). These groups are not mutually exclusive: linkages exist among groups and, additionally, actors may shift from group to group. Significantly, the table does not include a category for 'perpetrators' in recognition that perpetrators may, either through self-definition or definition by others, fall within all of the categories.

Within each of these groups, interests can vary further according to the

TABLE 8.1 Intersections between functions and position

Functions	International community	Local power-brokers	Survivors, victims and bystanders
Naming crime	• set and enforce boundaries of international law • express moral condemnation • save face for failures	• absolve (or blame) current leaders of responsibility • (de)legitimize new states	• receive public acknowledgement of what happened • discover way to talk about personal suffering
Blaming individual perpetrators	• stabilize successor states by individualizing guilt • pave way for normalization of international economic and political relations	• (de)stabilize successor politics by individualizing guilt • enable new power-brokers to assert their authority over violators • pave way for support from international community	• achieve revenge • save face among neighbours and international community
Punishing guilty and deterring potential perpetrators	• demonstrate the existence and force of international law • deter potential perpetrators worldwide	• displace threats of personal revenge • legitimize local efforts to try crimes • deter potential perpetrators locally	• achieve revenge • achieve retribution • force expiation of guilt • give significance to suffering • prevent recurrence of suffering
Delivering reparations to survivors	• demonstrate the existence and force of international law • deter potential perpetrators worldwide	• address needs of survivors • displace threats of revenge	• receive partial remedy for suffering • improve welfare for self and other survivors • receive public acknowledgment of guilt

Reforming lawlessness	• (re)establish the position of international law in a lawless world	• (re)establish the rule of law in lawless societies	• (re)establish the principle that law exists above power and force
Recording for history	• establish official record of the efficiency and efficacy of international institutions • use record to warn potential perpetrators worldwide • educate globally	• establish official record of (il)legitimacy of government • use record to warn potential perpetrators locally • educate locally	• establish authoritative 'living record' of what happened • retrieve and record a collective memory and identity • expose the truth • remember or forget • educate within families and communities

nuances of *position* – that is, proximity, attitude, job and social status. This chapter examines the ways in which each function of the war crimes tribunals serve the needs of each of the three groups of actors, remembering that not all actors within each group are the same. In sum, the thesis is that for each of its potential functions, a tribunal is most likely to address the interests of the international community, and least likely to hear the interests of survivors. Tribunals should therefore be understood as a necessary – although insufficient – response to the aftermath of conflict and the need for healing.

Naming crimes   The naming of crimes can serve important, though vastly different, interests of the three groups of actors. For the international community, the naming provides a historical opportunity to establish, refine and/or enforce the boundaries of international law. For example, by naming the crime of genocide, the tribunals are the first international criminal tribunals to define the meaning and application of the Genocide Convention, a post-Second World War treaty. By naming the crime of rape as a 'crime against humanity', they are the first international criminal courts to refine when and how rape in war can be prosecuted as such (although rape in conflict has been prosecuted previously as torture, inhumane treatment, crimes against personal dignity, and other national or international criminal offences – Blatt 1992). By naming superior officers' actions as criminal, the tribunals are defining the limits of command responsibility; by naming foot soldiers' actions as criminal, they are setting the limits of the defence of 'superior orders'. Who is most interested in the potential of the war crimes tribunals to fulfil this function? Those who have made it their profession to promote the existence and enforcement of international law – lawyers, scholars, judges, activists and diplomats.

The naming process and the content it brings to international law is 'shaped by the requirements of the international community' (Roht-Arriaza 1995: 5). At this juncture in history international war crimes tribunals present, as Carlos Nino has noted, opportunities for 'collective examination of the moral values of public institutions' (Nino 1996: 131; see also Franck 1997: 140) and, in this vein, for the building and assessment of international institutions, including trans-soverign courts (see Helfer and Slaughter 1997). The post-war era has opened a space in which 'universal' values can be discussed and (re)examined (cf. Gordon 1998). Where no consensus exists as to what constitutes 'justice', a tribunal may present a 'transformative opportunity' for the development of international norms (Osiel 1997: 2). Where consensus already exists, such as in the case of non-derogable clauses in international treaties, a tribunal may be an occasion to renew adherence to a particular norm and to re-educate the public as to its importance. The tribunal for the former Yugoslavia has worked particularly well in this regard, generating 'unprecedented interest in humanitarian law' (Meron 1997: 7) and in directing new generations to focus on the enduring importance of these principles.

The naming of crimes, even without the trials themselves, also provides the international community with a stage from which to express its moral condemnation. International leaders can thus reaffirm by words, if not by deeds, a vision of a just world in which violations of human rights are not met with impunity. Such naming can serve the international community's interest in saving face, in explaining its own failure to take early, decisive action to stop the slaughter, or later steps to minimize the carnage once it had begun. 'At least we are doing something now,' the powerful countries behind the tribunal can declare. Those who were troubled by the equivocal response of their country or institution to the bloodshed may find solace in these words.

Local power-brokers have their own interest in saving face, in explaining their present and past actions to their own constituents and to the international community at large. Those currently in government are interested in using the naming of crimes to absolve current leaders of responsibility; those outside government seek to use the naming of crimes to discredit and undermine the present leadership. Depending on one's attitude towards the accused and the current leadership, the naming of crimes can either legitimize or de-legitimize the new governments or states arising out of conflict. While local leaders care little about international law and institutions, they do have an interest in (re)establishing their own legitimacy and authority.

The naming of crimes carries an entirely different meaning for survivors. Individual survivors are searching for a way to be whole again. Some want to forget what is too painful to remember. For them, the war crimes tribunal is a show to avoid. Others want never to forget. They need to hear their stories told aloud, and to see others hearing their stories. For them, the naming of crimes may suffice as public acknowledgement of what happened. Without such acknowledegment, survivors feel invisible, erased, forgotten.

The language of the tribunal can provide victims with a way to speak about the unspeakable. 'Language and culture encode ways of seeing the world that facilitate common understanding of experience' (Senehi 1996; see also Narayan 1989). Without a language to express themselves, many survivors play out their feelings through the 'hidden transcripts' of anger, aggression and disguised discourses of dignity, such as gossip, rumour and creation of autonomous, private spaces for assertion of dignity (Scott 1990). The legitimized, distant words of law open a door for some to remembering, providing words to talk about personal suffering. The naming may help survivors redefine themselves 'as a collective self engaged in common struggle' (Gugelberger and Kearney 1991).

Most survivors, however, do not see themselves in the work of judicial processes. Their individual situations do not find their way into a legal case, either because there are too many crimes to try, or because their experiences, although horrible and morally reprehensible, do not constitute crimes under international law. There is no crime of destruction of souls, deprivation of childhood, erasure of dreams. There are crimes of murder, torture and inhumane treatment, but there is no crime of being forced to watch helplessly while one's loved one suffers – the injury many survivors swear is most severe (see Mertus et al. 1997).

Even when the tribunal does name their crime, the survivor may barely recognize it as the process and language of law transmutes individual experiences into a categorically neat something else. Law does not permit a single witness to tell their own coherent narrative; it chops their stories into digestible parts, selects a handful of parts, and sorts and refines them to create a new narrative – the legal anti-narrative. Women who have survived rape and sexual assault, for example, describe the harm committed in words far different from the sterile language and performance of law, no matter how the crime of rape is configured (see Lusby 1995; Ray 1997). So too, the Convention on Torture and the legal steps necessary to prove abuses under its provisions tell a different story from the one concentration camp victims would choose to reveal. The law at times limits examination of such witnesses in order to protect them and to ensure that their suffering is not put on trial (see Chinkin 1995; Ni Aolain 1997; see also *Rules of Evidence and Procedure*, especially Rules 70 and 75). Yet some witnesses long for the opportunity to finish their story, to name the crimes for themselves. To do so, they must look beyond the legal system.

Even in the rare cases in which survivors see themselves in the formal legal process, the naming is unlikely to result in a satisfactory public acknowledgement of the crime. While the international community and the prosecutorial staff may recognize the crime, the accused and his or her supporters are unlikely to do so. For example, Dusko Tadic, the first man tried before the Ad Hoc Tribunal for the Former Yugoslavia, failed to acknowledge these most egregious crimes for which he was charged; his supporters denied and continue to deny them as well.

Blaming individual perpetrators The function of blaming individual perpetrators serves varied interests that may directly conflict. While the international community seeks stability (defined narrowly as the continuation of the present government and the absence of war), local power-brokers and survivors may have something very different in mind.

In order to maintain its own credibility, the international community needs to secure peace and maintain stability in the former Yugoslavia and Rwanda. The blaming of individual perpetrators, the international community hopes, will help the people of Rwanda and the former Yugoslavia to stop 'cry[ing] out for justice against the [enemy] group' (Tetreault 1997: 197). Without individualized guilt, the injustice of the past may go on for ever, as a cycle of vengeance perpetuates itself, and the new emerging states will never have the chance to make the transition to democracy, which requires, at the very least, the absence of conflict and, as asserted below further, the establishment of the rule of law (Malamud-Goti 1989; Tobin 1990; Meron 1997: 2–3). Only through a fair investigation of the accused and equitable adjudication of the charges against them can a society teach the general populace about the rule of law and the notion that even state actors can be held accountable (Orentlicher 1990: 2544).

Politically charged trials may backfire and undermine the establishment of the rule of law (Orentlicher 1990: 2544). The populace may view such trials as unfairly selective and biased. The entire institutional framework in which the justice system operates may be deemed illegitimate, thereby eroding acceptance for any democratic institutions (Symposium 1990: 1024). Censure by an international tribunal instead of a national court, however, is thought to be less susceptible to accusations of national bias and therefore more likely to be accepted locally and internationally as legitimate (O'Shea 1996). The success of the tribunal for the former Yugoslavia, for example, has depended upon whether the prosecutor's decisions are based on available evidence and whether the judges refrain from doing anything that detracts from the appearance of impartiality (Schrag 1997: 21).

The naming of individuals also serves to pave the way for normalization of international economic and political relations. When individual perpetrators have been named and the accused are not among those in power, members of the international community can feel that it is legitimate to resume business as usual. This interest is particularly acute among leaders and states possessing a strong economic interest in resuming or beginning relations with successor leaders and/or successor states. For example, Germany has strong and growing economic interests in Croatia, Bosnia and Serbia: Croatia because of trade and investments; Croatia, Bosnia and Serbia because of a desire to return refugees and undocumented arrivals from the former Yugoslavia. Germany's interest in securing the absence of war in the Balkans may be coloured by these economic interests.

Like the international power-brokers, local leaders have an interest in securing peace and maintaining stability, so as not to interfere in seemingly more important matters like reconstructing communities, building governments and amassing new power and wealth. Conversely, some local power-brokers have an interest in undermining peace, re-cementing the dividing line between foes and friends, preparing for the next phase of war. Depending on their ultimate goal, local power-brokers may view the blaming of individuals as a component of forgetting and moving on, or remembering and fighting onward. The blaming will stabilize successor governments only if those currently in government are not among the blamed. If they are blamed, instead of supporting the process of blaming, the successor regimes may seek broad amnesties and deals in exchange for offering up sacrificial lambs.

The blaming process of the tribunals will also enable local leaders to claim and assert their authority over the violators. This step can be stabilizing or destabilizing, according to whether the blamed are inside or outside the present government, and the degree to which the blaming conflicts with popular will (see Weschler 1990). When the accused are identified with the old power structure, the blaming can underscore the discontinuity between the old and new regimes and promote confidence in the new leadership (Zalaquett 1989). When those blamed are inside the present government or when the blaming conflicts strongly with popular will, those on the outside can seize the opportunity for destabilization, pushing instead their own agendas. This phenomenon is complicated when popular will is itself conflictual as, for example, in Chile, where the public disagrees as to whether and how Pinochet should be held accountable for the atrocities committed during his regime.

Blaming plays a much different role for survivors. Although they may long to feel secure, many survivors have long since stopped believing in their own governments and, perhaps, in governmental authority in general. The stability of the newly emerging state is not at the top of their wish list. When the war crimes tribunals make public their indictments, some refugee camps erupt in celebration – not because their leaders have won a victory, but because one of their tormentors is receiving his due. For them, the individualizing of guilt meets their desire for revenge. (For the need for revenge in Rwanda, see Destexhe 1996.) The problem, as noted above, is that the tribunals will never be able to spread their net wide enough to catch every crime, to quiet every call for vengeance; they will be able to try only a small fraction of the cases. Many survivors worry about the failure of the tribunals to arrest the 'big fish', those most responsible for planning and orchestrating the violence. The desire for revenge thus remains strong, threatening to perpetuate the cycle of conflict.

For the survivors who are part of groups that have been accused of crimes, blaming serves another distinct purpose: helping them save face among neighbours and the international community. It is not me, the individualized indictments will allow them to say, it is someone else. In this manner, the tribunals will help the enormous population of bystanders to regain their own sense of identity and worth (Staub 1989). As with survivors, bystanders can regain subject-hood and identity by telling their stories. Their stories are important then as a hearing of history as 'experience' and 'myth', even if they are not factually true (See Rushdie 1990; Cohen 1997). However, like survivors, bystanders cannot rely on the tribunals alone for the telling. Since the list of potential defendants is short, bystanders need to rely on other tellings if they are to argue persuasively 'It was not me' and to tell their own experiences remembered, that is, their own version of history.

Punishing the guilty   The function of punishment could potentially serve the parties' divergent interests. Given the circumstances and nature of the war crimes tribunals and life on the ground in emerging societies, it is unlikely that punishment will entirely serve anyone's interests.

   In addition to demonstrating the existence and force of international law, the international community sees tribunals as essential for general deterrence of war crimes (see Orentlicher 1990: 2542). There are two strands to the general deterrence argument. The first is that the existence and operation of international tribunals will deter potential perpetrators worldwide, as they will know that they could be held accountable for violations of international law. The second is that establishment of fair legal institutions and the adjudication of abuses of prior regimes assists nations in making the transition to democracy (Malamud-Goti 1989: 89) and, the argument implies, democracies are less likely to commit gross human rights abuses. As Diane Orentlicher asks:

> If law is unavailable to punish widespread brutality of the recent past, what lesson can be offered for the future? A complete failure of enforcement vitiates the authority of law itself, sapping its power to deter. This may be tolerable when the law or crime is of marginal consequence, but there can be no scope for eviscerating wholesale laws that forbid violence that has been violated on a massive scale. (Orentlicher, 1990: 2542)

If violators are not tried, Orentlicher contends, the absence of trials may 'undermine the legitimacy of a new government and breed cynicism toward civilian institutions' (ibid.).

   The last strand of the general deterrence argument enjoys greater acceptance (see generally Symposium 1990). Democratization programmes throughout Central and Eastern Europe and Latin America, for example, view as a centrepiece of their operations the establishment of the rule of law over brute force and mechanisms to hold prior regimes accountable (see e.g. Stephan, 1986; Mertus 1999). Whether the application of international law to conflict has any deterrent effect generally is open to debate. While formal states may respect international law in order to retain the respect and cooperation of other states and of international bodies, paramilitary troops and rebel regimes do not usually care much about popular opinion – particularly not during the heat of battle. On the contrary, paramilitary groups may be interested in creating an image of law-breaker instead of that of law-abider. Nevertheless, the argument for the deterrence function contends that consistent and fair application of international law in conflict situations, accompanied by credible threats of international investigations, trials and punishments, may provide some deterrent effect. As the tribunals now stand as *ad hoc* bodies, with no authority to publish crimes anywhere except for Rwanda and the former Yugoslavia, their ability to deter crimes in war elsewhere is particularly limited (this argument has been used to promote the creation of a permanent international criminal court; see Sadat Wexler 1996: 707–13; McCormack 1997: 682).

Local power-brokers are more interested in specific deterrence – that is, preventing perpetrators from repeating their acts. Those who are in power hope that punishment will displace threats of personal revenge, build confidence among the citizenry and legitimize local efforts to try crimes. At the same time, they do not want the punishment to become too complete, lest it interfere with the objective of 'national reconstruction' and 'national pacification' (and, for some, even result in their own arrest) (Zalaquett 1989). Thus they are willing to support the trials superficially, as long as the international busy-bodies do not dig too deep. The international community is cognizant of the potential of punishment to destabilize the emerging governments, and thus it has held back from supporting prosecutions against some of the 'biggest fish' responsible for the conflicts. As a result, the deterrent effect of the tribunals within the countries themselves is circumscribed.

Survivors have little interest in deterrence. Instead, they see the punitive function of war crimes tribunals as a means to achieve revenge and retribution, to force expiation of guilt. Although many survivors do not advocate group blame and do not seek revenge against the entire group called the 'enemy', many survivors confess a desire for vengeance against the particular individual(s) who harmed family members and other members of their communities (see Mertus et al. 1997). That the punishment they demand may destabilize their homeland is of little concern.

Apart from mere vengeance, which may seem an illegitimate interest, punishment can substantiate the suffering of victims, aiding the process of reclaiming an entitlement to subject-hood. Punishment itself serves as important public recognition of the crime. Yet the tribunals can try relatively few cases and thus the process can result in few instances of punishment. Tribunals can never try the many cases in which the harm has no name as a crime – the harm of lost time, dreams shattered, the suffering that comes from endless waiting, the humiliation of asking for the help of someone else. The limited reach of the tribunals will leave survivors still longing for revenge and meaning. Stories of sexual abuse are not only particularly difficult to tell, they are difficult to hear as well (see generally Herman 1992). Not only did Dusko Tadic deny the accusations of rape made against him, the prosecutorial team faced a very difficult task in asserting such charges. Ultimately, the charges of rape failed (for an overview of the defence, see Scharf 1997a: 175–206).

Delivering reparations to survivors Very little effort has been made to use tribunals as means of delivering reparations for survivors. The international community has paid lip-service to reparations. As criminal courts of limited jurisdiction, the war crimes tribunals for Rwanda and the former Yugoslavia do not have authority to issue what are normally seen as civil remedies. Should they have the power and will to do so, reparations would, like punishment, demonstrate the existence and force of international law. Moreover, reparations in the form of economic penalties against responsible individuals and governments – to be turned over in the form of compensation to survivors – may be at least as effective as deterrent as criminal punishments (perhaps more effective, as the international community may have more success in enforcing economic measures against commanding officers and governments that supported war criminals than in enforcing penal measures).

Neither have local power-brokers emphasized the issue of reparations. As long as they are not held responsible for reparations, emerging leaders would have much to gain from them. Reparations would, like punishment, displace threats of revenge. Monetary reparations could also improve the welfare of survivors, thereby alleviating the pressure on local governments to provide for their needs. Reparations have the potential to benefit the entire community, freeing resources to be used for other aspects of reconstruction. A family that receives reparations would no longer seek state assistance for minimal needs and, perhaps, would be able to use the reparations to rebuild their own home and contribute to community reconstruction.

Survivors in Rwanda and the former Yugoslavia have a great interest in reparations. Although nothing can compensate for the loss of loved ones, dreams destroyed and days lost, reparations serve to dignify survivors with a partial remedy for their suffering. Practically speaking, reparations may mean an improvement in living conditions and general welfare. Above all, however, reparations constitute a public acknowledgement by the violator of guilt. A violator's admission of guilt, more than punishment of the violator itself, can mark a turning point in survivors' search for meaning and closure.

After some fifty years, the Japanese government in 1993 admitted to enslaving Korean, Chinese and Filipina women as prostitutes during the Second World War (the so-called Comfort Women). The living survivors refused Japan's offer of a lump sum of compensation for their suffering, instead pressing Japan for individual compensation. Individual compensation is important, the survivors and their advocates argued, because it signals recognition of guilt for each individual act. To date, survivors in Rwanda and the former Yugoslavia have not demanded similar compensation, although they may in the future.

The full potential for reparations thus has not been explored. The Inter-American Court of Human Rights, among other international bodies, has set a useful precedent in approaching the question of reparations. These experiences should be utilized in developing compensation mechanisms as an adjunct to the war crimes tribunal.

Reforming lawlessness International war crimes tribunals have been widely trumpeted as important components in re-establishing the rule of law. As José Alvarez explains: .

> International conventions and particularly the judgments are said to provide 'cathartic group therapy' to reestablish lost national and international consensus. The contrast between the rules of law by which the defendants are judged and the shocking barbarity of what they are shown to have done is said to encourage a unified sense of outrage against the guilty, accompanied by satisfaction in the civilized process that brands criminals. (Alvarez 1998)

The international community, local power-brokers and survivors have an interest in (re)establishing the principle that law exists above power and force. The international community is most interested in (re)establishing the force of international law in a lawless world; local power-brokers want to (re)establish the force of law in their own lawless societies. Survivors, for their part, acutely sceptical about anything called law, do not care what is (re)established where, as long as they do not have to live through another conflict (unless, some will concede, it is a conflict of their own choosing – a 'just' war).

The adjudication of war crimes based on principles of international law may take small steps towards (re)forming global lawlessness. Although their *ad hoc* nature undercuts the call for universal lawfulness, the very existence of these tribunals helps to (re)establish the rule of international law. It sends a message to the world that some international norms exist above brute power.

Still, justice before the tribunals will not necessarily trickle down to local law. In other words, just because the international community seems to be getting its act together on justice, this does not mean that the domestic courts and other institutions within Rwanda and the former Yugoslavia are willing and/or able to follow suit. Although local indictments have been issued and trials for war crimes have been held in many of the new states of the former Yugoslavia and in Rwanda, observers note the numerous obstacles that exist for local courts to hold fair trials (see e.g. Human Rights Watch/Helsinki 1997).

Survivors continue to pay bribes to local authorities for their daily needs; local syndicates continue to control the markets for many goods; illegal trade in weapons continues to flow across borders; the media continue to be dominated by one-sided propaganda and free speech belongs to the brave few who risk community (and, in some cases, state-condoned) harassment. While calling for justice against war criminals, many governments act with intransigence or, some survivors feel, conspire with the principal war criminals, failing to arrest and even harbouring them within their own borders. In such a world, survivors are discovering that the principle of lawfulness exists somewhere 'out there', far away from their lives. Tribunals are a necessary but not sufficient step to reforming lawlessness.

Recording for history The recording function of the tribunals is important for the international community and local power-brokers; for survivors, it is imperative. The record that will emerge from the trials, however, will be of the form and substance that best serve the interests of the international elite. If the tribunals are regarded as a success, the efficiency and force of international institutions will be applauded by the international community. Beyond the mere verdicts, the tribunals will showcase the accomplishments of international law. A positive record could be used to warn potential perpetrators of the force of international law. It may serve to build a global citizenry, teaching about the limits of evil and the triumph of international humanitarian and human rights principles. Finally, war crimes trials that successfully litigate international human rights principles may be said to provide – in Mark Osiel's words – a 'model of closure' based upon 'Durkenheimian veneration of settled consensus over moral fundamentals' (Osiel, 1997: 53).

Those in government locally will use the record to prove the legitimacy of their rule and the illegitimacy of their predecessors. Local history will underscore the extent to which the new governments cooperated with the tribunal and advanced justice. (Conversely, those outside government may try to use the record to prove the illegitimacy of the present regime.) The record could become the backbone of a call for national healing and a warning to potential perpetrators. Schools texts could be rewritten to educate future generations about the evils of the past, and to prepare them for a better future. Of course, there is no guarantee that the local histories will ring of reconciliation – they could just as well warn young people of the enemy 'other' and emphasize the need to fortify the collective identity against future attack.

No matter how even-handedly a tribunal record is compiled, it is likely to suffer from gaps that no judicial proceeding can fill: 'The courtroom's demands for the drawing of bright lines that skilled historians usually avoid, along with the perpetrator-driven nature of the rules of evidence, the requirements of substantive law, and the respective roles, as traditionally conceived, of prosecutor, defense attorney, and judge, all undermine the goal of rendering a nuanced history that [local or international] academics might respect' (Alvarez 1998: 43), or that locals might follow as their own Truth. The handling of the first case before the Ad Hoc Tribunal for the Former Yugoslavia, that against Dusko Tadic, illustrates the awkward nature of using a court hearing to tell history (Dusko Tadic, Case No. IT-94–I–T). The judgment from that case begins with a hodge-podge of incomplete renderings of the historical and geographic background of Bosnia and the break-up of the Socialist Republic of Yugoslavia. All sides are likely to find something missing or mis-reported in this history and, thus, it is unlikely to serve as an unbiased historical account for any audience.

Survivors have the greatest need for a record. Investigations and trials can 'reveal the extent of repression, restore the reputation of innocent victims, and confer an official authority-conferring imprimatur to state-sanctioned abuses, thereby making repetition of past mistakes less likely and permitting those societies to re-define themselves in light of real, and not falsified history' (Alvarez, 1998: 8, n. 24, citing Roht-Arriaza 1995: 7–8). According to Naomi Roht-Arriaza, the prosecutorial process and the record it provides may help survivors to put 'the past at rest' (Roht-Arriaza, 1995: 8). Yet the kind of record most survivors need to put the past at rest is one that a tribunal cannot provide.

The few survivors that will be called before the tribunals may be too afraid to testify as they are not assured of being provided with adequate protection once they leave The Hague. Survivors of all crimes – and, in particular, survivors of rape and sexual abuse – have a pressing need for protection of their identity (Chinkin 1994). In some cases, the entire family of the survivor must be assured long-term protection (including relocation and change of identity) if the survivor is to be safe to speak. So far, the tribunals for the former Yugoslavia and Rwanda fall short of respecting these needs (Richter-Lynotte 1996). In the case of both tribunals, a debate continues to fester over the proper balance between protection for witnesses and fairness to the accused (see Ellis 1997; Scharf 1997).

Above all, witnesses need a full and public account of what happened – an account in which they see their own memories, an account that exposes the Truths. These Truths have taken on a life of their own. They are so thick with history, power and fear that the actual truth does not matter any more. Allowing competing Truths to float through the air in the same space, unjudged and unquestioned, can be a revolutionary act. The Truths may always exist. But the telling can narrow the gap between Truths, creating a common bridge towards something else – towards an existence beyond these Truths. Since legal institutions attempt to discover truth, they are incapable of fulfilling the need to hear competing Truths.

Survivors need to feel a part of whatever record is created. Only then will they feel that others hear and acknowledge their suffering. Only then can they begin to remember or start to forget. Their record may be used to educate future generations, but its greatest utility lies in the telling. The court record, however, merely presses the words of survivors into the language of law. The adjudicatory process does not fulfil the kind of participatory function that facilitates healing for survivors.

Conclusion

The tribunals may serve important functions and address the interests of many parties. They will stop short, however, of addressing the concerns of survivors. The tribunals cannot be 'fixed' to address the missing, but instead additional avenues must be created to address the concerns of survivors. Public truth commissions in which witnesses and survivors speak, memory projects that collect and publish without judging the accounts of survivors, popular education campaigns that encourage survivors to test their voices – these and other such efforts are needed to supplement the work of the tribunals. Channelling all resources in the direction of the tribunal alone disserves the people of Rwanda and the former Yugoslavia. War crimes tribunals can, at best, generate incomplete truth. More is needed to promote long-term healing and transformative social change.

Bibliography

Alvarez, José (1998) 'Ruse to closure: Lessons of the Tadic judgment', *Michigan Law Review*, vol. 96, no. 7: 2031.

ASIL (1994) *Proceedings of the 88th Annual Meeting*, pp. 239–58, Washington, DC: American Society of International Law.

Aspen Institute (1989) *State Crimes: Punishment or Pardon*, Queenstown, MA: Aspen Institute.

Blatt, D. (1992) 'Recognizing rape as a method of torture', *NYU Review of Law and Social Change*, vol. 19, no. 4: 821.

Chinkin, C. (1994) 'Rape and sexual abuse of women in international law', *European Journal of International Law*, vol. 5: 326.

— (1995) 'Amicus curiae brief on protective measures for victims and witnesses submitted by Dean and Professor of Law Christine Chinkin', *Criminal Law Forum*, vol. 7, no. 1: 179.

Cohen, P. A. (1997) *History in Three Keys: The Boxers as Event, Experience and Myth*, New York: Columbia University Press.

Destexhe, A. (1996) *Rwanda and Genocide in the Twentieth Century*, New York: New York University Press.

Ellis, M. (1997) 'Achieving justice before the International War Crimes Tribunal: challenges for the defense counsel', *Duke Journal of Comparative and International Law*, vol. 7, no. 2: 519.

Franck, T. (1997) 'Three major innovations of international law in the twentieth century', *Quinnipiac Law Review*, vol. 17, no. 1: 139.

Gioseffi, D. (1993) *On Prejudice*, New York: Doubleday.

Gordon, J. (1998) 'The concept of human rights: the history and meaning of its politicization', *Brooklyn Journal of International Law*, vol. 23, no. 3: 689.

Gugelberger, G. and M. Kearney (1991) 'Voices for the voiceless: testimonial literature in Latin America', *Latin American Perspective*, vol. 18: 3–14.

Helfer, L. and A.-M. Slaughter (1997) 'Toward a theory of effective supranational adjudication', *Yale Law Journal*, vol. 107, no. 2: 273.

Herman, J. L. (1992) *Trauma and Recovery*, New York: Basic Books.

Human Rights Watch/Helsinki (1997) 'Bosnia and Hercegovina: politics of revenge: the misuse of authority in Bihac, Cazin, and Velika Kladusa', *Human Rights Watch/Helsinki Reports*, vol. 9, no. 9: 31–6.

Lusby, K. (1995) 'Hearing the invisible women of political rape: using oppositional narrative to tell a new war story', *University of Toledo Law Review*, vol. 25, no. 4: 911.

Malamud-Goti, J. (1989) 'Trying violators of human rights: the dilemma of transitional democratic governments', in *State Crimes: Punishment or Pardon*, Queenstown, MD: Aspen Institute, p. 89.

McCormack, T. (1997) 'Elective reaction to atrocity: war crimes and the development of international criminal law', *Albany Law Review*, vol. 60, no. 3: 681.

Meron, T. (1997) 'Answering for war crimes', *Foreign Affairs*, February.

Mertus, J. (1999) 'Mapping civil society transplants: a preliminary comparison of Eastern Europe and Latin America', *University of Miami Law Review*, vol. 53, no. 4: 921.

Mertus, J. et al. (1997) *The Suitcase: Refugees' Voices from Bosnia and Croatia*, Berkeley: University of California Press.

Narayan, K. (1989) *Storytellers, Saints, and Scoundrels: Folk Narrative in Hindu Religions and Teachings*, Philadelphia: University of Pennsylvania Press.

Ni Aolain, F. (1997) 'Radical rules: the effects of evidentiary and procedural rules on the regulation of sexual violence in war', *Albany Law Review*, vol. 60, no. 3: 883.

Nino, C. S. (1996) *Radical Evil on Trial*, New Haven, CT: Yale University Press.

Orentlicher, D. (1990) 'Settling accounts: the duty to prosecute human rights violations of a prior regime', *Yale Law Journal*, vol. 106, no. 8: 2537–615.

O'Shea, S. (1996) 'Interaction between international criminal tribunals and national legal systems', *New York University Journal of International Law and Politics*, vol. 28, no 2: 367.

Osiel, M. (1997) *Mass Atrocity, Collective Memory and the Law*, New York: Transaction Publishers.

Ray, A. E. (1997) 'The shame of it: gender-based terrorism in the former Yugoslavia and the failure of international human rights law to comprehend the injuries', *American Law Review*, vol. 46, no. 3: 793.

Richter-Lynotte, E. (1996) 'The real evidence to protect', *Monitoring the War Crimes Tribunal*, no. 5, September/October, London: Institute for War and Peace Reporting.

Roht-Arriaza, N. (1995) *Impunity and Human Rights in International Law and Practice*, New York: Oxford University Press.

Rules of Procedure and Evidence of the Ad Hoc Tribunal for the Former Yugoslavia, UN Doc. IT/32 Rev.2 (1994).

Rushdie, S. (1990) *Haroun and the Sea of Stories*, New York: Viking Penguin.

Sadat Wexler, L. (1996) 'The proposed permanent international criminal court: an appraisal', *Cornell International Law Journal*, vol. 29, no. 3: 665.

Scarry, E. (1985) *The Body in Pain: The Making and Unmaking of the World*, New York: Oxford University Press.

Scharf, M. (1997a) *Balkan Justice*, North Carolina: University of Carolina Press.

— (1997b) 'A critique of the Yugoslav War Crimes Tribunal', *Denver Journal of International Law and Policy*, vol. 25, no. 2: 305.

Schrag, M. (1997) 'The Yugoslav War Crimes Tribunal: an interim assessment', *Transnational Law and Contemporary Problems*, vol. 7, no. 1: 15.

Scott, J. C. (1990) *Domination and the Arts of Resistance: Hidden Transcript*, New Haven, CT: Yale University Press.

Senehi, J. (1996) 'Language, culture and conflict: storytelling as a matter of life and death', *Mind and Human Interaction*, vol. 7, no. 3: 150–64.

Stephan, A. (1986) 'Paths towards democratization: theoretical and comparative considerations', in C. O'Donnell et al. (eds), *Transitions from Authoritarian Rule: Comparative Perspectives*, Baltimore: Johns Hopkins University Press, pp. 64–8.

Staub, E. (1989) *The Roots of Evil: The Origins of Genocide and Other Group Violence*, New York: Cambridge University Press.

Symposium (1990) 'Transitions to democracy and the rule of law', *American University International Law Review*, vol. 5, no. 4: 965.

Tetreault, M. A. (1997) 'Justice for all: wartime rapes and women's human rights', *Global Governance*, vol. 3: 197.

Tobin, J. (1990) 'Accountability and the transition to democracy', *American University Journal of International Law and Policy*, vol. 5, no. 4: 1033–63.

Weschler, L. (1990) *A Miracle, a Universe: Settling Accounts with Torturers*, New York: Pantheon.

Zalaquett, J. (1989) 'Confronting human rights violations committed by former governments: principles applicable and political constraints', in Aspen Institute, *State Crimes: Punishment or Pardon*.

Justice for Women Victims of Violence:
Rwanda after the 1994 Genocide

Binaifer Nowrojee and Regan Ralph[1]

Throughout the world, sexual violence is routinely directed against women in situations of armed conflict. This violence may take gender-specific forms, like sexual mutilation, forced pregnancy, rape or sexual slavery. Being female is a risk factor and women and girls are often targeted for sexual abuse on the basis of their gender, irrespective of age, ethnicity or political affiliation.

Although rape and other forms of sexual violence are clearly recognized as violations of international law, justice has been slow to follow. The differential treatment of gender-based violence makes clear that the problem, for the most part, lies not in the absence of adequate legal provisions, but in the international community's willingness to tolerate sexual abuse against women.

Widely committed and seldom denounced, rape and sexual assault of women in situations of conflict have been viewed more as the spoils of war than as illegitimate acts that violate humanitarian law. As a consequence, women, whether combatants or civilians, have been targeted for rape while their attackers go without punishment. Rape has long been mischaracterized and dismissed by military and political leaders as a private crime, a sexual act, the ignoble act of the occasional soldier; worse still, it has been accepted precisely because it is so commonplace.

Since 1990, the international community has adopted a more institutionalized response to atrocities committed in conflict than in the past. In particular, two International Criminal Tribunals have been created by the UN Security Council to hold perpetrators of the violence accountable in an international procedure in the former Yugoslavia and in Rwanda.[2] In July 1998, the international community agreed on the creation of a permanent International Criminal Court. The precursors to such tribunals were the International Military Tribunal at Nuremberg and the International Military Tribunal for the Far East (the Tokyo Tribunal).

Not until the international outcry arose in response to reports of mass rape in the former Yugoslavia did the international community seriously confront rape as a war crime and begin to take steps to punish those responsible for such abuses through the *ad hoc* UN International Criminal Tribunal for the Former Yugoslavia. Many hoped that the gains made in recognizing rape as a crime in the former Yugoslavia would be continued when a second *ad hoc* International Criminal Tribunal for Rwanda was created in 1994. However, until international pressure was exerted, little or no attention to the plight of Rwandan rape survivors was given by the international community.

Rape Regularly Used in Conflict

Rape is a particularly effective weapon with which to terrorize and degrade individuals and their communities in order to achieve a specific political end. Although men are also raped, rape is inflicted predominantly against women. Often, gender intersects with other aspects of a woman's identity such as ethnicity, religion, social class or political affiliation. The humiliation, pain and terror inflicted by the rapist is meant not just to degrade the individual woman but also to strip the humanity from the larger community of which she is a part. The rape of one person is translated into an assault upon the community through the emphasis placed in every culture on women's sexual virtue: the shame of the rape humiliates the family and all those associated with the survivor. Combatants who rape in war often explicitly link their acts of sexual violence to this broader intended social degradation. In the aftermath of such abuse, the harm done to the individual woman is often obscured or even compounded by the perceived harm to the community.

Silence and Impunity

Silence about abuses against women hides the problems that devastate, and sometimes end, women's lives. Governments often excuse and fail to take action against those responsible for sexual violence in conflict situations. Also neglected by governments and international organizations have been the range of abuses that women suffer because many of these violations do not conform to the standard ideas of what constitutes human rights abuses.

The stigma attached to sexual violence worldwide further exacerbates the lack of justice. In many places women who have been raped dare not reveal publicly that they have been raped for fear that they will be marked as rape victims and may be ostracized by their families and community. Women know that integrating into their communities and resuming their lives will be more difficult if their rape is known. As a result, many women survivors of sexual violence are reluctant to seek medical assistance or to report what happened to them. The difficulty of collecting information on rape is compounded by fear of reprisal from the perpetrator. Women are often reticent to talk because some of the perpetrators may still live among them.

The failure of investigators to document gender-based crimes further shrouds the widespread nature of the crime. Because the testimonies are not collected, the abuse of women is overlooked. As a result, indictments for war crimes often do not include rape, further confirming to rape victims the futility of reporting the crime.

The lack of documentation of violations of women's rights reinforces the silence: without concrete data, governments have been able to deny the fact of and their responsibility for gender-based abuse. Where human rights violations against women remain undocumented and unverified, governments pay no political or economic price for refusing to acknowledge the problem and their obligation to prevent and remedy abuse. One of the first challenges faced by the women's human rights movement has been to transform women's experiences of violence and discrimination into fact-based proof of the scale and nature of such abuse and the role of governments in its perpetration.

Just as human rights groups have historically been the primary force in ensuring accountability for politically motivated human rights abuse, women's rights advocates are the vanguard in the fight for justice for gender-based violations. Thus, for example, they have won recognition that traditional notions of the political actor must be modified to acknowledge the political nature of women's efforts to challenge their subordinate status and the violence and discrimination that reinforce it.

In the past, in the absence of support from their domestic legal systems, human rights organizations and intergovernmental agencies, women often chose not to seek redress for fear of risking reprisal and social ostracism in cultures that often blame the victim. As the international human rights system becomes more responsive to gender-based human rights violations, women who have previously been silent about their experiences of abuse are speaking up. Their testimonies add to the evidence of the scale and prevalence of sexual violence during conflict in a way that the international community simply cannot afford to ignore.

Rape as a Violation of International Law

Sexual violence in situations of armed conflict constitutes a clear breach of international law. Under international law, perpetrators of sexual violence can be held accountable for rape as a war crime: as a crime against humanity, or as an act of genocide, if their actions meet the defining elements of each. Traditionally, in conception and enforcement, the crime of rape was regarded in international humanitarian law not as a violent attack against a woman, but as a challenge to honour. The word honour implies dignity and esteem, but concerning women, it also alludes to chastity, sexual virtue and good name. The reference to rape and other forms of sexual violence as an attack on women's honour is problematic in that it fails to recognize explicitly rape and other forms of sexual violence as an attack on women's physical integrity. The categorization of rape as a crime against honour as opposed to physical integrity diminishes the serious nature of the crime and further contributes to the widespread misconception that rape (i.e. an attack on honour) is an 'incidental' or 'lesser' crime in comparison to crimes such as torture or enslavement.

Rape as a War Crime

The Geneva Conventions of 12 August 1949 and the Protocols Additional to the Geneva Conventions prohibit rape in both international and internal conflicts. In internal conflicts, common article 3 of the Geneva Conventions prohibits 'violence to life and person, in particular murder of all kinds, mutilation, cruel treatment and torture' as well as 'outrages upon personal dignity, in particular humiliating and degrading treatment'. Protocol II Additional to the Geneva Conventions, which also governs internal conflicts, expressly forbids 'violence to the life, health and physical or mental well-being of persons, in particular murder as well as cruel treatment such as torture, mutilation' and 'outrages upon personal dignity, in particular humiliating and degrading treatment, rape, enforced prostitution, and any form of indecent assault', as well as 'slavery and the slave trade in all their forms'.

Rape as a Crime against Humanity

Rape – like murder, extermination, enslavement, deportation, imprisonment, torture, persecution on political, racial and religious grounds and other inhuman acts – is a crime against humanity. Crimes against humanity arise when such serious crimes as these are committed on a mass scale against a civilian population. After the Second World War, the Control Council for Germany enacted Control Council Law number 10 as a basis of establishing a uniform legal basis for the prosecution of war criminals in Germany. In the second set of Nuremberg war criminal trials, conducted under the authority of Control Council Law number 10, and in Article

6(c) of the Nuremberg Charter, rape was specifically enumerated as a crime against humanity, although it was not prosecuted at any of these trials.

Rape as a Genocide Crime

Rape and other acts of sexual violence can also be genocidal acts. Genocide is distinguished from other international crimes, not by the scope of the acts, but rather by the intent of the perpetrators in committing the acts to destroy a national, ethnic, racial or religious group. The crime of genocide has been codified in the Convention on the Prevention and Punishment of the Crime of Genocide and is defined as:

> any of the following acts committed with the intent to destroy, in whole or in part, a national, ethnic, racial or religious group, as such: (a) Killing members of the group; (b) Causing serious bodily or mental harm to members of the group; (c) Deliberately inflicting on the group conditions of life calculated to bring about its physical destruction in whole or in part; (d) Imposing measures intended to prevent births within the group; (e) Forcibly transferring children of the group to another group.

Rape as a Form of Torture

Rape can also constitute a form of torture under the Convention against Torture and Other Cruel, Inhumane or Degrading Treatment or Punishment, which defines torture as:

> any act by which severe pain or suffering, whether physical or mental, is intentionally inflicted on a person for such purposes as obtaining from him or a third person information or a confession, punishing him for an act he or a third person has committed or is suspected of having committed, or intimidating or coercing him or a third person, or for any reason based on discrimination of any kind, when such pain and suffering is inflicted by or at the instigation of or with the consent or acquiescence of a public official or other person acting in an official capacity.

Gender-based Violence during the Rwandan Genocide

During the 1994 genocide, Rwandan women were subjected to sexual violence on a massive scale, perpetrated by members of the infamous Hutu militia groups known as the Interahamwe, by other civilians, and by soldiers of the Rwandan Armed Forces (Forces Armées Rwandaises, FAR), including the Presidential Guard. Administrative, military and political leaders at the national and local levels, as well as heads of militia, directed or encouraged both the killings and sexual violence to further their political goal: the destruction of the Tutsi as a group. They therefore bear responsibility for these abuses.

Although the exact number of women raped will never be known, testimonies from survivors confirm that rape was extremely widespread and that thousands of women were individually raped, gang-raped, raped with objects such as sharpened sticks or gun barrels, held in sexual slavery (either collectively or through forced 'marriage') or sexually mutilated. These crimes were frequently part of a pattern in which Tutsi women were raped after they had witnessed the torture and killings of their relatives and the destruction and looting of their homes. According to witnesses, many women were killed immediately after being raped.

Other women managed to survive, only to be told that they were being allowed to live so that they would 'die of sadness'. Often women were subjected to sexual slavery and held collectively by a militia group or were singled out by one militiaman, at checkpoints or other sites where people were being maimed or slaughtered, and held for personal sexual service. The militiamen would force women to submit sexually with threats that they would be killed if they refused. These forced 'marriages', as this form of sexual slavery is often called in Rwanda, lasted from a few days to the duration of the genocide, and in some cases longer. Rapes were sometimes followed by sexual mutilation, including mutilation of the vagina and pelvic area with machetes, knives, sticks, boiling water, and, in one case, acid.

During the Rwandan genocide, rape and other forms of violence were directed primarily against Tutsi women because of both their gender and their ethnicity. The extremist propaganda that exhorted the Hutu to commit the genocide specifically identified the sexuality of Tutsi women as a means through which the Tutsi community sought to infiltrate and control the Hutu community. This propaganda fuelled the sexual violence perpetrated against Tutsi women as a means of dehumanizing and subjugating all Tutsi. Some Hutu women were also targeted with rape because they were affiliated with the political opposition, because they were married to Tutsi men or because they protected Tutsi. A number of women, Tutsi and Hutu, were targeted regardless of ethnicity or political affiliation. Young girls or those considered beautiful were particularly at the mercy of the militia groups, who were a law unto themselves and often raped indiscriminately.

As Rwandans begin the onerous task of rebuilding a country ravaged by bloodshed and genocide, the burden is falling heavily on Rwandan women. Rwanda now has a high proportion of widows and female-headed households. Regardless of their status – Tutsi, Hutu, displaced, returnees – all women face overwhelming problems because of the upheaval caused by the genocide, including social stigmatization, poor physical and psychological health, unwanted pregnancy and, increasingly, poverty.

In Rwanda, as elsewhere in the world, rape and other gender-based violations carry a severe social stigma. The physical and psychological injuries suffered by Rwandan rape survivors are aggravated by a sense of isolation and ostracization. Rwandan women who have been raped or who suffered sexual abuse generally do not dare reveal their experiences publicly, fearing that they will be rejected by their family and wider community and that they will never be able to reintegrate or to marry. Others fear retribution from their attackers if they speak out. Often, rape survivors suffer extreme guilt for having survived and been held for rape, rather than having been executed.

This sentiment is further reinforced by some Tutsi returnees, exiles who returned from Zaire, Burundi or Uganda after the genocide, who do not face the trauma of having survived the genocide, although they share the horror of what happened. Some of the returnees view the genocide survivors with distrust and suspicion. These survivors voice resentment against the returnees, including those in government, and criticize them for, among other issues: neglecting the problems of the genocide survivors; falsely denouncing the survivors as genocide 'collaborators'; illegally appropriating the land and property of the survivors; and being politically extremist in their blanket denunciation of the Hutu.

Victims of sexual abuse during the genocide suffer persistent health problems. According to Rwandan doctors, the most common problem they have encountered among raped women who have sought medical treatment has been sexually transmitted diseases, including HIV/AIDS (although it is often impossible to know if this is due to the rape). Since abortion is illegal in Rwanda, doctors have also treated women with serious complications resulting from self-induced or clandestine abortions arising from rape-related pregnancies. In a number of cases, doctors have performed reconstructive surgery for women and girls who suffered sexual mutilation at the hands of their attackers. Unfortunately the stigma surrounding sexual abuse often dissuades women from seeking the medical assistance they need.

A large number of women became pregnant as a result of rape during the genocide. Pregnancies and childbirth among extremely young girls who were raped have also posed health problems for these mothers. The 'pregnancies of the war', 'children of hate', '*enfants non-désirés*' (unwanted children) or '*enfants mauvais souvenir*' (children of bad memories), as they are known, are estimated by the National Population Office to be between

2,000 and 5,000. Health personnel report that some women have abandoned their children or even committed infanticide, while others have decided to keep their children. In some cases, the mother's decision to keep the child has caused deep divisions in the family, pitting those who reject the child against those who prefer to raise the child. In other cases, the child is being raised without problems within the community.

In addition to the social and personal trauma resulting from the injuries suffered from sexual violence, women are also facing dire economic difficulty. As a result of the genocide, many women lost the male relatives on whom they previously relied on for economic support and are now destitute. Women survivors are struggling to make ends meet, to reclaim their property, to rebuild their destroyed houses, and to raise children: their own and orphans. Some Hutu women, whose husbands were killed or are now in exile or in prison accused of genocide, are dealing with similar issues of poverty as well as with the recrimination directed at them on the basis of their ethnicity or the alleged actions of their relatives.

On top of mounting poverty, Rwandan women also face pressing problems due to their second-class status under Rwandan law. Although the Rwandan constitution guarantees them full equality under the law, women still suffer discrimination when it comes to customary inheritance, among other areas. Inheritance norms are not codified and are governed under customary law. Although there are a number of contradictory court judgments interpreting customary law, general practice has established that women cannot inherit property unless they are explicitly designated as beneficiaries. Accordingly, thousands of widows and daughters currently have no legal claim to their late husbands' or fathers' homes, land or bank accounts because they are women. Widows whose husbands worked for state enterprises or large companies are also facing great difficulties in obtaining their husbands' pensions. A complicated application procedure, coupled with the intimidation of dealing with the authorities, has deterred many women from pursuing valid pension claims. Hutu widows who were married to Tutsi men are facing particular problems from their Tutsi in-laws, who threaten them and drive them off their property. The government has initiated a legal commission to address these issues and to introduce legislation to allow women to inherit equally with men, but the reforms are expected to take a long time.

Rwandan survivors of sexual violence are particularly troubled by the lack of accountability for the abuse they suffered. They want the perpetrators of the violence against them to be held responsible. However, the Rwandan judicial system is facing systemic and profound problems that make the likelihood of justice for genocide survivors a remote possibility. There are also serious concerns about the lack of justice for the over

100,000 prisoners accused of genocide who are currently held without trial in prison. Five years after the genocide, the judicial system has prosecuted only a small proportion of those held in prison, and charges for sexual violence (although it is listed as one of the most serious crimes deserving of the death penalty under Rwanda's genocide law) remain few. Although the lack of justice is not confined to victims of gender-based abuse in Rwanda, it is clear that rape victims face specific obstacles, including the fact that police inspectors documenting genocide crimes for prosecution are predominantly male and are not collecting information on rape. These problems within the law enforcement and judicial systems, coupled with the reluctance of women to come forward because of stigma and fear, greatly reduce the likelihood of rape prosecutions.

Extending Justice to Rwandan Women: The International Criminal Tribunal for Rwanda

In late 1994, the United Nations Security Council created the International Criminal Tribunal for Rwanda (Rwanda Tribunal), which is charged with bringing the organizers of the genocide to justice. The International Criminal Tribunal for Rwanda was created by the United Nations Security Council Resolution 955 of 8 November 1994. The resolution stipulated that the Tribunal would be vested with the authority to prosecute persons responsible for serious violations of international humanitarian law committed in Rwanda and by Rwandan citizens responsible for such violations committed in the territory of neighbouring states between 1 January 1994 and 31 December 1994. Arusha, Tanzania was declared the seat of the Tribunal by resolution S/1995/148 of 21 February 1995. The Tribunal began its work on 26 June 1995, which was the day of the first plenary session of its eleven judges in The Hague, Netherlands.

The Tribunal has the power to prosecute persons who committed genocide, crimes against humanity, and violations of Common Article 3 of the Geneva Conventions and of the Additional Protocol II of the Geneva Conventions, which govern internal armed conflicts. Genocide includes acts committed with the intent to destroy, in whole or in part, a national, ethnic, racial or religious group.

At the outset, the Rwanda Tribunal progress was slow due to serious resource constraints. By mid-1996, however, the Rwanda Tribunal finally received adequate financial commitments for a budget that would allow it to hire a full staff. Yet, even in 1999, these positions had not all been filled and the Rwanda Tribunal remained understaffed. Of the investigators, the majority remain men. Accusations of mismanagement and incompetence have consistently plagued the Rwanda Tribunal. In April 1998, Amnesty

International released a report criticizing the shortcomings of the Rwanda tribunal including delays and inadequate witness protection.[3] With regard to the investigation and prosecution of gender-based crimes, the Rwanda Tribunal's problems have been magnified.

Despite the drawbacks, however, the Rwanda Tribunal deserves credit for the strides that have been made since its inception. Thirty defendants have been indicted. Of those, however, the Rwanda Tribunal has publicly charged only three persons with rape: Jean-Paul Akayesu, Arsene Shalom Ntahobali and Omar Serushago. Most notably, the first conviction of the Rwanda Tribunal of Jean Paul Akayesu included rape charges, and the judgment was a significant step forward in setting international precedent for punishing sexual violence under international law. The rape charge against Serushago was dropped after he pleaded guilty to four counts of genocide and crimes against humanity, and not guilty to one count of rape.

The Akayesu Judgment

On 2 September 1998, the Rwanda Tribunal found the former mayor Jean-Paul Akayesu guilty of nine counts of genocide, crimes against humanity and war crimes. The verdict was the first conviction handed down by the Rwanda Tribunal, the first conviction for genocide by an international court, the first time an international court has punished sexual violence in a civil war, and the first time that rape was found to be an act of genocide to destroy a group.[4]

The Rwanda Tribunal was initially reluctant to indict Akayesu for encouraging and permitting rape in the area under his control. When Akayesu was first charged in 1996, the twelve counts in his indictment did not include sexual violence – despite the fact that Human Rights Watch, and other rights groups, had documented widespread rape during the genocide, particularly in his area. A lack of political will among some high-ranking tribunal officials, as well as faulty investigative methodology by some investigative and prosecutorial staff of the Rwanda Tribunal, accounted for this omission.

Under pressure from Rwandan and international rights groups, the Office of the Prosecutor finally amended the charges against Akayesu to include sexual violence in June 1997. During the Akayesu trial, Rwandan women testified that they had been subjected to repeated rape by militia in and around the commune office including in view of Akayesu. They spoke of witnessing other women being gang-raped and murdered while Akayesu stood by, reportedly saying to the rapists at one point 'don't complain to me now that you don't know what a Tutsi woman tastes like'.

Recommendations

The Akayesu judgment was a hard-won victory, but the Rwanda Tribunal still has much more work to do. There is room for improvement to ensure that the issue of gender-based violence is treated seriously at all levels in the Rwanda Tribunal and to improve the technical competence of its staff members. These suggestions are made in recognition of the importance of the work of the Rwanda Tribunal and in support of its aspirations. Although the Office of the Prosecutor has made a stated commitment to prosecute rape, the Rwanda Tribunal has still not effectively incorporated gender-based violence in the Tribunal's work as a matter of course. The incorporation of sexual violence into the prosecutorial strategy of the Rwanda tribunal since its inception has been characterized by sporadic initiatives, the dedication of individual Tribunal staff members committed to this issue, and the continued prompting of international pressure.

The prosecution of sexual violence in an international court is a relatively new development. For many of the reasons already discussed, most international law was not drafted with much specificity on prosecuting sexual violence crimes, and there is little direction or precedent on how best to approach the prosecution of such crimes. Accordingly, a prosecution strategy for the prosecution of sexual violence under international law requires a creative legal team that can seek ways to incorporate the issue of sexual violence into all aspects of its legal arguments. It also requires a competent and experienced legal team willing and able to push the envelope at times.

The Rwanda Tribunal has veered between adopting an integrated approach to its investigative methodology by initially having all investigators responsible for collecting evidence and at other times creating specific teams devoted to investigating sexual violence. The lack of strong commitment to any one approach has detrimentally affected the collection of evidence, resulting in lost opportunities that may never be regained for the security reasons mentioned above. For instance, in July 1996, a sexual assault committee to oversee the implementation of sexual assault investigations was created. This committee never undertook any significant work because no serious authority or resources to undertake or direct the investigations were ever allocated. In 1997, the Rwanda Tribunal created a second sexual assault team. However, by the end of 1997, this team was still not fully staffed and it was unclear how its work would be integrated into the larger team effort.

Discriminatory attitudes among some Tribunal staff about gender-based crimes remains a problem. There still remains a widespread perception among some Tribunal investigators that rape is somehow a 'lesser' or 'incidental' crime not worth investigating. Whether characterizing these crimes as less egregious than and/or distinct from other international crimes, citing insurmountable legal obstacles linking rape to the perpetrators, or justifying its oversight because of scarce resources, staff consistently relegate crimes of sexual violence as subordinate to other violations of international law. For example, the creation of a token sexual assault committee in July 1996 following the public pressure was symptomatic of the lack of seriousness that this issue was accorded. The high turnover of staff at the Rwanda Tribunal further exacerbates this problem, because training or institutional awareness of this problem are offset by continually changing secondees and staff. The Rwanda Tribunal regularly loses staff members, some of whom are particularly dedicated to drawing attention to this issue. In order to preserve institutional memory and to ensure that new staff members receive direction in the prosecution of sexual violence, a routine orientation procedure needs to be put into place.

Some of the methodology and investigative procedures used by the Tribunal have not largely been conducive to collecting rape testimonies in the Rwandan context. Although some of these shortcomings in methodology were later addressed, as the security situation in Rwanda worsened, the Tribunal lost its window of opportunity to collect some testimonies because of a growing lack of access to some areas of the country and to increased fear on the part of potential witnesses following threats and reprisals against survivors. Often, Tribunal investigators have used interviewing techniques that are poorly designed in terms of gaining the confidence of the women, eliciting rape testimonies and ensuring protection from retaliation. In the Rwandan context, it is essential that women are approached through an interlocutor whom they trust, such as someone from the community or a women's organization with whom they are familiar. Interviews must be conducted in privacy and not in a large group of people. Rwandan women have also indicated that they are more comfortable telling their testimonies to women investigators, and when necessary with women interpreters, in large part because of the stigma attached to rape. In some areas, women even specified that the woman translator had to be another genocide survivor and not a returnee, because of the tension between the survivors and returnees. The Tribunal has not always conducted its investigations with regard to these factors, and as a result has not documented some rape testimonies that may have led to more rape indictments.

If women agree to testify, effective protection for rape victims must also be guaranteed by the Tribunal. Many women fear reprisals if they testify. These fears are not unwarranted. Witnesses and survivors of the genocide continue to be killed in the country and abroad. For other women, the stigma of rape will deter them from coming forward if they cannot be assured that their privacy will be protected. Unless the Rwanda Tribunal takes greater steps to ensure that adequate privacy and security is provided to rape survivors who agree to testify, it discourages, and even endangers, women who agree to testify.

Conclusion

The difficulties experienced by Rwandan rape survivors in receiving justice, both nationally and internationally, starkly demonstrates the fact that justice for women requires more than the creation of courts and the passage of laws. Without national and international pressure, little or no attention has been paid to the plight of Rwandan rape survivors by the international community, and even now, serious questions remain as to whether substantive justice will ever be delivered to Rwanda's women survivors of the genocide.

However, the work of the Rwanda Tribunal and the Akayesu judgment are significant steps forward in beginning to break the silence on gender-based violence. Even more significant was the inclusion of gender-based crimes in the Rome Statute for the International Criminal Court in July 1998. The statute includes, under both crimes against humanity and war crimes, the following: 'Rape, sexual slavery, enforced prostitution, forced pregnancy, enforced sterilization, or any other form of sexual violence of comparable gravity.' By explicitly enumerating these crimes, as well as gender-based persecution, victims of gender-based crimes can no longer be denied justice because an international tribunal claims not to have jurisdiction. But as the lesson of Rwanda indicates, continued oversight to ensure that this issue does not get forgotten will be necessary if the promise of the International Criminal Court is to be made a reality for the thousands of women victims still waiting for justice.

Notes

1. Binaifer Nowrojee is counsel with Human Rights Watch's Africa Division and Regan Ralph is executive director of Human Rights Watch/Women's Rights Division. This chapter relies heavily on material previously published in Human Rights Watch, *Shattered Lives: Sexual Violence During the Rwandan Genocide and its Aftermath*, September 1996 and Human Rights Watch, *The Human Rights Watch Global Report on Women's Human Rights*, August 1995.

2. In the case of Yugoslavia, the Security Council established first a commission of experts pursuant to resolution 780 (1992) and then the International Criminal Tribunal for the Prosecution of Persons Responsible for Serious Violations of International Humanitarian Law Committed in the Territory of the Former Yugoslavia since 1991. The Commission of Experts conducted investigations into violations of international humanitarian law against persons, including extrajudicial executions, torture and other

violations of international humanitarian law, particularly in detention camps. Special emphasis was given in these investigations to allegations of rape and sexual assault. The Report of the Secretary-General pursuant to paragraph 2 of Security Council resolution 808 (1993), discussing the competence of the International Criminal Tribunal for the former Yugoslavia, refers to crimes against humanity as being inhumane acts of a very serious nature, such as wilful killing, torture or rape, committed as part of a widespread or systematic attack against any civilian population on national, political, ethnic, racial or religious grounds, and states that 'in the conflict in the territory of the former Yugoslavia, such inhuman acts have taken the form of so-called ethnic cleansing and widespread and systematic rape and other forms of sexual assault, including forced prostitution'. 'Report of the Secretary-General pursuant to paragraph 2 of the Security Council resolution 808' (1993) (S/25704), paragraph 48 as quoted in the Preliminary Report submitted by the Special Rapporteur on Violence against Women, its Causes and Consequences, pp. 64–5.

3. Amnesty International, *International Criminal Tribunal for Rwanda: Trials and Tribulations*, April 1998, AI Index: IOR 40/03/98.

4. Section 731 of the Akayesu judgment read: '[With regard to] rape and sexual violence, the Chamber wishes to underscore the fact that in its opinion, they constitute genocide in the same way as any other act as long as they were committed with the specific intent to destroy, in whole or in part, a particular group, targeted as such.' Section 733 noted: 'The rapes of Tutsi women in Taba were accompanied with the intent to kill those women. Many rapes were perpetrated near mass graves where the women were taken to be killed. A victim testified that Tutsi women caught could be taken away by peasants and men with the promise that they would be collected later to be executed. Following an act of gang rape, a witness heard Akayesu say "tomorrow they will be killed" and they were actually killed. In this respect, it appears clearly to the Chamber that the acts of rape and sexual violence, as other acts of serious bodily and mental harm committed against the Tutsi, reflected the determination to make Tutsi women suffer and to mutilate them even before killing them, the intent being to destroy the Tutsi group while inflicting acute suffering on its members in the process.'

10

The Truth According to the TRC

Mahmood Mamdani

I would like to begin with an empirical observation. Structurally, the TRC was divided into two halves, the Amnesty Committee and the rest of the Commission. They differed in two important respects: both in their manner of appointment and in the weight given to their decisions.

The main Commission was appointed through a transparent process. Its starting point was a selection panel, comprising members of civil society and government, appointed to consider 299 nominations from different stakeholders. After interviews, the panel submitted a short-list of 25 to the president. He, in turn, appointed 17 commissioners on 29 November 1995. The Amnesty Committee was appointed after, and independently of, the main Commission. It was also appointed without a transparent process: the president appointed three commissioners and two judges to it on 24 January 1996.

The Amnesty Committee focused on perpetrators, the main Commission on victims. The Amnesty Committee's decisions were binding, both on the Commission's majority and on the government. In contrast, the main Commission's decisions carried the status of recommendations. The rest of the Commission has wound up its work. Its report has been published with haste, as the *Report of the Truth and Reconciliation Commission*. The Amnesty Committee continues to function, with less fanfare.

One may ask: why the difference? The answer is, I think, clear: the amnesty was part of the political compromise that ushered in a post-apartheid South Africa. It was written into the interim constitution. Its terms were embodied in the very structure of the TRC. Without an amnesty for the political leadership of apartheid, there would have been no political compromise. What, then, was the point of the rest of the Commission? Was it so much sugar-coating the bitter pill of compromise, an add-on? I do not think so.

The TRC could have been called the Amnesty Commission, but it was not. Popularly, it was known as the Truth Commission, not even as the

Reconciliation Commission – I now think, rightly so. For I think the real power of the Commission was exercised through the work of its main body. That was the power to define the terms of a social debate, and in doing so define the parameters of truth-seeking. To recognize the scope of these powers, one needs to make a clear distinction between a social debate and an intellectual debate. The TRC's version of truth was reported as news in the media. It was discussed on talk shows and television programmes. It framed the outlines of a social debate. My question is: what kind of truth did the TRC produce, and will its version of truth hold? Will the TRC's version of truth become the founding myth of the new South Africa?

A Reflection on Truth

A myth is not a lie. It is based on truth. Only, its tendency is to de-contextualize the truth, and to present a version of truth as the truth. For a start, I think it is worth distinguishing between two kinds of truth: individual and institutional. The former opposed truth to power; the latter links truth to power.

There is a powerful tradition in Western history, one that links the Old Testament to the Enlightenment. It is a tradition of speaking truth to power: the prophet faces the pharaoh. Here, truth is an individual truth, and the opposite of truth is a lie. A more complicated relation between truth and power is articulated by the critics of the Enlightenment, from Marx to Foucault. In Marx's notion of institutional ideology, the relation between truth and untruth is more like that between light and shadow, less the opposition between truth and lie. The focus on the institutionalized production of truth is perhaps the sharpest with Foucault's claim that power relations undergird the institutional production of knowledge. When does truth become a partial truth, masking certain relations of power, or privilege?

A related emphasis is to be found in Martin Luther King's call for direct action as a call to bring hidden tensions to surface as truth, not to bury them. From this point of view, there are two kinds of truth: truth that brings unresolved tensions to light, and truth that obscures, hides, veils, masks the unpleasant face of reality. Truth which opens a social debate as opposed to truth that stifles a social debate in the name of maintaining social peace.

My claim is that the truth of the TRC makes most sense when understood as an institutionally produced truth, as the outcome of a process of truth-seeking, one whose boundaries were so narrowly defined by power and whose search was so committed to reinforcing the new power, that it turned the political boundaries of a compromise into analytical boundaries of truth-seeking. By reinforcing a political compromise with a compromised truth, I will argue, the TRC has turned a political into a moral compromise, and obscured the larger truth. I do not question the wisdom or the morality of the political compromise. But I do question the wisdom and the morality of defining the truth for narrow political reasons.

My argument is two-fold: while the political compromise is justifiable, the moral and intellectual compromise is not. Further, the moral and intellectual compromise may boomerang, undercutting the very political compromise it hoped to reinforce.

The Truth of Apartheid

What is the truth of apartheid? Rather than an Orwellian claim to the truth, I suggest a more modest beginning: an acknowledgement that truth may be not in the singular, but in the plural, and that there may not be one but several versions of truth. Whose truth comes closest to capturing the experience of the most?

I will argue that the TRC's version of truth was established through narrow lenses, crafted to reflect the experience of a tiny minority. This tiny minority included two groups, on the one hand perpetrators, being state agents, and on the other, victims, being political activists. The TRC defined over 20,000 South Africans as the 'victims' of apartheid, leaving the vast majority in the proverbial cold.

The search for truth involved a circuitous route, one that involved both analogy-shedding and analogy-seeking. This journey preceded the establishment of the TRC. The analogy that was shed was that of Nuremberg. This process has recently been recounted as a 'conversion' by a leading ANC activist, Kadar Asmal, along with two authors. His argument, in a nutshell, is that Nuremberg stands for victor's justice, and is incompatible with 'a negotiated revolution'. Where there was no victory, any attempt to exact a victor's justice would lead to 'justice with ashes'.

I would like to make two observations on the argument. First, Asmal assumes that all justice is victor's justice. From this point of view, all justice is the same as revenge. If so, it is then hardly surprising that justice should appear as the price of reconciliation. I will argue that there are different forms of justice, that one needs to distinguish not only between criminal and social justice, but also between victor's justice that turns the tables and survivors' justice that equalizes chances. Whereas the former may be based on revenge, the latter needs to be based on empathy.

Second, Asmal and his colleagues are right that the Holocaust and Nuremberg are an inappropriate metaphor for apartheid, but for a different reason. The metaphor would be misleading because it abstracts from the real problem. Whites and blacks in South Africa are not akin to Germans and Jews, for Germans and Jews did not have to build a common society in the aftermath of the Holocaust. There was Israel, and America. South African whites and blacks, however, do have to live together in the aftermath of apartheid. Faced with identities inherited from the past, they must forge new and common identities. To paraphrase a friend of mine, if the survivors of the Holocaust marched to the tune 'Let My People Go', the survivors of apartheid march to a different tune, 'Let My People Stay'.

If Nuremberg was the analogy that was shed, the analogy that was enthusiastically embraced was that of dictatorships in Latin America. If the price of shedding Nuremberg as an analogy was to drop the demand for justice, the price of embracing the Latin analogy was to diminish the truth of apartheid. For the basis of the diminished truth was the claim that apartheid was no more than a harsh and cruel dictatorship, a gross denial of human rights. The analogy that underscored this claim was enthusiastically embraced through two conferences that prepared the ground for the legislation that set up the TRC.

During these conferences, a consensus was forged that the two situations presented numerous similarities. Didn't both experience gross human rights abuses in the confrontation between power and resistance? Didn't both get mutually exhausted in protracted, endless struggle? Didn't both attain a mutual recognition, a political wisdom, that the waste of life and resources need not continue in the absence of outright victory? Were not both constrained by a global situation simultaneously underlining the need for compromise and facilitating it? Didn't both face the vexing question of how past perpetrators and their victims may live together in a new society?

The similarities existed, but they did not exhaust the whole truth. The flip-side of the analogy, the side that did not fit, was that the Latin analogy obscured what was distinctive about apartheid. For the violence of apartheid was aimed less at individuals than at entire communities, and entire population groups. And this violence was not just political. It was not just about defending power by denying people rights. The point of torture, terror, death, was even more far-reaching: its aim was to dispossess people of means of livelihood. The point is that the Latin analogy obscured the colonial nature of the South African context: the link between conquest and dispossession, between racialized power and racialized privilege. In a word, it obscured the link between perpetrator and beneficiary.

The Latins did not face the question that South Africa does: how would the continuing beneficiaries of apartheid, a substantial minority, and its continuing victims, the majority, live together? To answer that question, one would need a different commission, one that would redefine the truth from the point of view of the majority. It would have to produce a truth that would capture both the distinctive violence of apartheid and the distinctive relation between the beneficiaries and the victims of apartheid.

Imagine that there was a truth commission in the Soviet Union after Stalin, and this commission said nothing about the Gulag. What credibility would it have? The South African Gulag was called forced removals. Between 1960 and 1982, an estimated 3.5 million people were forcibly removed, their communities shattered, their families dispossessed and their livelihoods destroyed. These were not inert outcomes of socio-economic processes, but outcomes of active violence by state agents. These 3.5 million victims comprise faceless communities, not individual activists. They constitute a social catastrophe, not just a political dilemma. Were these not gross violations within the terms of reference set by the law? Why then did the TRC not include these among the 'victims'?

The law also asked the TRC to frame this gross denial of rights after 1960 within a historical context. Is not that context a history of conquest and dispossession, including both the dispossession of land through land laws and the Group Areas Act, and the militarization of labour, through pass laws? An understanding of gross violations that would have included the violence done to the 3.5 million victims of forced removals, and an understanding of context that would have highlighted the colonial violence leading to the dispossession of land and the militarization of labour, would have produced a different kind of truth. It would have illuminated apartheid as a reality lived by the majority, a reality that produced racialized poverty alongside racialized truth, both equally undeserved. It would have redefined our understanding of the victim of apartheid.

It would have gone beyond notions of individual harm and individual responsibility, and located agency within the workings of a system. The result would have been to explain apartheid as an evil system, not just to reduce it to evil operatives. One is tempted to ask: why did not the Truth Commission follow this route? The answer, I think, is once again relatively simple. Like Land Laws, Pass Laws, Group Areas Acts and other benchmarks in the legal umbrella of apartheid, forced removals too were not illegal under apartheid. We are forced to ask whether the TRC had come to share the legal fetishism so characteristic of the apartheid regime, in that it considered as a gross violation only that which was a gross violation under the laws of apartheid! What is the moral and political effect of this tendency that seeks to equate the violation of rights with the violation of the law?

We may recall Hannah Arendt's question in a different but related context, related because the Nazi regime shared apartheid's fetishism with the law. What happens, Hannah Arendt asked, when crime is legal? When criminals can enthusiastically enforce the rule of law? Let me cite one example. During the early 1950s, courts in South Africa would at times rule against the Department of Native Affairs' summary evictions and expulsions of Africans in urban areas. In 1956, Prime Minister Hendrik Verwoerd passed through Parliament the Native (Prohibition of Interdicts) Act. It prohibited any court of law from interfering with removal orders against Africans anywhere in the country. The courts obliged, claiming to uphold the rule of law. Verwoerd celebrated, 'The courts have nothing more to do than to accept and explain the laws.'

One wonders: did Verwoerd's bill limit the agenda not only of apartheid's courts but also of the post-apartheid Truth and Reconciliation Commission? Perhaps the greatest moral compromise the TRC made was to embrace the legal fetishism of apartheid. In doing so, it made little distinction between what is legal and what is legitimate, between law and right.

It is not that the TRC ignored beneficiaries. It actually held institutional hearings. But it understood as beneficiaries only those who gained from corrupting the system, who were able to turn links to public power to private advantage. Benefit too was defined as a corruption outside the law. By defining beneficiaries of apartheid as beneficiaries of the corruption of apartheid, it ignored systemic benefits derived through the law. So, in the end the TRC focused on torture, murder and rape, all outside the law, ignoring everything that was distinctive about apartheid and its machinery of violence.

An Insight into the Politics of the TRC

While the TRC was set up following the political compromise of 1994, its mandate did not just reflect the compromise. The two parts of the TRC point to two parts of its mandate. While the Amnesty Committee confirmed the compromise, the main Commission was given active powers to tell the story from the point of view of victims. The point of that story would be to educate the beneficiaries of apartheid, those who had historically formed its social base. (Here, too, apartheid was different from Latin dictatorships, in that it was also a political democracy for whites who had elected it with a greater majority every four years.) The political project that was the TRC was not confined to confirming the political compromise of 1994; it was also meant to build a bridge between the compromise and a future beyond it. If the point of the compromise of 1994 was a political reconciliation between state agents (perpetrators) and political activists (victims as a minority), the post-apartheid future would require a social reconciliation between beneficiaries and their victims, the vast majority. The irony is that not only did the TRC fail to build the ground for a social reconciliation, one wonders whether it may actually have eroded the ground for it. To understand why, we need to look at the contradictory effect of the truth as defined by the TRC.

The TRC invited beneficiaries to join victims in a public outrage against perpetrators. If only we had known, it seemed to invite beneficiaries to say, we would have acted differently; our trust has been violated, betrayed, abused. So, beneficiaries too were presented as victims. But, in spite of the best of intentions, their intended salvation had a paradoxical and unintended outcome.

On the one hand, the more beneficiaries were outraged at gross violations, the less they felt responsible for these. Not only did they see no need to be forgiven, they actually experienced forgiveness as a humiliation. Hence the growing opposition to the TRC process in the white community in general, and the Afrikaner community in particular. One wonders to what extent the near-total hostility of Afrikaners to the work of the TRC was triggered by the focus on perpetrators, to the exclusion of beneficiaries, which tended to translate apartheid as an exclusive Afrikaner project in the public eye.

On the other hand, the more beneficiaries appear complacent, indifferent, callous and lacking in empathy, the more victims are outraged. They feel forgiveness to be undeserved. The more they feel so, the more they demand: justice. So, the TRC ends up fuelling the very demand it set out to displace: justice!

Justice

The TRC began with several misconceptions. One, it was so preoccupied with a highly individualized notion of truth and responsibility that it failed both to focus on apartheid as a form of power and to underline the victimhood of the vast majority of South Africans. Two, the TRC began with the presumption that truth and justice can be alternatives. The critical response to the TRC underlined the opposite: that truth is not an alternative but a prerequisite for justice. The real alternative is not between truth and justice, but between forms of justice. Finally, the TRC systematically underestimated the task at hand by defining 'reconciliation' as the point of the transition of 1994. Reconciliation is a code word for a diminished truth. To reconcile is to restore, to return to a status quo ante. But the South African transition – unlike that in many a Latin dictatorship – is about creating something that has never existed before. Where there has been a political community based on conquest and dispossession, the task is to create a political community based on consent and justice. The task is nothing less than to get yesterday's conquerers to see the light and to be reborn as political equals. The challenge is to arrive at a form of transition that leads not to a political divorce, but to a political community of consenting adults.

I have argued both that this justice cannot be a turning of the tables, a victor's justice, and that one needs to explore alternative forms of justice, based on consent, what I have termed survivors' justice. It is worth recalling a statement from Gandhi: treat the thief as if, when the light came on, you recognized him as your father! Surely, this was not an invitation to tolerate theft or its ill-gotten gains as nepotism. But it was an invitation to make an analytical distinction between the agent and the act, to empathize with the former while confronting the latter. In short, only social justice that underlines the empathy between a community of survivors can lay the foundation of a new political community based on consent.

It is this bridge that the TRC needed to build, but failed to build. To lay the groundwork for social justice, it would have had to impart a different kind of education to beneficiaries. It would have had to educate them of the link between wealth and power, by painting apartheid as a regime of violence that dispossessed the majority of means of livelihood, just as surely as it laid the basis for enriching a privileged minority. Only by teaching beneficiaries that they benefited from the workings of apartheid – whether they intended it or not – could it hope to convince them of their moral responsibility. For while beneficiaries do not bear moral responsibility for gross violations of apartheid, they do bear moral responsibility to redress its consequences. In the absence of that education, the tragedy is that, even after the work of the TRC, the beneficiaries can still say: 'We did not know about it!'

Conclusion: A Mixed Record

The TRC's great achievement has been to discredit the apartheid regime in the eyes of its beneficiaries. This is no small achievement. History tells us that to drive a wedge between perpetrators and beneficiaries of an order has been the political requisite for every successful revolution.

In its eagerness to reinforce the new order, however, the TRC wrote the vast majority of apartheid's victims out of its version of history. The unintended outcome has been to drive a wedge between the beneficiaries and the victims of apartheid. In doing so, the TRC has failed to open a social debate on possible futures for a post-apartheid South Africa. That debate will need to be opened in South Africa. To reflect on the experience of the TRC is to ponder a harsh truth, that it may be easier to live with yesterday's perpetrators who have lost power than to live with beneficiaries whose gains remain intact.

Conclusion: The Cause of Justice Behind Civil Wars

Francis M. Deng

In my position of having to conclude a book that was opened with a chapter by Wole Soyinka, I am reminded of a piece of advice that my ageing mother gave me when she came to visit me in Washington. I told her that I was going to an important conference. As I was leaving, she said to me, 'Now, remember what your [deceased] father used to do. He would listen to everybody and then have the last word.' The problem is, she was talking about her husband who was a paramount chief, which I am not. So, while I speak last, I realize that I do not have the last word.

As I thought about how I should address my topic, 'The Cause of Justice Behind Civil Wars', which I thought would be close to the themes of this book, I felt torn. I wondered whether I should try to reflect some of the themes in the previous chapters by way of a synthesis or a conclusion. In the end I decided that it would be grossly unfair to what had already been said. I feared I would produce a poor version of truly inspiring discussions of the issues. And so, I decided that I would fall back on my initial idea and try to adhere to the theme of my title.

In doing so, I thought I should build on some of the work I have been doing. One is the work of the Brookings Institution's Africa Project, which I head. The other has to do with my mandate as special representative of the UN secretary-general on internally displaced persons, a global assignment. The third is the work of the Africa Leadership Forum. When General Olusegun Obasanjo (head of state of Nigeria since May 1999), the founding chairman of the forum, was in prison in Nigeria, he wrote a letter asking me to be the acting chairman while he was incarcerated.

First I will present the policy orientation that should guide our perspective on the issues we have been writing about. I will then outline what I believe to be the problem areas connected with these issues, try to identify their root causes, look at some guidelines for possible solutions, and elaborate on the sharing of responsibility for action. I will also refer to some of the lessons we have learned from the work on the mandate on internal displacement and the relevance of that experience to the ongoing quest for a normative framework of good governance in Africa. I will then conclude with a few remarks highlighting the need for balancing globalization with localization, through a process that builds on African indigenous values and institutions and links all levels of human interaction, from the local to the global.

Policy Orientation

With respect to policy orientation, it seems to me that there are two trends in the post-Cold War period that are relevant in this context. One is the strategic withdrawal of the major powers, which has resulted in a degree of marginalization of developing countries, especially in Africa. It has also meant that the responsibilities that used to be shouldered by the superpowers and their major allies are now falling on the shoulders of the Africans, who do not have the capacity or, in some cases, the political will to deal with their own problems. That is a negative development. But there is a positive side to the situation. Instead of distorting problems, particularly in the area of conflicts, as episodes in the superpowers' confrontation around the world, we are now forced to look at problems in their proper context. That means that we have to dig deeper into our own context to understand the sources of these conflicts. Along with that is a demand for assuming responsibility for our own problems, instead of looking to others to solve them for us. There is a necessity dictated by circumstances that we should become more self-reliant in dealing with our problems. I see these two major trends as relevant to what we are concerned with here, although I realize that I am broadening the scope to give a much broader, and yet deeper, meaning to what we mean by the search for the truth, healing and social justice.

Digging deep to know the truth leads to empathizing with each other, which I believe has a bearing on healing, because to understand, as they say, is to forgive, though not to forget. To empathize with your opponent is to try to fit yourself into his or her shoes, to know the truth from both points of view, and understand why people behave the way they do. Along with that would be seeking equitable remedies because, if you have understood the other point of view and have empathized with that point of view, you come to seek alternative solutions that address the cause of justice from both points of view.

Let me illustrate with an anecdote. I was in a meeting in South Africa connected with the Graça Machel study on children in armed conflict. We had a small dinner honoured by President Nelson Mandela and Archbishop

Desmond Tutu. Wole Soyinka was there too. In the discussion that ensued, there was a strong criticism of African leaders that was shared by a number of people. With the powerful voices of Machel and Soyinka, you can imagine how critical of African leaders the group was. President Mandela, looking at the situation from a different perspective, argued that he had been impressed by the qualities of leadership he had found in many African leaders, which the world does not recognize. The critics responded by saying that he was being too indulgent. Their general tendency was to be unrelentingly hard on African leaders. I could see Mandela getting a little restless and impatient with that line of criticism. At one point, almost bringing the discussion to a close, he said, 'You know, every person by virtue of being a human being, however bad, has a good side.' He then proceeded to argue that in dealing with people, it is important to explore and build on that good side. That requires bridging the differences and finding the common ground. The immediate response of the critics was, 'Ah, but you are a saint.' I disagreed with the critics and agreed with Mandela. Initially, I did so in a moderated language, but after Mandela left, I turned on the critics more sharply: 'How can you turn into *just* a saint a man who is inspiring his nation and the entire humanity to live up to certain human ideals? By considering him a saint, you make him almost irrelevant to our daily life, when he is, in fact, influencing and guiding human behaviour at all levels.' An animated discussion continued. As Archbishop Tutu got up to leave, he remarked, 'This has been a stimulating theological discussion and Francis, if you ever want to be ordained, I'm ready.' I saw a glimpse of hope for another calling there.

This leads me to another policy issue. I believe that we should postulate some overriding norms or goals to guide our analysis, values that we should look up to. There was a time when I would have been reticent to speak of values because my earlier legal training made me suspicious of such terms as falling into the realm of metaphysics and therefore irrelevant to hard legal analysis. But then I was fortunate, I would say, to go to Yale Law School, where Myres McDougal and Harold Lasswell attached considerable importance to values. In their jurisprudence of law, science and policy, values were defined in concrete terms, embracing such deference values as power, rectitude, affection and respect, and welfare values like wealth, well-being, skills and enlightenment. Another major principle to which I was introduced by the Yale School of Jurisprudence was the concept of human dignity as an overriding goal of community and social processes. Again, human dignity was one of those concepts that I had been conditioned by earlier legal training to dismiss as metaphysical. The Yale school gave it a more empirical meaning by defining it in terms of the broadest shaping and sharing of values. Put in those terms, as a goal, we should try to maximize the production of values and broaden the basis of sharing them so that as many people as possible participate in the processes. These are universal principles which different societies and cultures observe in varying degrees.

In every society there is an aspiration for human dignity articulated differently in different cultural or social contexts, which, for a variety of reasons, falls short of the universal ideal. No society can claim to have achieved the optimum goals of human dignity. We try to achieve them through a variety of ways, international human rights being the most recognized of those ways. But even the international human rights instruments do not fully achieve the ideal. There are societies that culturally fall much shorter, either because they discriminate against others of a different culture, gender, race or who otherwise fall outside the community by some definition. So, the promotion of human dignity is a cause to which we are all committed and are struggling to accomplish, but which we are still far from achieving.

Problem Areas

With these policy objectives in mind, what are the problem areas that we need to address? This was the question I posed to myself when I was designing the Brookings Institution Africa Project. The question was: standing as I did in my country, the Sudan, looking at the continent of Africa, what are the major problem areas, those that call for serious study, and on which policies can be formulated and acted upon? I did not have to think much to come to the conclusion that managing conflicts or conflict resolution came first, followed by issues of human rights, democracy and equitable development, with cultural considerations cutting across those themes. I am sure the order would be reversed by economists, to whom economic issues would probably rank highest. But it is my firm belief that basic security ranks highest in the order. It is a matter of life and death. People need to be secure enough to go about the normal tasks of everyday life. In conflict situations, particularly when conflicts become violent, it is difficult, if not impossible, to have any meaningful discourse on human rights, democracy or development. But rather than prioritize them, I would say that they are all interactive, interrelated and inseparable. As much as possible, they should be seen as elements of an integrated whole.

The story of Africa is well known. The crises of the continent take the form of violent conflicts, dictatorships, gross violations of human rights, flawed development, and lack of intercontinental integration or even co-operation. There is a tendency today to see the positive side of Africa, and we have heard much recently about an African Renaissance. Wole Soyinka even told us that African Renaissance has always been around. According to him, it has been renewed, would atrophy, and then be rejuvenated; but it has always been there. Some of this, of course, has to do with a quest for optimism, which is essential for doing anything meaningful. One has to feel that one can do better in order for one to try at all. But there is also the risk of complacency, of assuming that things are fine, and that there is nothing to worry about.

In my country, the Sudan, we have an incurable disease of optimism in everything we say or do. We Sudanese tend to believe that when all is said and done, there is nothing really wrong with us. Whether we speak in the comparative context of Africa, the Arab world, or any other part of the world for that matter, all things considered, we are among the best. With that racial and cultural arrogance, the Sudan stands there atrophying, while others, who want to improve their lot, come passing by, forging ahead. It is only now that we Sudanese are beginning to realize that we were living in a dream of fake pride, arrogance and complacency.

The lesson for Africa is that even if things are beginning to improve on the continent, it is still healthy for us to keep spotlighting the problems and seriously think about what we can do to address our ills at their roots.

Addressing the Root Causes

What are the root causes of our problems? We have a tendency to begin the history of our crises with colonial intervention. This tendency is now being questioned, particularly because it connotes denial of responsibility and placing the blame on others. If this is true and we revise history to escape responsibility, then that is wrong. But it is important for us to understand why things are the way they are, because things do not just happen without cause and effect. There is a connection between what is happening right now, where things began, and how they led to where we are. Only by understanding that causal connection can we find pertinent solutions.

In many of our countries today, we experience serious crises of identity, which have much to do with ethnicity, and, in some cases, race, religion and culture. The fallacy I want to talk about concerns the over-generalizations or over-simplifications by those who say that there is no such thing as ethnicity and that it is a construct exploited by self-serving politicians, and those who see everything in ethnic terms. I would like to agree with those who see fault with both of these extreme points of view. Of course ethnicity is a reality to reckon with. Human beings are born as individuals in a context that involves families extending into lineages, kinships and clans. Beyond the clan, we live in communities that can be broadened into villages and, ultimately, what some call tribes, and others concerned with political correctness prefer to call ethnic groups. To say that this has no relevance at all is to deny the very existence of the human being, born in context, certainly not as a sole individual belonging to nowhere. At the same time, there is no question that ethnicity is a potential that can be used or exploited for various causes, some positive, some negative.

There is another assumption about ethnic identity that I would like to question. We are told that identity is what people believe themselves to be, their self-perceptions, rather than what they are objectively. In other words, the fact that I believe myself to be of a particular group should qualify me as a member of that group. The fact that what I think I am and objective realities about me do not harmonize is said to be irrelevant. I am supposed to be what I think I am. While this is valid to a degree, I think it can be carried to an extreme. I say this because I come from a country where I see a clear dichotomy, or should I say discrepancy, between what people believe themselves to be and what by objective criteria they are. I happen also to believe that what people believe themselves to be, though to a large extent fictional or mythical, has been more a source of division and conflict than what they objectively are. A Sudanese, for example, can say he is an Arab. By the definition of the Sudanese, he is a Muslim and an Arab, and the two are considered inextricably combined. If he were typical, representing the frame of mind of the people who think themselves Arabs, he would trace his genealogy to Arabia and be very proud of his Arabian ancestors. He would even believe in the purity of his blood as an Arab. There is of course, a grading of people according to what the Arab-Sudanese call *asl*, the purity of origin, unlike those whose identity has been adulterated or polluted by mixing with what they consider to be slave blood, which is black.

In the Sudan, we use a variety of colours for describing people. If you are very dark, like me, you are blue; you cannot be called black because that is the colour of slaves. Since I am not, technically speaking, a slave, I cannot be black, so I am blue. Then you have people who are green, people who are brown; people who are red, and people who are yellow. Just as there are no blacks in the Sudan, there are no whites. The ideal colour for the Sudanese is probably green, the proper colour for the true *wad ballad* – son of the land. If you become too light, then you run the risk of being *Khawaja*, European, a *nasarani*, infidel, or worse, a *Halabi*, Albanian, which is associated with gypsy. Being too dark connotes black origin and therefore slave background.

All this is not as nonsensical or ridiculous as it may sound. It represents a history in which people were stratified according to race, religion and culture. There were very serious consequences associated with the classification. If you were a heathen and black, and assuming you were not already a slave, you were a legitimate target for slavery. But if you became a Muslim, that liberated you. And, of course, if you were culturally Arabized and could fantasize that you had some loosely credible Arab ancestry, that was even better.

In this respect, the Arab-Islamic assimilation process compared favourably with what existed in the Anglo-Saxon approach to slavery. In the Islamic system, if a slave master had a child with a slave woman, that child was born free and equal to all the other children of free mothers. If you were in a situation where you were given an opportunity to exit from a status of indignity, to climb and cross categories, why wouldn't you? So, you have a nation that started with a few Arab men coming from outside, whose religion was the mighty Islam, mixing with African women, whose progeny had the potential of being either slaves or saved and lifted to something much higher, respected and honoured. The choice clearly favoured the Arab-Islamic identity. That is how the psychology of being Muslims and Arabs developed in the northern Sudan, even though most northern Sudanese look like many Africans, and certainly like most African-Americans, who have a touch of non-black element in their racial mix.

A southern Sudanese student came to the United States in the early 1960s, when migration in this direction was not as much as it is today. He was eager to see what were then known as the American Negroes. So, his host family, which was white, took him to Harlem. They drove around. He looked out for the Negroes, the Blacks, but could not see any. He then asked his host family where the Negroes were. They responded, 'Don't you see them all over here?' He said, 'But these aren't Negroes, these are Arabs.' Your typical Sudanese Arab is your typical African-American.

A friend of mine, who was our ambassador to the UN, very much a typical Sudanese Arab, was approached by an African-American in the Delegates' Lounge. He asked the ambassador where he was from. When the ambassador said he was from the Sudan, the African-American remarked, 'What are those Arabs doing to you?' Of course, he assumed that the ambassador was African, black. That is to me the crisis of Sudanese identity. It is a crisis for the north as much as it is a crisis for the country.

At a personal level, the crisis represents a tension between what people think they are, and what they truly are by objective standards. Subjectively, the northern Sudanese are generally at peace with themselves. As already alluded to, they consider themselves better than any other race or ethnic group, an ethnocentrism commonly shared by most, if not all, indigenous groups. But when northern Sudanese go to the Arab world, or to other countries, they are confronted with the objective reality that they are not aware of. Even in the Arab world, Sudanese Arabs get discriminated against as Africans. Some of them go back to the Sudan hating any mention of Arabs and Arabism. They do not want to be associated with Arabism any more. Also, northerners come to the West and are called blacks, which offends them because they do not recognize themselves to be black. That too is a crisis for them. Another crisis expresses itself at the national level. The dominant north defines the nation, which is diversified racially, ethnically, religiously and culturally by their own Arab-Islamic self-perception. Defining the country as Arab and Islamic is not simply a label, for policies, domestic and foreign, get shaped accordingly. You have then a discrepancy or a disconnection between the way the nation is composed in its multiple identities and the way in which it is perceived by the dominant group in accordance with its own identity.

As others begin to assert their own identities, the crisis becomes a contest for the soul of the nation. That is the situation in the Sudan today. The south, having initially fought for secession, is now saying that it is a case not of wanting to secede, but of restructuring the nation to reflect its true composition, which is predominantly non-Arab. The new frame of mind is, 'We belong to the country as a whole and most of us are indeed Africans. The Arabs, who have shaped the identity of the country, are the minority. What we want is a new Sudan, restructured so that we all have a sense of belonging on equal footing.' That line of thought, supported by credible military action, becomes threatening to the established identity that was Arab and Islamic. This generates the fear that Abdullahi An-Na'im and Svetlana Peshkova are talking about.

As they say, we have to understand the fear of the other group. There is a deep-seated fear on the part of the Arab north that these blacks, once slaves they looked down upon, are now rising and wanting to take the nation and redefine it in a way that would reverse the order of things and put the blacks on top. Fundamentalism in the Sudan is directly related to the fear of the north that the tables are being turned and the blacks are threatening to take over. Therefore they invoke Islam, which makes them a majority, to justify policies that are radical and discriminatory against the non-Muslims and even the non-Arab Muslims in the north.

It is important to reiterate that in the Sudan, Islam goes hand-in-hand with being an Arab, not just culturally, but also racially. The Nigerian Muslims go to the Sudan on their way to Mecca for pilgrimage, and yet northern Sudanese barely recognize them as genuine Muslims. Because they do not speak Arabic and are not racially Arab, they do not quite qualify as Muslims. For some reason, when speaking of Iran and some of the Asian countries like Indonesia, Malaysia and Pakistan, northern Sudanese seem more inclined to accept that Muslims can be non-Arab. But when it comes to Africa, the ideal Muslim is one who is also Arabic-speaking and is Arabized culturally, if not racially or ethnically Arab. The self-perception of the northern Sudanese as Arab, and their fears that the non–Arabs are threatening to take over the country and Africanize it, may be unreasonable, but we have to understand their own sense of identity and the roots of their insecurity.

The question then is, do you leave people's self-perceptions as they are, even though they are erroneous, or do you tell them, as I try to do with the northern Sudanese, to stand in front of the mirror and ask themselves some tough questions? The latter may be a step towards bridging the gap, but it is also difficult, because you are basically telling someone that he is not what he thinks he is.

I was quite intrigued in Burundi when I went there in my capacity as representative of the UN secretary-general on internally displaced persons. As I addressed large audiences, I saw that some faces looked typically Tutsi, the way we are told Tutsis look, and some looked very typically Hutu, as they are supposed to look. Many of them fell in between and I could not identify them with either stereotype. So I asked some ministers if they could always tell a Tutsi from a Hutu. The answer I got from the foreign minister was, to begin with, a confident 'Yes,' but then he added, 'with a margin of error of 35 per cent.'

I believe that although it is difficult and perhaps painful to tell people that they are not what they think they are, if they must create a nation with others on equal footing, and their false self-perception impacts negatively on their relationship with their compatriots, then identity is no longer a personal matter to be left to one's own self; we have to pose some serious questions about the gap between what you think you are and what you truly are, if that gap is relevant to public policy.

There are also themes of historical perceptions where subjectivity and objectivity leave a gap. This has to do with the much talked-about collective memory. In my discussions with people wherever I have been in connection with the mandate on internal displacement resulting from conflict situations, I have heard two contrasting versions of history. This is true of Azerbaijan, Burundi, Bosnia, Rwanda, Sudan, Sri Lanka and Tajikistan, to mention only a few. One version of history sees the conflict between the groups as continuous. They see themselves as having always been in conflict, going back a long way. This is often reflected in the journalistic reports about those conflict situations. The other version is that they have always lived together harmoniously, intermarried, and shared the same occasions of happiness and sadness. 'We do not understand where this division is coming from,' is a typical remark.

In a way, it's not surprising that these two versions of history coexist and alternate. As a number of contributors have said, memories of conflicts continue even after they get resolved. People who are adjacent to one another must find ways of managing their differences. Of course, they must from time to time come into conflict, but they must also develop norms for resolving their conflicts. The cycle of conflicts and their resolutions is continuous. When you have been in conflict and have resolved it, but something happens to trigger another conflict, you remember past conflicts. And so, both themes are real: the chain of causations of conflicts that you remember when you are in a conflict psychology and the situations of harmony that occur when you have successfully resolved a specific conflict. It then becomes a question of when you look at which of the two as your point of focus.

In the 1970s, I conducted research among the Dinka for a book about their perceptions on past, present and projected future. Their accounts inevitably touched on their relations with their Arab neighbours to the north. The Ngok Dinka and the Missiriya Arabs were neighbours and interacted with one another long before colonial intervention. As the leaders of the Dinka, members of my family maintained close ties with their Arab counterparts to mediate their coexistence on an otherwise hostile and volatile border. At one time in the mid-1970s, a conflict erupted between the Arabs and the Dinka. Hundreds of people were killed and feelings were very high; people were extremely embittered. I conducted my first set of interviews with the Dinka at that time. Dinka perceptions of their origin and historical experiences, from creation, to early migration, to the current situation, to visions of the prospects for integration or separation, did not reflect anything in common between the Dinka and the Arabs. God had created them differently, the Dinka black and the Arabs brown. All the negatives were associated with Arab identity, while the Dinka associated themselves with the positive side of things. Separation was seen as the only answer: to hold otherwise would offend God.

Then the first vice-president and I, together with others, intervened and mediated an end to the conflicts. We held a successful peace conference, which restored peace and memory of the good old days, the history of cooperation that had existed between the two groups. It was after this peace agreement and reconciliation that I conducted the second set of interviews. The story had changed dramatically. 'We were always one people,' had become the theme. Even the myths of creation were reconstructed. The Dinka and the Arabs were created as twins. In fact, sometimes they added the white race, making for triplets: 'Don't you see how we have mixed? People have intermarried. There are many people among us who are of Arab origin and there are many of our people among the Arabs.' The future was seen as one not of separation, but of integration. It was a total change.

This anecdote shows that whichever aspect of history people want to focus on, they can find supportive evidence. Certainly, current events have much to do with the choice. But leadership has a vital role to play in creating negative or positive images that influence the choice.

In this connection, there is also an incident in our oral history during the nineteenth-century upheavals associated with slavery and inter-tribal warfare. It was a total breakdown, what the Dinka called the time when the world as they knew it was spoiled. When peace was re-established, a major peace conference was held in which my great-grandfather, who was what under the colonial administration became known as the paramount chief, asked his people to dig a big pit. He asked them to gather the surrounding rubbish, put it into the pit, and cover it. Rituals were performed and the general agreement proclaimed that the past be forgotten. Whatever had happened was buried, not to be invoked again. That is one incident the Dinka often quote in the aftermath of serious crises. The moral principle of forgiving and forgetting behind this incident contrasts with what we have been saying in favour of digging for the truth.

Over the years, I have collected Dinka songs, as I mentioned at one point. A popular Dinka poet/singer, who has composed songs about the north–south crisis, says in one song that while the tradition of burying the differences, forgetting and forgiving wrongs, will be followed one day, when peace is restored, there are a few things that will never be forgiven or forgotten. He singles out the problem of those who change their colours for political opportunism. In particular, he argues that changing religion to please those in power will not be buried, because God cannot be deceived: he will always see the truth. What is important about this is not so much the specific cases that are considered unforgivable or unforgettable, but the fact that there is a category of cases that will not be buried, but must be revealed. I think this is relevant to what we are talking about here.

What is also significant about this is that there are traditional ways of dealing with inter-communal conflicts. We in the Sudan have a group of experts called *ajaweed*. These are elders, mostly tribal chiefs, who are experienced in mediation. They are usually called upon to mediate in conflicts between groups other than their own. The process of mediation begins with an open discussion in which everything is aired. The parties express their grievances against one another in lengthy and often embittered speeches, which make one wonder whether an agreement is possible. After an exhaustive exchange, in which the mediators labour against all odds to explore a common ground, there comes a point when the leaders come together and agree on the principles for resolving the conflict and living together. Rituals of reconciliation are then performed and the conflict is formally declared resolved.

This does not mean that the conflict is ended for ever. Max Gluckman, one of the pioneering experts on African law, used to say that African conflicts never get fully resolved. When I first heard him say that, at Yale Law School, it offended me because I thought this was a distortion of the African reality. Of course we resolve our conflicts, I thought to myself. I eventually realized that what he was talking about was memory of old conflicts being triggered by new ones. A conflict gets resolved, then erupts again opening old wounds. Each time a conflict erupts, the past becomes part of the evidence to be weighed in finding a resolution that is appropriate to the specific case under consideration.

Guidelines for Solutions

If there is a reason for why things are the way they are, then there have to be solutions, whether temporary or lasting. That is why I think the crises confronting Africa today should also be seen as offering opportunities for addressing the problems of the continent. We have in the past tended to cover up much of what divides us in our countries. We know that the colonial state created diversities by breaking up ethnic groups and bringing together groups that were not part of the same identity. Paradoxically, they also kept them apart and even used them in their divide-and-rule policies. Certainly, the colonial state did not design policies for harmonizing relations among the various groups, except for the maintenance of strict law and order, which prevented or limited inter-tribal warfare. We also know that after independence, the response of the African countries was to insist on a sacrosanct principle of preserving the borders as they were inherited from the colonial powers. In order to retain some semblance of unity within those borders, Africans tended to strengthen centralized control, leading to authoritarian rule under the one-party system. Human rights and democracy were sacrificed in the name of national unity. In order to give development priority as a unifying goal, most independent African states adopted what they euphemistically called African socialism, which entailed state control of national wealth and the means of production. The overriding goal of maintaining national unity became a source of most of the evils the continent has suffered. The principles of self-determination that brought independence to the continent did not go far enough. Independence gave individuals who had learned the rules of governance from their colonial masters the opportunity of seizing power from them and using the same tools of state domination. Then came Cold War politics, which reinforced those leaders, as long as they were on the right side of the ideological divide, by giving them the necessary resources and building their capacity to impose their rule on the people.

If we are to revisit this whole arrangement with an open mind and ask ourselves seriously what solutions can address our problems of diversity and disparity, then it seems to me that we have to raise some tough questions about the meaning of self-determination in the context of ethnic pluralism in independent Africa. It does seem that of all the African countries today, the one that speaks about self-determination for ethnic groups, even if it amounts to independence, is Ethiopia. It seems to me that the Ethiopian policy is a shrewd move that can in fact reinforce national unity. By making people feel that they have the right to self-determination, even if they want to break away, and then do the best you can to make unity appeal to them, you are almost assured that they will remain within unity. But when I said this once at a conference, an Ethiopian official took offence because he thought that I was belittling the seriousness of their intentions to give self-determination to their ethnic groups. Whether they are sincere about self-determination, or use it as a tactical ploy for appeasing or pacifying ethnic groups, I think theirs is an experiment that should be looked at very closely.

Associated with that is the use of indigenous cultures and identities in the broader sense of political and economic development. It seems to me that the worst thing that can happen to a people is to deny them the cultural content of their identity. It is that identity that makes people the human beings they are. Identity implies history and the legacy of how the forefathers dealt with societal problems. That collective memory is passed on to successive generations as an ancestral legacy and a resource for building the future. For a people to adopt wholesale what has evolved elsewhere, reflecting the logic of another culture, means at best being a copy of that outside culture. To me, it is a denial of the dignity of being a human being as well as a denial of the capacity to function at one's best; it almost means taking a fish out of water and expecting it to swim or survive.

In our contributions here we have from time to time referred to indigenous ways of doing things, including methods of resolving conflicts. This is relevant to political, cultural and economic development. Indigenous cultures have a potential role to play that we have not explored fully. African leaders have tried all along to resort to indigenous cultures, but early post-colonial leaders used culture as a pretext for doing things that were in fact not as African as they claimed. Such notions as the one-party system and African socialism were justified by reference to African cultural ways. We heard African leaders talk about humanism in Zambia; in Ghana, Kwame Nkrumah talked about consciencism; Sese Mobutu in Zaire talked about *authenticité*; and in Tanganyika (later Tanzania), Julius Nyerere linked his ideology of *ujamaa* with indigenous cultural values and did so with intellectual depth. All these reflect both the desire for cultural relevance and a manipulative way of using culture that, except perhaps for Nyerere, did not go deep enough. I think this is an area that needs to be revisited by in-depth work on the part of African and Africanist scholars.

In this context, the issue of ethnic and cultural pluralism needs to be emphasized. Managing diversity is an issue that we have tended to push under the rug, but I believe it will continue to challenge us. We need to find genuine ways of interpreting democracy to accommodate diversity. When you have elections in which people vote with their identities, while the official claim is that ethnic differences either do not exist, or, if they do exist, are negative reflections of tribalism, then you are definitely not building on your cultural resources in a positive way.

When we talk about assigning responsibility for these problems, we have to bear in mind that things have changed and that responsibilities are being reapportioned accordingly. There is now a tendency to see the problems as internal in the first place (most of the conflicts we are talking about are internal) and therefore as problems of governance. I cite my friend and colleague Bill Zartman to the effect that management of conflicts is essentially a function of governance. This is why it is important to reconceptualize sovereignty not as a principle of exclusion, a barricade against external scrutiny, as sovereignty has conventionally been perceived, but rather as a principle of domestic responsibility. But since sovereignty is a principle of international relations, responsibility implies accountability at various levels, from the national, through the regional, to the international. As the national context often lacks the capacity to check leaders, neighbours, sub-regional and continent-wide organizations should assist in making accountable leaders who are not accountable within their own countries. The UN comes as a last resort, representing the international community in its totality. Even there, we have to disaggregate the international community by asking what it means. Here is where the role of the major powers comes in. Even the UN often depends very much on the major powers, in particular the United States. It is here that we have to fine-tune the responsibilities of different actors in this global sharing of responsibilities, a process in which the international responses to the crisis of internal displacement have lessons to offer.

Lessons from Internal Displacement

I will simply comment on the lessons from internal displacement by saying that this is a concrete example of how a crisis that is affecting some 25–30 million people in about 40 countries worldwide has been until recently dismissed as an internal matter that the United Nations should not get involved in. When I was appointed in 1992 as representative of the secretary-general on internally displaced persons, my initial assignment was to study the problem, to advise the international community, particularly the United Nations High Commissioner for Human Rights and the General Assembly, on whether and how to get involved in this problem. We have since focused on developing a legal framework based on existing human rights law, humanitarian law, and refugee law by analogy. We have also tried to develop a collaborative institutional arrangement within the United Nations system, because the options of creating a new organization or designating an existing one to assume full responsibility were ruled out. I have also been visiting countries that are affected by displacement, so far 13 countries, of which five are from Africa, to engage governments and other actors in a dialogue on behalf of the internally displaced. In collaboration with a team of legal experts, we developed a set of guiding principles, which the UNHCR has taken note of and the Inter-Agency Standing Committee has formally endorsed to be used to guide people in their work.

What should be emphasized about internal displacement is that in most instances, the affected countries suffer from an acute crisis of national identity. This creates vacuums of responsibility for the displaced population and other victims of conflict situations. Instead of the government seeing the victims as citizens who should be protected and assisted, they are often seen as part of the enemy and are therefore deprived of shelter, basic food, medicine – virtually all necessities for a reasonably decent living. In essence, these are a people dispossessed, abandoned by their own governments. What is happening in the Sudan today, with respect to the famine in the south, is a good example of the national identity crisis I am talking about. The southern Sudanese are not being seen by the government as citizens to whom they owe responsibility for protection and assistance to be saved from the drought- and war-related famine, by providing them with food or at least facilitating access to international relief agencies. They are perceived as the people of the rebel leader, John Garang, and therefore as the enemy, or part of the enemy. It is part of the war objective to eliminate them or at least to destroy their resource base so that the movement is denied the support of the local population.

Sudan is only an extreme example of what prevails worldwide, which I witnessed in varying degrees in virtually all the countries I visited. In one country, I did what I normally do, that is to begin my mission by talking to the national leaders, then going down the hierarchy of authority, before visiting the displaced. I then go back to debrief the leaders. In this country, I asked the displaced what message they wanted me to take back to their leaders. The answer I got from one woman, speaking for the rest, was, 'We have no leaders there. Those are not our people.' In another country, a man responded to the same question by saying, 'To those people we are not citizens, we are criminals, and our only crime is that we are poor.'

When people see themselves in relation to their government as outsiders, to whom do they turn but the international community? And if the international community then says that this is an internal affair, what happens to them? If we conceptualize sovereignty to mean that to claim legitimacy, a state must live up to a minimum standard of responsibility for the protection and general welfare of citizens, failure to do so should mean forfeiting sovereignty and risking outside intervention by a more caring international community. But the threat must be credible to be useful or meaningful. How realistic is it to presume that state failure will trigger external intervention? This is where the dynamics of regional involvement become relevant.

Africa's Search for a Normative Framework of Good Governance

Africans are being told to put their house in order: 'Your problems are your problems in the first place, take a good shot at it first and we will help you from a distance.' The neighbours of the countries that are affected are beginning to say, 'Your problems are not entirely your own internal affairs; they also affect us.' This indeed is the case with ECOWAS, with SADCC countries and to some extent, with the IGADD countries. The Great Lakes region is traumatically experiencing the need for a sub-regional security arrangement. In all these sub-regions, neighbours are saying, 'We have a vested interest in your problem. If you do not allow us to help you solve the problem amicably in a peaceful way, we will find some other way of getting involved.' That is why next to the national level, the sub-regional level becomes vital. Then follows the continent-wide level. This, in essence, has been the main finding of our Brookings research work, but it is also connected with the efforts of the Africa Leadership Forum in developing a normative framework for good governance in the continent.

Some of you will undoubtedly have heard of the proposed Conference on Security, Stability, Development and Cooperation in Africa (CSSDCA), which was developed by the Africa Leadership Forum (ALF) at the in-itiative of General Olusegun Obasanjo, head of state of Nigeria and the founder of the ALF. Working in collaboration with the OAU Secretariat and the Economic Commission for Africa (ECA), ALF, building on the European experience, initiated a process that culminated in the 1991 conference in Kampala, Uganda, and adopted the Kampala Document, stipulating the principles of the CSSDCA. The Kampala Document was submitted shortly afterwards to the OAU to be formally adopted by the heads of states. That is where the process stalled; it became too threatening to a number of governments. The most outspoken against the CSSDCA were the most vulnerable, those whose internal governance is so flawed that such a normative framework would expose them. So they played a shelving game, by tactically sending it back for further studies by the Secretariat of the OAU. Since then, it has remained on the shelves of the OAU, supposedly being studied. The question now is whether it is possible to move the CSSDCA process forward, by identifying the obstacles, exploring alternative ways of overcoming them, and developing partnership with other actors that could ultimately bring pressure to bear on the governments to be more responsive to Africa's quest for an appropriate policy framework.

Conclusion

Let me conclude by emphasizing that we should seize the opportunity of the African crisis to think through our problems again and come up with fresh ideas for solutions. We should address the problem in a way that bridges the various levels of analysis, from local to global. Here, I think we have to recognize that the mirror side of globalization is localization. We have been focusing so much on the processes of globalization, while the contemporary world, whether in Africa or elsewhere, is also undergoing a process of fragmentation, localizing perspectives. Much of this represents a quest for recognition and for making use of local resources in the processes of building nations. This is a challenge that calls for serious attention on the part of researchers.

The policy objective ought to be to develop benchmarks or yardsticks for measuring performance, which the international community can hold up to countries and say, 'By these recognized standards or criteria, this is how you are performing.' Let governments be shamed by how they see themselves reflected in the chart of performance. I believe this is an agenda in which the research community can do a great deal.

Digging into the truth is an important first step. The post-Cold War period encourages us openly to look for the truth in a way we were not able to do before. By digging into the truth, we will reveal the different perspectives that need to be reconciled or harmonized. By so doing, I believe we will have a better understanding of how best to pursue the overriding goal of human dignity, defined as the broadest shaping and sharing of all values, material, moral and spiritual.

Index

Abacha, General Sani, 7, 15, 28, 44, 49, 64
Abiola, Chief Mashood, 7, 22, 28, 39, 47
abortion, arising out of rape, 168
accountability, 52–3; for sexual abuse, 169; in Europe, 134; in Latin American experience, 127–41; of General Pinochet, 152
Achebe, Chinua, 57, 58–62, 65, 103; *Anthills of the Savannah*, 60–2; *The Trouble with Nigeria*, 106
Addis Ababa Agreement, 81
Adedeji, Professor, 90–1
Adekunle, Colonel, 93
Africa: Balkanisation of, 1; study of, 18
Africa Leadership Forum, 184, 199
African Renaissance, 187
African Studies, 2, 69, 111–12
agriculture: flight of men from, 104; in Nigeria, 97; women's role in, 102, 103, 104
Ahazuem, Jones, 113
Ahmed, Mohamed (al-Mahdi), 80
Akayesu, Jean Paul, 171, 174
Albert, I.O., 94
Alfonsin, Raul, 129, 130
Alvarez, José, 156
Amadiume, Ifi, 6–7, 113
amnesty, 5, 14, 63, 128, 130, 131, 132, 136; conditional, 134
Amnesty Committee (South Africa), 13, 176, 181
Amnesty International, 170–1
An-Na'im, Abdullahi, 6, 8–10, 191
Anaoku, Chief Emeka, 56
Anglo-Egyptian Condominium, 80
anti-Semitism, 32

apartheid, 13, 14, 53; legal fetishism of, 180–1; truth of, 178–81
Arabs: conflict with Dinka, 193; in slave trade, 28–30; in view of Sudanese, 189; Sudanese, 190, 192
Arendt, Hannah, 180
Argentina, 128–30, 131
Aristide, Jean-Bertrand, 133, 139
Armah, Ayi Kwei, 59
Armstrong, R.G., 42
art: in the service of social justice, 7; role of, 58
Arusha process, 79, 88
Asmal, Kadar, 178
attack trade, women in, 117
Awolowo, Chief Obafemi, 96, 106
Aylwin, Patricio, 131
Azikiwe, Nnamdi, 122

Babangida, Ibrahim, 44
Balewa, Tafawa, 42
Banjo, Victor, 47–8
Belgium, 25; occupation of Rwanda, 78
Benin, 34, 36
Berlin, Treaty of, 51
Berlin Conference (1874–6), 78
Biafra, 2–3, 6, 16, 38–55, 112; as lesson, 17; as metaphor, 3, 51, 113; collapse of, 90; economic blockade of, 96; forced recruitment to army in, 116–17; revolution in, 105; war literature of, 56–67; warfare and reconstruction in, 110–26
Biafran Organization of Freedom Fighters (BOFF), 51
Black Consciousness, 51
Black nationalism, 32
blaming of perpetators, 145, 150–3

Bolivia, 133
Bosnia, 6, 14, 118, 151, 158
Boulding, Kenneth, 57
Brazil, 133
Brookings Institution, Africa Project, 184, 187, 199
Burundi, 78, 91, 106
burying differences, 194
Busby, Margaret, 62

Cardoso, Fernando Henrique, 133
Carrington, Walter, 43
children: in armed conflict, 185; unwanted, result of rape, 168
Chile, 130, 144, 152
Chingono, Mark, 112
Christianity, 50, 82; conversion to, 29
civil rights movement in USA, 72
civil society, role of, 72–5
civil wars, and cause of justice, 184–200
civilians, protection of, 3
Clinton, Bill, visit to Africa, 38–9
closed districts policy (Sudan), 81
closure, models of, 157
Cold War, 38, 195; end of, 83
colonialism, 17, 26, 195; boundaries imposed by, 33
Comfort Women, compensation for, 156
command responsibility for war crimes, 133
compensation for victims, 156
complicity, webs of, 134, 152
Confederation of Central Africa, proposed, 84
Conference on Security, Stability, Development and Cooperation in Africa (CSSDCA), 199
conflict: management of, 195, 197; mediation of, 75–8, 87–8; nature of, 8–10; role of, 76; transformation of, 75–8
Congo, 4
Convention against Torture ..., 166
Convention on Genocide ..., 166
corruption, 58, 65
Council for the Development of Social Science Research in Africa (CODESRIA), 69
crimes against humanity, 128, 133; rape as, 165–6

Croatia, 151
Czechoslovakia, lustration laws, 134

democracy, 8, 11, 13, 15, 53, 65, 83, 127, 134, 137, 153, 187, 195; in Africa, 15; transition to, 153
Deng, Francis, 17–18, 77
derivation, principle of, 97
dictatorships: Latin American, as analogy, 179; transition from, 127
dignity, human, 186–7
Dina Committee Report (Nigeria), 96
Dinka community, 193–4
disappearances, 127, 128, 129, 134
displaced persons, 184, 185, 192
displacement, internal, 14; lessons from, 197–9
diversity, managing of, 197
DuBois, W.H., 34

East Germany, 134
Eastern Europe, 134
ECOWAS, 199
education: as individual reconstruction, 121; Western, 92, 94
Egypt, 80
El Salvador, 131–2
Emecheta, Buchi, 49, 51, 57, 65; *Destination Biafra*, 62–3
Emezue, Sydney, 9
empathy with opponent, 185
Engels, Friedrich, 103
Enterprise Promotion Decree (Nigeria), 96
Ethiopia, self-determination in, 196
ethnicity, 188–9, 195, 196, 197
evil, inevitability of, 52
executions, extra-judicial, 128
Ezeigbo, Akachi, 7–8

Fanon, Frantz, 53
feminism, 62, 102
Final Solution, use of term, 23
forced removals of populations, in South Africa, 180
forgetting, policy of, 136
forgiveness, 25
France, 30

Gallagher, M., 103

Gandhi, Mahatma, 183
Garang, John, 198
Garcia Meza, General, 133
Geffray, Christian, 111
Geneva Conventions, 165, 170
genocide, 6, 7, 11, 15, 17, 23–7, 40, 44,
    45, 46, 48, 80, 83, 107, 166, 170;
    conventions on, 148, 171; conviction
    for, 171; in Bosnia, 11; in Rwanda,
    8, 82 (prosecution for, 139)
Germany, interests in Balkans, 151
globalization, 38, 185, 200
Gluckman, Max, 194
good governance, in Africa, 199–200
Goree, landmark of slave trade, 34
Gowon, General Yakubu, 9, 39, 40–1,
    43, 45, 46, 48, 49, 91, 93
Group Areas Act (South Africa), 180
Guatemala, 131
guilt, admission of, 156

Habyarimana, Juvénal, 79
Haiti, 133, 139
Hardy, George, 29
Harnet-Sievers, Axel, 9
Hausa-Fulani community, 90, 93, 94,
    95, 97, 98, 99, 107
healing, 15, 21–37, 52
historical perceptions, 192–3
history: from below, 113; oral, 54, 115;
    project of, 34
Hofmeyr, Isabel, 115
Holocaust, 17, 26, 178, 179
human rights, 4, 134, 139, 157, 187,
    195; law on, 198; organizations, 132,
    164; violations of, 127, 128, 130,
    131, 139, 164, 179
Human Rights Watch organization, 171
hunger, as instrument of war, 96
Hutu community, 22, 23, 24, 78, 79, 80,
    82, 84, 86, 106, 166, 167, 192;
    women targeted for rape, 167

identity, 196; crises of, 18, 188;
    national, 85 (crisis of, 82, 198);
    selection of, 9
Igbo community, 7, 39, 40, 42, 44, 47,
    50, 63, 64, 112; abandoned property
    issue among, 120; boundary
    adjustments affecting, 99;

demarginalization of, 107–8;
economic strangulation of, 96–8;
excluded from military positions,
    100; marginalization of, 17, 90–109
    (economic, 101–6; mechanisms of,
    95–101); massacre of, 43; military
    neutralization of, 100; murders of,
    46; ostracism of, 100–1; political
    emasculation of, 98–100;
    punishment of, 43; role of informal
    sector in, 105; role of women in, 9,
    101–4, 116–17
Igboland, 100, 118; economic problems
    of, 97–8; establishment of money
    economy in, 120; under-
    development of, 119
immunity, 131
impunity, 17, 128, 129, 130, 136, 163–4
indigenous cultures, 196; resolution of
    conflicts in, 196; democratic ethics
    in, 60; use of, 18
infanticide, 169
informal sector, 91; in Nigeria, 104–5;
    role of, in Biafra war, 51
inheritance, rights of women, 169
Inter-American Court of Human
    Rights, 156
International Committee on
    Reparations, 28
international community, interests of,
    150–1
International Conference on National
    Dialogue (Burundi, 1994), 88
International Criminal Court, 135, 162;
    creation of, 174
International Monetary Fund (IMF),
    53, 74
international treaties, 148
Internet, policing of, 50
Iraq, 16
Iroh, Eddie, 57, 65; *Forty-eight Guns for
    the General*, 63; *The Siren in the
    Night*, 63, 64; *Toads of War*, 63
Ironsi, Major-General Agui, 48
Islam, 28, 29, 81, 85, 190, 191

Japan, reparations for Comfort Women,
    156
Jones, Eldred, 23
judicial accountability, 10–13

judiciary, construction of, 139
justice: limits of, 142–61; managed, 48–50; pursuit of, 182–3; related to position, 145

Kenya, bombing in, 10
Ker, David, 61
King, Martin Luther, 177
Kriger, Norma, 111

land, dispossession of, 180
land-mines, problem of, 112
Lasswell, Harold, 186
law, international, 11, 127, 129, 136, 154, 156, 157; and rape, 164; and sexual violence, 171
Leacock, E., 103
legal system, function of accountability, 52–3
legitimacy of trials, conditions of, 137–8
Letelier, Orlando, 131
Liberia, 23, 39
Lumumba, Patrice, 23

Machel, Graça, 185, 186
Mamdani, Mahmood, 13, 69, 72, 75
Mandela, Nelson, 38, 185, 186; Nobel Prize speech, 53
marginalization: definition of, 90, 91, 92; eradication of, 107–8; in Nigeria, origins of, 93–5; of developing countries, 185; of Igbo, mechanisms of, 95–101
marriage, forced, 167
Massera, Admiral Emilio: imprisonment of, 129; release of, 130
Mazowiecki, Thadeusz, 134
McDougal, Myres, 186
memory, 5, 21–37; and intellectual responsibility, 46–8; as corrective, 6; burden of, 40; collective, 192; need for, 33; politics of, 1, 38–55; preservation of, 31; reach of, 6, 21; selective, 53
Mendéz, Juan, 10–11
Menem, Carlos, 130
Mertus, Julie, 11
methodology, 1, 3–4, 18; comparative, 2

Michnik, Adam, 134
migration, 106; rural–urban, 104
military, 129, 130, 131, 132, 135; courts, 137; role of, 127
Milosevic, Slobodan, 16
Mitterrand, Danielle, 31
Mobutu Sese Seko, 196
modernization, 92; theory of, 72
Moffitt, Ronnie, 131
Mohammed–Obasanjo regime, Nigeria, 93, 106
mosquito, as party symbol, 27
Mothers of the Disappeared organization, 12
Mozambique, study of, 112, 114
murder, 136, 150, 181; punishment of, 134

Nagel, Professor Thomas, 138
naming of crimes, 145, 148–9
National Commission on the Disappeared (CONADEP) (Argentina), 129
National Islamic Front (NIF) (Sudan), 80, 83, 84–6, 88
National Liberation Front (NLF) (Rwanda), 83
National Reconciliation Committee (Nigeria), 15
National Rehabilitation Commission (Nigeria), 44
Ngugi wa Thingo'o, 59
Nicaragua, 131–2
Nigeria, 7, 17, 22, 23, 36, 63; civil war in, 62, 65, 119–21 (ending of, 122, 124; study of, 112–16); creation of, 41–2; failure of industrialization in, 104; marginalization of Igbo people in, 90–109; military coups in, 57; reorganization of army in, 123; role of British industry in, 93; unity of, 40, 44; US policy on, 38, 42–3; warfare and reconstruction in, 110–26; women's experience of civil war, 116–19
Nino, Carlos, 148
Nkrumah, Kwame, 196
Nnoli, Owudiba, 57
non-governmental organizations (NGOs), 6, 11

non-violence, 77
Nowrojee, Binaifer, 11–12
Ntahobali, Arsene Shalom, 171
an-Numeiri, Jaafar, 80, 81
Nuremberg trials, 13, 133
Nyerere, Julius, 196–7

Obasanjo, General Olusegun, 184, 199
oil interests, 42, 43, 97
Ojukwu, Chief Chukwuemeka
    Odumegwu, 47, 49, 64, 65
Okereke, Grace, 63
Okigbo, Christopher, 23, 45
Omo Ebih Atrocities Tribunal, 48
Onyekwere, Mrs, 90
oral tradition, clichés of, 115
Orentlicher, Diane, 153
Organization of African Unity (OAU),
    9, 27, 28, 42, 57, 88, 122–3, 199–200
Osiel, Mark, 157
Ovevhamwen, Oba, 36

P'Bitek, Okot, 23
pan-African movement, 4
partitioning, 26, 27
pass laws, and militarization of labour,
    180
Peshkova, Svetlana, 6, 8–9, 191
Peters, Lenrie, 23
Phillipson Commission Report
    (Nigeria), 96
Pinochet, General Augusto, 130, 131,
    144, 152
Plekhanov, G.V., 58
pluralism, ethnic and cultural, 197
Poland, 134
polygyny, 117
post-colonialism, 59, 73
pregnancy, forced, 162, 174
punishing the perpetrators, 145, 153–5;
    destabilizing effect of, 154

Ralph, Regan, 11–12
rape, 9, 11, 12, 14, 118, 144, 150, 155,
    158, 162, 174, 181; as act of
    genocide, 171; as challenge to
    honour, 165; as crime against
    humanity, 148, 165–6; as form of
    torture, 166; as genocide crime, 166;
    as metaphor, 49; as private crime,

162; as violation of international
    law, 164–5; as war crime, 163, 165;
    collecting of testimonies, 173; in
    Bosnia, 9; in former Yugloslavia,
    163; in war, 163; lack of
    documentation, 164, 170; of men,
    163; perpetrators of, 171;
    prosecution for, 172; protection for
    victims of, 173–4; punishment for,
    12; reporting of, 163–4; silences
    about, 168, 170; social stigma of,
    168; used regularly in conflict, 163
    see also war marriage
reconciliation, 4, 27–32, 138, 158, 181,
    182, 194; analysis of, 63; law and,
    52–4
Reconciliation, Rehabilitation and
    Reconstruction, 43, 63, 107
reconstruction, social history of, 110–26
recording: for history, 17, 145, 157–9;
    need of survivors, 158
reforming of lawless societies, 145,
    156–7
refugees, 119; Bosnian, 142–3; policies
    on, 112; studies, 111
Rehabilitation, Reconciliation and
    Reconstruction, 63
relatives: killing of, 167; torture of, 150
reparation, 6, 16, 17, 21, 26, 27–32;
    delivery of, 145, 155–6; for slavery,
    22; in Rwanda, 155; in former
    Yugoslavia, 155
responsibility: for slavery, 32;
    intellectual, 38–55
Rettig, Jorge, 131
Rettig Commission, 131
Richards, Paul, 112
Richburg, Keith, 30–1
Rodt-Arriaza, Naomi, 158
Rutherford, Anna, 61
Rwanda, 3, 11, 22, 24–5, 75, 77, 84, 91,
    106, 118, 151, 157; ad hoc court for,
    135; need for revenge in, 152;
    proposed Protectorate
    Administration, 84; prosecutions for
    genocide in, 139; social movements
    in, 68, 78–80; violence against
    women in, 162–75; war crimes
    tribunal in *see* war crimes, tribunals
Rwandan Armed Forces (FAR), 84–6,
    166

Rwandese Patriotic Front/Army
(RPF/RPA), 79, 83, 84–6

Sabato, Ernesto, 129
Saro Wiwa, Ken, 38
Scarry, Elaine, *The Body in Pain*, 142
self-determination, 9, 50–2, 68, 195,
196
Senegal, *signares* of, 30
Serbia, 151
Serumaga, Robert, 23
Serushago, Omar, 171
sexual abuse, 158; telling of, 155
sexual mutilation of women, 162, 167
sexual slavery, 162, 167, 174
sexual violence against women, 9, 124,
174, 117–19, 124, 169, 174;
prosecution of, 172
sexually transmitted diseases, arising
out of rape, 168
Shagari, Shehu, 42
Shari'a law, 80, 85
Sierra Leone, 23, 112
silences about abuse of women, 163–4
slave trade, 6, 29, 81, 106; Arab
participation in, 28–30, 190;
Atlantic, 26; route of, 34–5
(preservation of, 31)
slavery, 17, 22, 25, 26, 29, 34, 80, 111,
194
Sobowale, Dele, 49
social justice, 4, 21, 22, 52, 56–67; as
means of healing and reconciliation,
57–65; attentuation of, 65; definition
of, 16
social movements, 2, 4, 6, 8, 68–89;
contradictory role of, 82–4;
definition of, 68, 69–75; in relation
to political parties, 71, 87; internal
inconsistency of, 76
socialism, African, 195, 196
Somalia, 39
South Africa, 3, 7, 53; transition in, 4
see also Truth and Reconciliation
Commissions
sovereignty: conceptualization of, 197,
199
Soyinka, Wole, 5, 6, 7, 8, 39–40, 44,
45–8, 56, 57, 58, 65, 185, 186, 187;
The Burden of Memory ..., 21;

Madmen and Specialists, 58–9;
Season of Anomy, 59; *A Shuttle in the
Crypt*, 58
Special Security Services (SSS)
(Nigeria), 64
Special Task Force (STF) (Biafra), 51
spying on private lives, 134
state, 74; interaction with civil society,
74; Islamic, 85; nature of, 8 (post-
colonial, 73); redefinition of, 9
sterilization, enforced, 174
structural adjustment, 53, 74; in
Nigeria, 105
subject-hood of victims, 143, 144, 153,
154
Sudan, 9, 75, 84, 187, 188; ascription
of skin colour in, 189; civil war in,
80, 81; identity crisis in, 198;
indigenous culture of, 33; role of
elders in, 194; social movements in,
68, 80–2
Sudanese People's Liberation
Movement and Army (SPLM/A),
81, 84–6, 88; split in, 77
survivors: and the naming of crimes,
149; need for record, 158; protection
of, 158–9

Tadic, Dusko, 150, 155, 158
Tarrow, Sidney, 71
Third Force, 47–8
torture, 14, 64, 128, 129, 134, 136, 148,
150, 165, 181; convention on, 150;
definition of, 166; rape as, 166
trials: conditions of legitimacy of,
137–8; prejudice against, 136–7;
truth, 10, 21–37; and forgiveness, 32–6;
brought to light by direct action,
177; defined within political
parameters, 178; from majority
viewpoint, 179; in relation to justice,
182; in the South African TRC,
176–83; incomplete, of war crimes
tribunals, 159; of apartheid, 178–81;
parameters of seeking of, 177; right
to, 11, 128; spoken to power, 177;
telling of, 137
Truth and Reconciliation Commissions
(TRC), 5, 11, 17, 139; case for,
135–7; for Yugoslavia, 14; function

of, 13–16; in Argentina, 131; in El
Salvador, 132; in Guatemala, 132; in
South Africa, 7, 13–14, 16, 25, 41,
134–5, 176–83 (*Report of the Truth
and Reconciliation Commission*, 176;
Amnesty Committee, 176, 181;
reaction of Afrikaners, 182); need
for fairness, 138
truth-telling, emphasis on, 134
Tutsi community, 22, 24, 78, 79, 84,
106, 167, 192
Tutu, Archbishop Desmond, 15, 135,
185, 186

Uganda, 23, 79
ujamaa, 196
UNESCO, 31
Union of Soviet Socialist Republics
(USSR), 10
United Nations (UN), 11, 24, 57, 74,
78, 88, 122, 131–3, 135, 197, 198;
resolution on Rwanda, 170
UN High Commissioner for Human
Rights, 198
UN Human Rights Committee, 128
United States of America (USA), 10,
16, 32; foreign policy of, 3 (on
Nigeria, 38, 42–3); State
Department, 42–3, 53
Universal Declaration for Human
Rights, 139
Uruguay, 133

Verwoerd, Hendrik, 181
Videla, General Jorge: imprisonment
of, 129; re-arrest of, 130; released,
130
violence, 83, 111; gender-based, in
Rwanda, 162–75; inevitability of, 52;
role of, 77; sexual, against women
see sexual violence

war crimes, tribunals, 5, 11, 14, 44, 49,
53, 54, 142, 144, 145–7, 150, 154; ad

hoc nature of, 156; backfiring of
trials, 151; functions of, 144–5; in
former Yugoslavia, 162, 163; in
Rwanda, 11, 12, 142, 145, 154, 155,
162, 163, 170–1 (turnover of staff
at, 173); incomplete truth of, 159;
international, 50, 52; language of,
149; need for, 153; Nuremberg, 12,
162, 165 (as analogy, 178); Tokyo,
162
war industry, profits of, 44
war marriage, 10, 119
war-affected populations, studies of,
112
warfare, social history of, 110–26
widows, difficulties of, 169
Wiesel, Elie, 31
witness protection, 12
witnessing, 12, 17
women, 59, 62, 86; among Igbo, 91
(role of, 102, 116–17; strategies of,
101–4); and social justice, 65; as
victims of war, 7; central role of, in
war, 7; empowerment of, 61;
experience of Nigeria's civil war,
116–19; justice for, 162–75;
relationship with soldiers, 10; role
of, 9, 51, 124; sexual violence
against, 117–19; work in markets,
117
women's organizations, 42
women's rights, 11
writer, position of, 59

Yoruba community, 90, 36, 93, 94, 95,
96, 98, 99, 107
Yugoslavia, 15–16, 151, 157, 158; ad
hoc court for, 135; war crimes
tribunal in, 142, 145, 149, 154, 155,
158

Zartman, Bill, 197
Zimbabwe, warfare in, 111
Zirakzadeh, Cyrus, 70